101 591 259 1

D1760365

ONE WEEK
LOAN

17 NOV 1998   ☲1 MAY 2001

16 APR 1999   11 JAN 2002
27 OCT 1999

☲3 MAR 2000   19 NOV 2003

2̄ OCT 2000

☲0 MAR 2001

Sheffield Hallam University
Learning and Information Services
Withdrawn From Stock

C
N

SU

MI

an

AI

MACMILLAN

© Susan Halford, Mike Savage and Anne Witz 1997

All rights reserved. No reproduction, copy or transmission of this publication may be made without written permission.

No paragraph of this publication may be reproduced, copied or transmitted save with written permission or in accordance with the provisions of the Copyright, Designs and Patents Act 1988, or under the terms of any licence permitting limited copying issued by the Copyright Licensing Agency, 90 Tottenham Court Road, London W1P 9HE.

Any person who does any unauthorised act in relation to this publication may be liable to criminal prosecution and civil claims for damages.

The authors have asserted their rights to be identified as the authors of this work in accordance with the Copyright, Designs and Patents Act 1988.

First published 1997 by
MACMILLAN PRESS LTD
Houndmills, Basingstoke, Hampshire RG21 6XS
and London
Companies and representatives
throughout the world

ISBN 0–333–60977–8 hardcover
ISBN 0–333–60978–6 paperback

A catalogue record for this book is available
from the British Library.

This book is printed on paper suitable for recycling and made from fully managed and sustained forest sources.

10 9   8   7   6   5   4   3   2   1
06 05 04 03 02 01 00 99 98 97

Editing and origination by
Aardvark Editorial, Mendham, Suffolk

Printed in Hong Kong

SHEFFIELD HALLAM UNIVERSITY LIBRARY
WL
331·133
HA
COLLEGIATE CRESCENT

Contents

List of Tables and Figures

Preface

In this book we examine the relationship between gender, careers and organisations in Britain during the 1980s and early 1990s. On the surface this seems a period of dramatic change. Until the 1970s women were usually located firmly at the bottom of most organisational hierarchies. In some cases women were still expected to leave work on marriage, in most cases they were expected to leave work when they had children, and they were nearly always employed in jobs that allowed them little opportunity for job mobility or promotion.

In their influential study of gender and white collar work carried out between 1979 and 1981, Crompton and Jones (1984) suggested that traditional forms of gender inequality were likely to change as growing numbers of women working in white collar jobs began to seek promotion into more senior posts. In the 1980s and 1990s there was indeed considerable evidence that the position of women in British organisations was improving. During this period the number of women in the labour market increased, as it has done for much of the post-war period, but more importantly women began to acquire credentials at an increased rate (Crompton and Sanderson, 1990) and have consequently come to make up a significant proportion of new entrants to professional jobs (Crompton, 1995; Fielding, 1995). There is also considerable evidence that increasing numbers of women are being promoted to senior management level within many organisations (Davidson and Cooper, 1992). Connected to these changes, and following from the Equal Pay Act and the Sex

Discrimination Act in 1975[1], many organisations have developed an array of additional, non-statutory equal opportunity policies that aim to encourage changes in organisational practice, in order to improve the position of women workers (as well as that of other under-represented groups). Indeed, in 1991 a large group of major employers banded together under the auspices of the government-backed organisation Business in the Community to launch 'Opportunity 2000', a joint initiative designed specifically to improve women's career opportunities.

There are, however, plenty of reasons not to be swept away by these sorts of observation. It is easy to find counter examples that testify to the persistence of gender segregation and inequality. For example, although growing numbers of women are becoming qualified in professions such as law and accountancy, some of the occupational areas in which women have traditionally used credentialism to secure professional employment have been radically restructured and/or contracted, as in for example teaching (Crompton and Sanderson, 1990) and nursing (Walby *et al.*, 1994). There is also strong evidence that a 'glass ceiling' effect prevents women from moving into the most senior jobs within organisations (Chapman, 1989) and that well-credentialed women are channelled into specialist 'niche jobs' that prevent them from using their skills, acquired expertise and experience to their full potential (Crompton and Sanderson, 1990; Savage, 1992; Crompton, 1995). These 'niche' jobs often entail using professional skills but not *managing* other professionals. Furthermore, many of the new 'women's jobs' that have appeared in recent years involve temporary or part-time contracts offering women only marginal career status and opportunities. Finally, whatever the statements of intent, equal opportunity policies are not always implemented in practice (Halford, 1992) and even when they are implemented may have ambiguous and possibly contradictory implications for women's position; for example, targeting childcare provisions at women could be seen to reinforce gender-specific 'familial' roles in an organisational context (Cockburn, 1991).

To what extent, then, are gender relations within organisations *really* changing? This book explores the changing position of women and men within one high street bank and two local authorities, and on the nursing staff of two hospitals. Initially, we wanted to compare men's and women's career paths in these different organisational settings (partly along the lines pioneered by Crompton and Jones, 1984), and were most interested in the gendered experience and meaning of career, and in comparing the career trajectories of men and women. This interest lies at the heart of this book. However, the study of 'career' pathways, narrowly defined, has become only one aspect of a much broader analysis. From the outset we were also interested in the organisational practices and cultures that affected careers within our case study organisations. Indeed, one of our aims was to shift attention away from movement between occupations – which has been the main focus of social mobility research – to movement within organisations. As our research progressed, it became even clearer that in order to understand changing patterns of career mobility, it was not enough just to compare the movement of men and women between different jobs within organisations. It was also vital to consider the pervasive gendering of a whole variety of organisational processes that define the terrain on which mobility takes place. After all – to rehearse a tension that has always characterised sociological research in this area – occupational mobility cannot be under-stood just by looking at the individuals who are (or are not) mobile but needs to be analysed in terms of the positions between which people move and through which the nature and meaning of mobility are understood and contextualised (see Savage, 1996, for further discussion).

This raises a number of questions. How do the meaning, status and power of jobs change as women move into them (Reskin and Roos, 1990)? How does the restructuring of organisations affect job and career opportunities within them? How, in turn, is organisational change related to gender divi-sions and gendered careers? Thus the analysis of women's and men's careers that we elaborate in this book is embedded within a much broader inquiry into the gendering of contem-porary organisations and into an analysis of the dynamics of organisational change. This latter point raises far more than a simple consideration of the changing proportions of men and women in different jobs or following different career paths. Rather, recent organisational restructuring has changed the ways in which gender is embedded in various organisational roles and activities. This in turn means that the terrain on which career mobility takes place has itself been redefined. Our examination of these issues is found in Chapter 3, where we provide an account of the gendered restructuring of the organisations we studied and develop our theoretical argument about the nature of restructuring.

In Chapter 4 we explore the consequences of such change for women's and men's career paths. We show that restructuring has significantly redefined the 'career', and provide some evidence from our organisations that traditional 'male' careers are being threatened whilst emergent 'female' careers are being formed (although the reader will see that there are significant differences between the organisations).

Through our discussions in Chapters 3 and 4 it becomes clear that recent organisational restructuring has changed the 'personal' qualities and attributes that are valued in our organisations, and hence that are rewarded in career terms. Of course, this has major implications for people working in these organisations. In Chapter 5 we focus directly on individuals' responses to recent change, their interpretations of what was expected of them and their reflections on their place within the organisations in which they worked.

This raises some broader questions. As one would expect, when individuals discuss their 'careers', they do so in the context of broader concerns and social relationships. Perhaps the most widely remarked on instance of this within popular and academic accounts of gender and careers concerns the relationship between domestic and familial ties and employment careers. In Chapter 6 we explore individuals' accounts of these relationships and the ways in which these are being (re)shaped by organisational change. We consider both the practical arrangements between 'home' and 'work' commitments, and the symbolic ways in which the domestic, and particularly the 'maternal', are embedded in organisational life. This leads us to a more abstract discussion, at the end of Chapter 6, about the ways in which embodiment – specifically gendered embodiment – features in organisational discourse and practice. These points are extended in Chapter 7, where we take up the issue of sexuality, exploring the complex interaction of gender and sexuality in workplace relationships and hierarchies through a notion of an organisational 'politics of the body'.

The reader will now see how this book has finally ended up as a rather broad inquiry into the linkages between gender and organisation. In order to orient readers to the many issues which this book takes up, we provide two introductory chapters. Chapter 1 situates our analysis within broader theoretical debates about the relationship between gender and organisations. This introduction reflects on the various issues and theoretical perspectives within contemporary debates on gender and organisation, and provides a rationale for the particular positions we take in this book. Chapter 2 presents an introduction to the case study organisations and to the research methods we used in our study. The fact that we have included many of the basic details of our research in Chapter 2 means that subsequent chapters can be more fully devoted to developing points of substantive interest. Readers who skip this chapter (which is not, strictly speaking, central to the arguments we make) should bear in mind that basic factual material about the organisations and occupations we studied, as well as a discussion of our research methods, is contained in this chapter and that cross-reference to it might be necessary.

Overall, perhaps the single most important contribution that we hope this book makes is to bring a wealth of new empirical material to bear on the many hotly contested current debates about gender and organisation. As far as possible, we have allowed the people we spoke to during the course of our research to comment on the changes they saw happening around them *and to them*. It has become commonplace within the social sciences to point out that people are knowledgeable agents (Giddens, 1984), and in this book we take this point very seriously by making people's accounts central to our study.

Acknowledgements

First and most importantly, we would like to thank the Economic and Social Research Council for funding this project (grant number R00023277301). Readers will detect that the project changed somewhat as it progressed, in terms of both institutional support and intellectual direction, and we are grateful that the ESRC as it was constituted then was able to fund and support necessary modifications. The project was not the easiest to co-ordinate, since Susan Halford was initially based at Sussex University (later at Southampton University), Mike Savage at Keele University (later at the University of North Carolina and later still at Manchester University), and Anne Witz at Birmingham University (later at Ruhr-Universität Bochum, Germany). This situation led to British Telecom earning a good commission from our project, but more seriously it meant that we have to thank a number of London-based friends who lent us their houses and flats for our regular meetings. Chris Howlett and Claire Higginson gave us the benefit of their flat in Hackney, whilst Caron Jones offered a nearby alternative in Walthamstow.

We would also like to thank the organisations that allowed us access and the individuals who helped our research, whether by answering questions, filling in questionnaires or being interviewed in depth. We cannot name any individuals, since this would reveal the identity of the organisations involved, but we do wish to record our gratitude to everyone to whom we spoke and who helped us in the course of our research.

One of the distinctive features of our project was that we invited an 'expert panel' to guide us in the preparation and conduct of our research. This expert panel comprised both academics, people working in policy fields and members of the case study organisations themselves, and allowed a rare opportunity for the interplay of academic and policy-oriented ideas. We cannot name all the participants, since again this would reveal the identities of the organisations, but we can thank Sara Arber (University of Surrey), Steven Bubb (Association of Metropolitan Authorities), Margery Povall, Ed Puttick (Equal Opportunities Commission) and Dianah Worman (Institute of Personnel Management). Many other people have also given advice, comments and support of various sorts: we would like to single out Lisa Adkins, Sarah Cant, Rosemary Crompton, Sue Gilbert, Gill Court, Joy Kendrick, Dave Laflin, Pauline Leonard, Ann-Therese Lotherington, Linda McDowell and Jane Wills.

Versions of parts of this book have been presented at a variety of conferences and seminars. We would like to thank everyone who gave us feedback on these occasions. Susan Halford presented papers in the Geography Departments at Southampton University, Reading University and Cambridge University; at the Social Science Research Institute in Tromsø, Norway; and at the Institute of British Geographers Annual Conference. Mike Savage presented papers to the Rural Economy and Society Study Group Annual Conference; the British Association Conference at Keele University; the Department of Sociology and Social Anthropology, Keele University; and the Department of Sociology, Buckinghamshire College of Higher Education. Anne Witz presented papers to a National Day School on sexual harassment in the National Health Service, University of Central Lancashire; the Faculty of Social Sciences Seminar, University of Plymouth; a conference on 'Organisations, Gender, and Power' organised by the Industrial Relations Research Unit, Univeristy of Warwick; and a workshop on 'Transformation in Gender Relations', Sozialforschungsstelle Dortmund, Germany. Susan Halford and Mike Savage gave papers to the 9th Urban and Regional Change Conference, Sheffield University; the Gender Studies Institute, London School of Economics; and the Department of Sociology and Social Policy, Southampton University. Susan Halford, Mike Savage and Anne Witz gave a paper to the British Sociological Association Annual Conference, University of Central Lancashire.

Finally, many thanks to Frances Arnold and Catherine Gray at Macmillan Press for their enthusiasm, support and patience.

1 Gender and Organisations: Theoretical Issues

Introduction

The recent growth of interest in exploring the relationship between gender and organisations has generated a range of theoretical positions and encouraged a widening focus that draws new and exciting issues into the debate (see, for example, Cockburn, 1991; Mills and Tancred, 1992; Savage and Witz, 1992). In this chapter we aim to clarify the main perspectives on the relationship between gender and organisation, and also to explain the rationale that we have taken in carrying out our research and presenting our findings in this book. We take the view that theoretical elaboration takes place alongside, rather than just before, social research. Thus the arguments that we develop here were clarified *through* our empirical research rather than simply being *illustrated by* our research.

This chapter proceeds by evaluating three alternative approaches to the study of gender and organisations. We label these *contingent*, *essentialist* and *embedded* (these terms will be elaborated below). We selectively review literature on gender and organisations under each of these headings and explain why we find the first two approaches deficient. We go on to develop the final perspective, which sees gender relations as embedded within organisations, drawing in particular on the writings of Acker. The arguments we present here are an elaboration of those of Witz and Savage (1992), who claim that:

1

The modern Western bureaucracy, as dissected by Weber, is only one way of organizing social relations and it *depends upon* particular configurations of gender relations... It is vital to develop a perspective on gender and bureaucracy which foregrounds *gender relations as an embedded property of organisations* rather than valorising gender differences as dichotomous sets of attributes or distinctive orientations and modes of action, which are simply 'brought to' organisations (1992: 3 and 26; emphasis added).

In order to elaborate this perspective we also explore the significance of sexuality and embodiment in organisations. Towards the end of this chapter we clarify the relevance of these issues for our study of gender and organisations, and also indicate how they may be conceptualised in this context. Thus this chapter aims to set out some of the key concepts and theories that are developed throughout the book using our own empirical research material.

The critique of gender-neutral organisation

Until the 1980s there had been a general neglect of gender within organisational theory and organisational sociology.[1] Indeed, mainstream organisational theory tended to ignore gender and feminist theory tended to ignore organisations. This is rather surprising since 'Most organisations remain patriarchal, if only by virtue of their domination by men' (Hearn and Parkin, 1983: 219). The gendered composition of bureaucratic organisations is so striking that it would seem an important, even essential, topic of investigation for the organisational theorist. Equally, the increased participation of women in large workplace bureaucracies and, more generally, the increasing bureaucratisation of public life means that in order to understand male domination in modern society 'feminism and organisational theory need each other' (Ferguson, 1984: 4). However, this mutual dependency has until recently remained unrecognised.

Of course, the study of women and employment has been a major topic of mainstream economics since the 1960s (Mincer,

1962; Becker, 1965) and of feminist research since at least the 1970s (Beechey, 1977; Hartmann, 1979). However, this and subsequent research was primarily concerned with the gendered character of *occupations* (clerical work, nursing, management or construction work) rather than of *organisations* (the bureaucracies that might employ workers in many occupations, organise them into hierarchies and shape movement between them). It focused on issues such as women's labour force participation (for example, movement in and out of the labour market related to childbirth/care and arguments that women formed a reserve army of labour for capitalism) and processes of occupational segregation within the labour market (how women and men become confined to certain occupations), rather than on organisational processes *per se*. In particular, early feminist work offered a critique of the idea that women's labour market activity was the result simply of their familial position (as suggested by Becker, 1965) and established that labour market processes (reflecting capitalist and/or patriarchal forces) led to occupational sex segregation (Acker, 1973; Hartmann, 1979; Barrett, 1980; Murgatroyd, 1982; Cockburn, 1983; Walby, 1986; Beechey, 1987). Interestingly, there were some rich empirical case studies of women's work in particular factories (Cavendish, 1982; Pollert, 1982; Westwood, 1984) but these focused more on the factory floor as the site of lived relations of class, gender and race, within relations of production, rather than on investigating these particular organisational sites in their own right.

Thus, with a few exceptions, this early feminist interest in explaining gender relations in the workplace and in the labour market tended to neglect the contribution that organisational factors might make to these issues. The relative lack of interest in organisation may be explained by the intellectual context in which 1970s research emerged. In Britain an important strand of feminist research was based around the development of a distinctive socialist–feminist programme that attempted to reconcile elements of Marxism with feminism (for example, Beechey, 1977; Barrett, 1980). One of the claims that these feminists took from the Marxist tradition was the idea that organisational processes were not *in themselves* important since they were simply

derived from capitalist social relations. An example of the consequences of this can be found in the 'dual systems' framework
pioneered by Hartmann (1979) and later developed by Walby
(1986, 1990). These writers argued that capitalism and patriarchy
existed as two independent social processes, which articulated in
complex and varying ways in differing historical situations. The
main object of Hartmann's and Walby's work was to establish the
significance of patriarchy as a stratifying system independent of
capitalism, with the result that the analysis of capitalism itself and
capitalist institutions was rather taken as 'given', that is, as dealt
with by (neo)-Marxist analysis. In Walby's (1986) formulation this
led to the argument that capitalists tend to employ women since
they are cheaper than male labour: that capitalism is in itself
(theoretically at least) gender-blind, working only through a pure
capitalist dynamic. Walby argues that this dynamic is modified in
given circumstances by the actions of men that seek to exclude
women from the workplace, especially through trade unionism
(see also Cockburn, 1983).

   The point we wish to establish is that socialist and Marxist
feminist analysis, and dual systems theory, allowed little conceptual
space for the salience of organisational processes to be registered.
With hindsight this can be seen to place certain limitations on
feminist accounts of the gendered division of labour. Organisational processes cannot be 'read off' from capitalist ones and have,
historically, been a crucial force shaping the subordination of
women in employment.

   On the other hand in organisational theory there has been a
distinct lack of interest in gender, at least until the mid-1980s.
Largely as a result of the professionalisation of management
education during the 1960s and 1970s, reflected in the growing
number of business schools located within universities, 'organisation theory' developed its own specialist literature, of which the
'sociology of organisation' was but a part. However, even this
subfield remained remarkably gender-blind until the publication
of Acker and Van Houten's (1974) critique of Mayo's famous
productivity experiments, carried out during the 1930s and
1940s. The results of these experiments at the Hawthorne plant
of Western Electric in the United States prompted a paradigm

shift in managerial theory away from 'Taylorism' towards a 'human relations' school of management. Whereas Taylor understood organisations as mechanistic, rational and amenable to scientific management, and workers as driven purely by economic incentives, the human relations school emphasised the importance of the informal, emotional and 'non-rational' aspects of human behaviour in organisations (see below for a further discussion). Acker and Van Houten's critique of Mayo's experiments shows that because his research (along with other established organisational and management theories) failed to take into account the different gender composition of the work groups studied, an important – perhaps even primary – explanation for his results was completely ignored. The group that showed the greatest increase in productivity was composed of women only and seems to have been treated differently by the researchers, who also failed to consider that there may have been wider, gender-specific factors in the women workers' lives that were relevant to the outcome of the research. It may have been these gendered factors, rather than anything else, that explained the differences between the two groups. Thus Acker and Van Houten established the dangers inherent in a gender-blind perspective on organisations and set a pressing agenda for research into the gendering of organisational processes.

Acker has developed her work since to further substantiate her arguments for the integral coupling of organisations and gender. In a recent article Acker (1992) highlights four major areas in which gender and organisations can be seen to intertwine. First is the construction of *divisions between women and men*, for example in terms of the jobs they do and how they are allowed or expected to behave. Second, she goes on, there is the construction of *images and symbols,* which explain, express and reinforce (or, rarely, oppose) those divisions. For example, successful organisation today tends to be defined as lean, mean and aggressive, which can be construed as metaphors of masculinity, and not empathetic, supportive or caring, all of which can be seen as metaphors of femininity (Acker, 1992). The third set of processes producing gendered organisation are *actual interactions* between embodied women and men, as well as those between women and between men, through which relations of dominance and subordination are enacted (or sometimes resisted). Finally, the fourth set of processes concerns the *internal mental work* that individuals undertake in order simply to participate and/or build successful careers in their organisation, for example performing a correct gender persona or hiding unacceptable forms of sexuality. These processes are built on and, in turn, help to reproduce what Acker (1992) terms 'the gendered substructure of organisation'.

Clearly, the agenda for investigating the gendered substructure of organisations is a broad one. Not least it raises fundamental questions about how to conceptualise both 'gender' and 'organisation' as well as the connections between them. In what follows, we will consider this question, evaluating what we see as the three established perspectives at present. First, there is a *contingent perspective*, which argues that bureaucracy is fundamentally gender-neutral and that any gendered patterns or processes that may exist are a superficial and/or accidental addition to this neutral core. Second, there is an *essentialist perspective*, which ties bureaucratic organisation intrinsically to masculinity and patriarchy. Third, there is the perspective that we advocate, the *embedded perspective*. This third way of conceptualising the relationship between gender and organisations suggests that the social relations of gender are embedded (in complex and historically mutable ways) within the social relations of bureaucratic organisation. Gender is not an accidental addition to a fundamentally gender-neutral organisational form. However, nor are gendered organisations a fixed reflex of male characteristics. We might see gender relations as part of the field of social relations within which organisations take shape, and as becoming part of the social fabric of organisations.

The contingent approach to organisation and gender

This approach suggests that if organisations happen to be gendered, this is the contingent outcome of specific historical processes rather than an intrinsic feature of bureaucratic organisation *per se*. One rendering of this view is the claim that gender inequalities within organisations are not due to organisational processes themselves but to other factors, such as the imperfect application of essentially gender-neutral bureaucratic procedures or the result of the different situations of men and women external to the organisation (for example, their differing family roles). Even whilst it might be acknowledged that in practice bureaucracies are not gender-neutral, the argument is that the *principle* of bureaucratic organisation is gender-neutral.

The best known argument of this kind is Kanter's (1977) pioneering analysis of gender and organisation. Kanter's central concern is to reject individualistic or sociobiological explanations for the gender inequalities apparent in the modern American corporation and to construct instead a social–structural account. Her starting point is the initial concentration of women in clerical posts and men in managerial posts at the time when bureaucratic organisations expanded in the early part of the 20th century. Kanter offers little explanation for this initial sex stereotyping, but argues that once it had been established it was the dynamics of *bureaucracy*, rather than gender relations, that acted to reinforce and perpetuate it. This is not to say that bureaucracy is inherently gendered but rather the opposite, that bureaucracy is only accidentally gendered. For example, one of Kanter's strongest claims is that two inherent features of bureaucratic managerial life – uncertainty and the need for good communication – require the creation of an environment where managers share common features ('homosociability'), thus reducing uncertainty and aiding smooth communication. In this context the tendency for male managers to appoint other male managers and to construct and perpetuate forms of male 'homosociability' is primarily a consequence of managerial imperatives in large bureaucracies (where at the moment the managers happen to be mainly men) and certainly not a consequence of patriarchal relations operating in bureaucratic context. Thus, Kanter claims:

> the fate of women is inextricably bound up with organisational structure and processes in the same way that men's life-at-work is

l by them. Differences based on sex retreat into the background as
... eople-creating, behaviour-shaping properties of organisational
locations becomes clear (1977: 9).

In other words, it is position in the organisational hierarchy, rather
than gender, that determines both opportunity and, linked to
opportunity, behaviour within organisations. If women, or men,
act in ways that appear to confirm their status in organisations, it
is not because of innate gender characteristics but because organisational dynamics encourage both senior and junior staff to
behave in different and specific ways. Thus Kanter argues that it is
the job which makes the person, not the person who makes the
job, and that it is power differences, rather than gender differences, that provide the key to understanding the different fates
and fortunes of men and women of the corporation.

This view draws upon an instrumental concept of power, as
something which is 'possessed' by virtue of hierarchical seniority.
Because it happens to be men who are dominant in organisations, they possess the power that enables them to subordinate
and control others in jobs lower down the organisational hierarchy, many of whom happen to be women. However, Kanter
argues that once women gain access to these senior posts, they
too will possess power, and a critical mass of women in managerial posts will disrupt the male character of homosociability.
Bureaucratic grounds for excluding women from management
will thereby be outdated, invalidated and unnecessary.

Kanter's analysis of the interstices between gender and power
is uncompromisingly optimistic. She believes that power wipes
out sex. The relative powerlessness of women in organisations
can be rectified (by increasing the numbers of women at the
top) whilst leaving bureaucracies themselves largely intact. The
one exception to this analysis that Kanter identifies is the case of
secretarial work and the boss–secretary relationship. This relationship, she argues, is structured by personal rather than bureaucratic relationships, and it is this which explains (women)
secretaries' lack of organisational power. The position of women
secretaries is the outcome of a 'bureaucratic anomaly... a repos-
itory of the personal inside the bureaucratic' (Kanter, 1977: 101).

It is precisely because the boss–secretary relation has not been rationally structured on the basis of rational–legal authority, but is instead a 'patrimonial relic', lingering on within a rational, bureaucratic shell, that the position of secretarial workers is so poor. Again optimistic, Kanter argues that once the boss–secretary relation is set on a more rational, bureaucratic footing, gender will not taint its form or content. Once more Kanter endorses the general argument that bureaucracy is inherently gender-neutral.

However, it appears doubtful that the gender differences and inequalities apparent in Kanter's corporations will really be 'bureaucratised out' in the way she suggests. The boss–secretary relationship that she describes as a 'patrimonial relic' continues to flourish within organisations, and efforts to use formal bureaucratic mechanisms to ensure equality of opportunity for women have had limited success. This has often been because of informal opposition to changing established practices and the construction of equal opportunities initiatives as an unwelcome interference, a politically correct side-show, to the proper and legitimate business of bureaucratic life (Cockburn, 1991; Halford, 1991).

This leads us to two particularly important points. First, there does not seem to be universal agreement about 'good' organisation. Rather, what constitutes good managerial practice or delivers organisational efficiency is a matter of dispute. Second, male homosociability may be more than simply a bureaucratic by-product of vertical occupational segregation, as Kanter suggests. Instead, organisational power relations may work through a gendered dynamic rather than a purely bureaucratic dynamic. The central weakness in the contingent approach such as Kanter's is the unquestioning acceptance of Weberian notions of bureaucracy. In Weber's view bureaucratic organisation is based on impersonal rules, procedures and hierarchies that work together as the most rational and efficient form of organisation. Within this type of organisation, traditional forms of power and discrimination, based for example on personal sex or class characteristics, disappear. Thus bureaucracy is, in essence, gender-neutral. By contrast, both the essentialist and the embedded perspectives claim that gender relations continue to be an integral part of the structuring of bureaucratic organisation rather than a superficial and/or outdated layer on top of an otherwise gender-neutral system. Both the perspectives to which we now turn 'unpack' the gendered subtext of organisation.

The essentialist account of gender and organisation

Standing in opposition to a contingent analysis of gender and bureaucracy is the suggestion that the bureaucratic form of organisation is inherently, or essentially, masculinist. That is, bureaucracy reflects a *specifically male* way of organising, so even if women are moving into more senior posts within bureaucracies, we should not assume that these organisations are losing their patriarchal character or masculinist underpinnings. In this approach the particular gender of the incumbents of bureaucratic posts is of little significance in determining the extent to which organisations are gendered, since bureaucracy is inherently male. Even if some women get into senior posts, they do so at the expense of co-option into male cultures: they will still be marked out from men and their organisational power will be undermined.

This view is developed most articulately by Ferguson (1984), Ferguson's account, like Kanter's, draws upon a Weberian view of bureaucratic organisations, except that she sees this as inherently masculine rather than gender-neutral. Ferguson makes this claim on the grounds that men are socialised into certain ways of being which they have 'bureaucratised into' the large organisations that they dominate. So whereas Kanter 'holds apart' gender and organisation, viewing rational bureaucratic forms of organisation as having absolutely nothing to do with gender, Ferguson collapses all forms of bureaucratic activity into the gender of its agents. Women, who are socialised into feminine ways of behaving and relating to others, are necessarily muted within this masculinist setting. Bureaucratic relationships between subordinates and superiors in organisations mirror the relationships that women have with men within the broader social relations of patriarchy, again endorsing the idea of an overlap between patriarchal and bureaucratic power. Ferguson's view is that:

> it is not just the case that women's voices are muted within the bureaucratic discourse, and their modes of acting and relating to others submerged within bureaucratic structures, but also that bureaucratic discourse and structure are masculinist and antithetical to feminist modes of organising (Witz and Savage, 1992: 20).

Ferguson believes that feminine ways of organising, based upon a special feminine capacity for friendship, stand in contrast to male bureaucratic forms of organisation. This perspective has been adopted by some feminist groups that have attempted to organise in ways which assiduously avoid bureaucratic procedures and instead emphasise non-hierarchical and co-operative forms of organisation (for examples see Dominelli, 1991; Brown, 1992; Halford, 1992).

It is important to make clear that Ferguson's argument does not rest on a *biological* essentialism, although accounts within this perspective on gender and organisations may do so. Rather, Ferguson claims that it is *social* processes that have attached fixed and coherent characteristics to the categories of 'man' and 'woman' and resulted in gender-specific modes of behaviour, action and, hence, organisation. However, even if not strictly essentialist, such universalising claims have become increasingly difficult to sustain in the face of powerful critiques of the category of 'woman' within much feminist writing, which have emerged particularly from black feminists (hooks, 1982; Hill-Collins, 1990) and also from post-structuralist and post-modern feminists (for example, Butler, 1990; Callas, 1992). Such writers argue that the notion of a universal and coherent category of 'woman' bears little relation to the diverse experiences of different women. Furthermore, it is claimed that dominant representations of 'woman' within feminist theory are in fact drawn from the experiences of white, mainly middle class and academic women whose universalising of their own experience effectively silences other experiences, constituting in itself another form of oppression. Ferguson's account might thus be criticised for valorising fixed gender identities, experiences and behaviour, and succumbing to a form of essentialism, assuming an essential femininity and an essential masculinity, albeit socially constructed (Spellman, 1988; Fuss, 1989).

The research described in this book has also led us to be wary of essentialist claims. Although this may sound banal, it is important to state that both the women and the men we spoke to had very different views and practices, and to collapse these into two stark categories would be to deny them their own voice on the issues addressed in this book and to refuse to recognise their agency in affecting their social environment. As we go on to explore, men articulated different forms of masculine identity – occasionally voicing criticisms of the patriarchal character of their organisations. Many women who had struggled hard to develop their careers, and to challenge their organisations, in varied, imaginative and sometimes unconventional ways, would not recognise the dismissal of their efforts as useless in the face of the male bureaucratic monolith. Essentialist assumptions do not help to illuminate the more messy and complex views of the people we talked to, and we have tried to develop a perspective that recognises that our respondents are knowledgeable agents with meaningful contributions to make to our analysis.

However, whilst we endorse the arguments against essentialism – of either a biological or a socially constructionist nature – we maintain that gender relations, masculinities and femininities, and associated values, opportunities and resources, constitute significant social, cultural and economic divisions in contemporary society (although these are complex, fractured and sometimes contradictory). Gender is a key constitutive component of the field of social, economic and political relations that make up the terrain within which ways of organising are forged and constructed. Indeed, the notion that gender is embedded in the constitution of all economic, social and cultural processes is gaining increasing currency within feminist theory (Connell, 1987; Acker, 1990, 1992; Adkins and Lury, 1994). That is to say, there are no 'pure', gender-free, economic, social or cultural processes, but that gender is always implicated:

> Gendered processes do not occur outside other social processes but are integral parts of those processes – for example class and race relations – which cannot be fully understood without a comprehension of gender. At the same time class and race are integral to gender relations (Acker, 1992: 251).

Following this general proposition, an alternative approach to the study of gender and organisations emerges which suggests that organisational designs, practices and cultures are constructed within economic, social and cultural processes that are always already gendered. Unlike Kanter we suggest that 'organisation' cannot be seen as somehow above or beyond society and social relations, either in practice or as an ideal type. We are not suggesting, as Ferguson does, that there is such a neat historical correspondence between bureaucracy and a universal masculinity, or a parallel between bureaucratic relations and a simple rendering of gender relations (i.e. men/dominating/in senior positions and women/subordinated/in junior positions). Instead, we should see gender relations within organisations as complex, dynamic and, potentially at least, unpredictable.

An embedded approach to gendered organisation

A key feature of the embedded perspective is that 'organisation' is seen to be a *socially situated practice*. Bureaucratic organisation exists within a field of dynamic social, economic and cultural relations. There is no finite end state of purely instrumental and technical procedures that can be achieved once the 'wrinkles' have been ironed out. Features of rationality, impersonality and continuity are certainly central to ideal-typical, and indeed self-referential, definitions of bureaucracy. However, 'rationality' must be understood within a gendered field of social relations, both historically and in everyday assumptions and practices.

Linked to this point, the embedded perspective emphasises that organisations cannot be understood as depersonalised systems. Of course, many organisational theorists from Mayo onwards have criticised the Weberian/Taylorist perspective on bureaucracy,

arguing that organisations can never separate off the human attributes of their employees (for example, Crozier, 1961; Morgan, 1986).
Inevitably, workers bring with them a range of human emotions
and behaviours that may not (or may) concur with official organisational functions or procedures. It is therefore common to suggest
that organisations have both a *formal* and an *informal* structure
(Crozier, 1964) where the formal structure refers to the technical
establishment of organisational designs and procedures that can be
expected to display the classic features of Weberian bureaucratic
organisation (rationality, impersonality, rule bound, and so on).
However, the 'human relations school' of organisational theorists
(amongst others) argues that alongside this there is an informal
structure in which individuals and social groups within organisations express and pursue particular interests and feelings, behaving
in 'personalised' ways distinct from the formal aspects of organisation. These ideas about the informal aspects of organisational life
have made an important contribution to organisational theory and
have been cited as an aspect of gender relations in organisations
(Ressner, 1987). However, the embeddedness of gender relations
within organisations must be seen as going deeper than the level of
the 'informal' or else this would leave cherished notions of the
rationality of 'formal' organisation untouched by a feminist critique.
This has become untenable following convincing critiques by
Pringle (1989b) and others, which show that whilst the
rational–legal, bureaucratic form *presents* itself, in Weber's analysis, as
gender-neutral, it in fact constitutes a new kind of patriarchal structure where 'The apparent neutrality of rules and goals disguises the
class and gender interests served by men' (Pringle, 1989b: 161).
There is, then, an unthematised, gendered subtext within Weber's
own account of rationality, and this relates to the way in which the
personal, the sexual and the feminine are excluded from any definition of 'rationality' (Pringle, 1989b; Bologh, 1990). It is vital, then,
to recognise how gender relations are embedded within both the
informal and formal relations of organisations.[2]

Acker's recent work provides an excellent account of the ways
in which gendered social relations are embedded in contemporary bureaucratic organisations (Acker, 1990, 1992). It is worth
quoting her position at some length:

To say that an organisation, or any other analytic unit, is gendered means that advantage and disadvantage, exploitation and control, action and emotion, meaning and identity, are patterned through and in terms of a distinction [or, we would say, distinctions] between male and female, masculine and feminine. Gender is not an addition to those processes, conceived as gender neutral. Rather, it is an integral part of those processes, which cannot be properly understood without an analysis of gender (Acker, 1990: 146).

Thus, Acker suggests, bureaucratic organisation has a 'gendered substructure'. That is, the social practices that are generally understood to constitute 'organisation' rest on certain gendered processes and assumptions. Acker defines this substructure as follows:

The gendered substructure lies in the spatial and temporal arrangements of work, in the rules prescribing workplace behaviour, and in the relations linking work places to living places. These practices and relations, encoded in arrangements and rules, are supported by assumptions that work is separate from the rest of life and that it has the first claim on the worker (1992: 255).

Here Acker is arguing that organisational designs and established norms are far closer to men's lives and assumptions about men (for example, men as rational, goal oriented and with a primary commitment to the workplace) than to women's lives and the assumptions made about women (for example, women as emotional and with a primary commitment to home and family). The particular power of the gendered substructure of organisation lies in the fact that it is rarely recognised as such. Established organisational designs and practices are usually simply assumed to be the best way of organising and as such gender-neutral (cf. Kanter, 1977). The gendered substructure is hidden under a shell of rationality and neutrality.

Acker's work is extremely helpful in pointing towards a number of issues that we will take up in our empirical analysis, where we seek to establish that the construction of male and female jobs, and career routes, is related to the symbols and cultural idioms deployed within organisations, and to explore how the sexualised interactions of male and female employees, linked to the ideas and values of the workers themselves, play a part in this. Acker points the way to a number of key insights that help us in this task. She shows how the social construction of 'organisation' means that organisation is *variable*, that it may be *contested* and that the *agency* of organisational members is central to the construction of 'organisation' as a lived practice.

Celia Davies' work also provides a fine example of the specific ways in which gender is embedded within the organisation of nursing (Davies, 1992). In common with the above account, Davies' analytical starting points are first that gender is 'built into the very design and functioning of organisations' (p. 230), and second that exploring gender in organisations does not mean simply the consideration of imported gender characteristics that women and men are assumed to bring with them as they enter an organisation, but rather seeing that gender relations are continually enacted *within* organisational contexts. Davies goes on to develop an historical account of the ways in which gender relations have been embedded into the organisation of paid work generally (using Acker's work as described above as an example) and in the organisation and management of health care more specifically. She argues that we will discover the experiential bases of gender-differentiated management styles – such as the 'coping management' style of nurse managers – not just by looking at women's experiences of gender relations outside the workplace, but more importantly by looking at their experiences of the gendering of the organisation of paid work itself.

Conceptualising 'organisation'

The embedded perspective that we have developed above contains some important implicit points about our theorisation of 'organisation'. We have established some of the ways in which we understand gender as an embedded property of organisational forms and relations, but what about 'organisation' itself? There is clearly considerable debate about what an organisation is and how organisations are changing. We wish to make explicit three points about our understanding of organisation.

First, we must not reify 'organisation' or portray organisations in 'ideal-typical' terms, as is the case within the Weberian tradition.[3] Kanter (1977) appears to regard bureaucracy as the universal zenith of good organisation. By contrast, a number of contemporary commentaries (arguably including some of Kanter's later work, e.g. Kanter, 1983) point to the declining salience of 'bureaucratic' forms of organisation in the modern world. Instead, it is claimed that transformations in the world economy will validate new, non-bureaucratic forms of organisation as instruments of firms' economic success in the current period. In this vein Lash and Urry's (1987) analysis of a shift from 'organised' to 'disorganised' capitalism captures in its very terminology the importance of transforming organisation, even though its direct significance is not addressed in their work. Other writers have argued that we are now witnessing the emergence of post-Fordist organisations, based not on the hierarchical, abstract principles of the 'modernist' bureaucracy (Clegg, 1990) but instead on de-layered, flexible organisation in which responsibility is delegated to workers. Furthermore, post-modern theorists suggest that far from discovering a new prescription for best organisation, we must recognise that there can no longer be one account of organisation, that organisation has to be embedded within specific cultural contexts, and that the old certainties of efficiency and rationality should be revealed as discursive expressions of power rather than abstract or neutral principles of 'good' organisation (Clegg, 1990; Morgan, 1990).

We do not share the view that an epochal and universal shift in global economics and forms of organisation is taking place. For example, rather than being a linear shift from one type of 'Fordist' organisation to a 'post-Fordist' one, different models of organisation co-exist simultaneously across the globe and in different industrial sectors. New forms of organisation (the 'flexible firm', etc.) have not totally eclipsed more established bureaucratic models; rather both forms of organisation co-exist (Sayer, 1989). These observations alert us to the fact that far from being a fixed arrangement of resources, or a universal goal, 'organisation', both in practice and discursively, is socially situated and subject to interpretation and redefinition. Existing accounts of gender and organisation tend to take 'bureaucracy' as fixed, elaborating on the gendering of static organisational forms. However, particularly at the present time, organisational forms are subject to change. The embedded perspective allows us to investigate the gendering of such restructuring and thus to consider the causes, content and implications of the changes described in our introduction with a greater degree of sophistication.

Thus we must recognise the specificities of different organisational forms, and this leads us to our second point, that the struggles and activities of organisational members to constitute and validate particular versions of 'organisation' are of crucial importance. Clegg's work is helpful here. Although Clegg does not himself point to the significance of gender, we endorse his view that:

> Organisations should not be conceptualised as the phenomenal expression of some inner principle such as economic exploitation or rationality... [but are] locales in which negotiation, contestation and struggle between organisationally divided and linked agencies is a routine occurrence (Clegg, 1989: 197–8).

Organisations are thus 'contested terrains', as are the specific configuration of gender relations therein.

Within our embedded perspective we suggest that existing organisational structures, practices and cultures are, in so far as they are stable, devices by which past forms of agency have been stored/sedimented so that they can be maintained/reactivated. This in turn shapes the activity of current organisational membership, which is itself constantly engaged in (re)structuring the organisation. Thus organisational structures, practices and cultures are devices by which past forms of agency are in a sense 'stored'. In as much as structures, practices and cultures remain constant, the effect of past agency is continuously reactivated, and even where change takes place it is on terrain defined by previous 'organisation'.

Each organisation has its own history, linked to the actions of its members as well as its wider social and political context, with the result that particular organisational forms and cultures are developed as the crystallisation of various forms of struggle, contestation and negotiation between various organisational members. These organisational practices, in all their diversity, become vehicles that allow the 'victors' at any one time period to sediment their success in a more durable form so that their advantages can be actualised − again − in the present.[4] Of course, in many cases the situation is confused by the fact that there may be no clear victors, or there may be contradictory outcomes, in which case different features of organisational life may be at odds or in conflict with each other. An example of this can be seen in the women's initiatives set up by local politicians during the 1980s to challenge gender inequalities in the design and practices of British local authorities. Once they tried to implement change across local authority organisations, these initiatives encountered great resistance mobilised through established bureaucratic procedures. However, they would occasionally find allies in unlikely places, with the result that their work would be embraced by one part of the bureaucracy at the same time as it was vilified by others (Halford, 1991).

The third and final point which we wish to emphasise in this section is that, from the human relations school onwards, it has been clear that organisations are 'peopled' institutions, animated by people who re-enact, reinterpret and (possibly) challenge existing practices and procedures. This is not to suggest that people entering organisations enter a field that is a blank space on which they can act freely. As we have argued above, historically established modes of organisation are vitally important in shaping current activities, in defining the terrain for new sets of conflicts and tensions. But, in turn, these conflicts and tensions may transform organisation, 'storing' different forms of agency and shaping future organisational activities and changes. This agentic account of organisation makes it difficult to draw hard and fast distinctions between organisational structures and organisational cultures. Clearly, at any one time structures such as grading systems, entrance requirements or administrative authority are identifiable and distinguishable from more nebulous values and expectations of practices determined in an unwritten way by organisational cultures and subcultures. However, organisational cultures also contribute to both the design and implementation (or non-implementation) of structures, and organisational structures will in turn contribute to the non-codified aspects of organisational life. For example, formal structures will influence the forms of social interaction that may take place (or are proscribed) within a given organisation, thus shaping – although clearly not determining – the generation of cultures and subcultures.

Thus far we have attempted to clarify our conceptual approach to the study of gender and organisation, debating and extending existing accounts within this field. However, as we signalled earlier, there are also at least two further areas of research that offer great potential for enhancing our embedded perspective on gender and organisation. First, there is a growing volume of literature addressing sexuality in an organisational context. The sexualisation of organisation is clearly relevant to gender in organisation (although it is not always presented as such). Any investigation of gender and organisation must consider this dimension. Second, the growing literature emphasising the significance of the body for social relations and social theory alerts us to the perhaps obvious point that gendered persons in organisations are also embodied. A very limited amount of attention has been paid to this topic within organisational studies, but it is a flourishing concern within sociology more generally and one which, we believe, has considerable potential for extending analysis of gender, sexualities and organisation.

Sexualities, gender and organisation

Sexuality is a demonstrably important aspect of organisational life (Hearn and Parkin, 1987; Pringle, 1989b; Adkins, 1995), and sexuality and gender are clearly intertwined with one another. In arguing that sexuality, as well as gender, is embedded within organisation we must clarify two central issues: first, the relationship between sexuality and organisation, and second, the relationship between sexuality and gender.

In the past decade increasing attention has been devoted to sexuality in an organisational context. This has emerged from two principal sources: one, radical feminist concern with the links between male power and sexual violence, which in turn led to the naming and study of 'sexual harassment' in the workplace as a mode of intimidation, verbal or physical, whereby men 'kept women in their place' (for example, MacKinnon, 1979; Stanko, 1988); the other, radical organisation theorists (ironically these were mainly men – as Burrell, 1984, notes) who declared that the issue of sex in organisations had been ignored for too long (Hearn and Parkin, 1983, 1987; Burrell, 1984). As Hearn and Parkin (1987) argued, the 'booming silence' about sexuality in the mountains of literature on organisations was surprising, given that workplace organisations often:

> include a mass of sexual displays, feelings, and innuendoes, as part of everyday organisational life, right through to sexual relationships, open or secret, occasional sexual acts, and sexual violations, including rape (1987: 3).

Far from desexualisation being seen as an historical corollary of rationalisation and civilisation under capitalism, as Burrell (1984) initially suggested, the sexualised underpinning of organisational power relations is now recognised. From this point it has been a short step to claims that sexuality is a crucial component of the organisational gender order. What has emerged out of both the radical feminist and radical organisation literature is a clear view that women's subordination at work is 'eroticised' or 'sexualised'.

Pringle's (1989b) study of secretaries was instrumental in placing the issue of sexuality and power at work at the centre of feminist analyses of gender relations in the workplace. Focusing on the relationship between (usually male) bosses and (usually female) secretaries, Pringle explored the way in which sexualised discourses of femininity, masculinity and family construct notions of what secretarial work involves and how secretaries

osses may interact. Rather than the role of secretaries
.g created as an economically rational response to the need
. *i* particular organisational tasks to be performed, their position
within organisational hierarchies and relationships has been
culturally and discursively constructed in non-rational, expres-
sive and sexualised ways. Unlike Kanter, Pringle does not see the
boss–secretary relationship as a patrimonial relic awaiting
modernisation, but as embedded within contemporary work
and organisational life.

The notion of pleasure is central to Pringle's analysis. Unlike
the radical feminist focus on the harassing aspects of sexualities
in organisations, Pringle draws attention not only to the plea-
sures that male bosses derive from their position *vis-à-vis* female
secretaries, but also to the ways in which subordinate women
derive pleasure from the relationship. In part Pringle suggests
that male bosses exploit women's pleasure as a form of control,
for example by establishing (through the personal nature of their
relationship) what their secretaries enjoy and using this in
manipulative ways. However, Pringle also takes a more psychoanalytic approach in suggesting that women's own desires and
fantasies may in some way be fulfilled through the boss–secretary relationship.

Pringle's arguments are extremely helpful in pointing to the
way in which cultural processes construct a sexualised
boss–secretary relationship. However, whilst we agree with
Pringle that sexuality is embedded in contemporary organisations, we have some concerns with her particular theoretical
position. Our most serious concern concerns the epistemolog-
ical assumptions underlying her arguments, which are never
entirely spelled out. Pringle appears to use two different episte-
mological frameworks in her account. One, derived from
Foucault and post-structuralism, points to the role of *discourse* in
constituting meaning and would seem to indicate a scepticism
regarding *structural* accounts of organisations. Yet Pringle also
draws upon elements of structuralist theories, especially where
she discusses the relationship between class and gender, and she
accepts the importance of structural constraints on individual
actions. For example, she describes the main reason for many

women taking on secretarial work as lack of any other opportunities (p. 157 ff.). In the introduction to her book Pringle remarks that 'the relationship between "discourses" and "structures" is a recurrent theme of this book' (p. 5). However, this is precisely the question that is rather left hanging in Pringle's account. In particular, the conceptual status that 'structures' are meant to have in those sections of analysis where Pringle adopts a more post-structuralist perspective is unclear.

Adkins and Lury (1996) argue that Pringle's post-structuralist perspective reduces both gender and sexuality in the workplace to cultural phenomena and suggest that there are at least two problems with this. First, Pringle fails to see how sexuality is embedded in *economic* as well as cultural processes in the workplace. Adkins' work on women workers in the leisure industries shows how women are constituted as a sexually *commodified* workforce, and that sexuality is central to the processes of production, appropriation and exploitation and not only a cultural phenomenon (Adkins, 1994). Pringle's work might well be used to confirm this point, although where she talks about the demands of production she seems to see these in purely economic terms, speaking of rationalisation, drives for efficiency and flexibility, and so on, bringing 'continuous changes in the demands for particular types and quantities of labour' (p. 157) but not speaking of the *sexualisation* of these 'demand' factors.

Arising from this, Adkins' and Lury's (1996) second criticism concerns what they see as the implications of *sexual voluntarism*, which infuse Pringle's account of sexuality in the workplace. Adkins and Lury claim that this leads Pringle to disassociate agency, pleasure and desire from the category 'gender', and the suggestion that women and men can both choose to play with sexual identities and activity. Adkins' and Lury's critique is harsh, playing down Pringle's recognition of structural constraints and gender inequalities and overplaying the voluntarism in Pringle's account of sexuality at work. Certainly, Pringle would like to establish 'women's rights to be subjects rather than objects of sexual discourse' (p. 100) within bureaucracies, but she well recognises that this does not currently happen and that transforming workplace sexuality in this way would pose a fundamental challenge to current constructions of female sexuality. Nonetheless, she believes that such a transformation is *possible* – maybe this is the key difference between Pringle and Adkins and Lury – and that in the meantime we must recognise that women might even derive pleasure out of sexuality as it is currently structured into organisational life.

Leaving this specific point aside, however, Adkins and Lury argue that it is Pringle's reliance on cultural and discursive processes that is the main problem, and that it is only by re-instating the social and the economic into the picture that the embeddedness of sexuality in the labour market (or in our case organisations) can be properly investigated. We share their concern, highlighting as it does some of the current conceptual ambiguity surrounding discussions of 'gender' and 'sexuality'. Many writers (within sociology, sexology and psychology) have placed gender and sexuality in a fixed relationship, suggesting that there is a single male and a single female sexuality, and that the primary axis of distinction is an active/passive dichotomy (Segal, 1994). Conversely, others have suggested that sexuality floats free from gender, being fixed in neither form nor experience.

Space does not permit an exhaustive overview of this debate, but our argument here does not endorse either position. Of course sexuality cannot be tied to gender in a fixed or universal way, but nor can sexuality be disassociated from gender. Acker (1990) views sexuality as 'part of the ongoing production of gender' (p. 250–1) whilst, in turn, we would suggest that gender is also part of the ongoing production of sexuality. We see no need to deny the reciprocity of this relationship. More generally, we take the view, along with Adkins and Lury (1996), that theories of gender, organisations and the labour market must guard against an over-valorisation of 'the cultural' in explorations of sexuality and power in workplace organisations, which has led to a 'retiring' of the economic and the social. If gender is seen as embedded in the very constitution of social and economic as well as cultural processes, and sexuality is seen as part of the ongoing production of gender, we then see this as the most fruitful way to move forward, working within a framework that seeks constantly to integrate an analysis of gender and sexuality into processes where the social, the economic and the cultural are constituted. However, we are not as confident as Adkins and Lury that 'the social', 'the economic' and 'the cultural' can be readily or distinctly separated (see Chapter 3 for elaboration of this point). An embedded perspective on gender and organisation must recognise the ongoing relationship between gender and sexuality as well as the sexualised underpinnings of aspects of organisational experience.

Gendered bodies and organisation

People in organisations are not 'abstracted from' their bodies, although on reading much organisational theory one might have got this impression! Within organisational theory, as elsewhere, the body has tended to take the status of an 'absent presence' (Shilling, 1993), at once obvious and yet analytically unproblematised, even obscured. However, once it is recognised that both gender and sexuality are embedded within 'organisation', this draws attention to the embodiment of organisational actors. Both gender and sexuality are inscribed on, marked by and lived through bodies. In this section we will suggest that bureaucratic organisation draws on particular constructions of embodiment which are both gendered and sexualised. In other words organisations validate or permit certain 'styles of the flesh' (to draw on Butler's, 1990, phraseology) and invalidate or banish others.

Female and male bodies do (usually) act as identifiers for differentiated treatment, opportunities and expectations in a way which dramatically extends the significance of biological distinctions between the sexes. Acker (1990, 1992) goes further and suggests that not only is the socially constructed gendered body significant in shaping the ways in which women and men are treated, but also that assumptions about embodiment are built into the very foundations of social institutions, particularly bureaucratic organisation. Following on from her argument that bureaucracies covertly privilege attributes linked to masculinity, and male work life arrangements, Acker suggests that bureaucratic organisation has naturalised the capacities and (common) uses of the male body. She says:

> it is the man's body, its sexuality, minimal responsibility in procreation and conventional control of emotions that pervades work and organisational processes. Women's bodies – female sexuality, their ability to procreate and their pregnancy, breast-feeding... menstruation and mythic 'emotionality' – are suspect, stigmatised, and used as grounds for control and exclusion... Whilst women's bodies are ruled out of order, or sexualised or objectified in work organisations, men's are not (Acker, 1990: 152).

We would be more circumspect here and prefer to say that bureaucracy endorses *certain* sorts of body usage and relationship that tend to privilege particular versions of male bodies or male styles of the flesh. That is to say, we do not support the notion of 'a' male body or body usage (see discussion of Frank, 1991, in Chapter 6).

The list of gender–embodied features which Acker gives in the quotation above is interesting since she mixes social constructions of what it means to have a female or male body (emotionality/lack of emotions) with actual bodily processes (menstruation, pregnancy). (Her use of the term 'sexuality' is unclear in this context.) This raises some important questions. Is the significance of the sexed body only a socially constructed one? What is the significance of material, physical bodily processes?

Like others, we believe that the distinction between the physical body and the socially constructed body is an increasingly difficult, perhaps even impossible, one to make (Martin, 1987; Gatens, 1990, 1996; Shilling, 1993). Instead, we follow recent injunctions to understand the body as not only socially constructed but also having a material dimension, including different capacities for reproduction, whilst recognising that 'materiality' is never a fixed substructure but only realised and always subject to transformation in particular ways in different places and at different times.

Having said all this, most of the discussions around this topic in this book are based on social constructions of the gendered body. At the time we designed our research we had no idea that these issues would be as important as they have turned out to be, and our methods were not appropriate for exploring the questions raised above in any depth. However, it is clear from our material that the body is a significant component of discourses around gender and sexuality in organisations and, furthermore, that one way of exploring both these dimensions without prioritising one or other is through a notion of a 'politics of the body' (Burrell and Hearn, 1989; Cockburn, 1991). In her study of men's resistance to equal opportunities for women in organisations, Cockburn reveals men's relation to equal opportunities for women in organisations as one which takes on board the principle of equal treatment by arguing that women must assimilate and strive to be indistinguishable from men, yet at the same time insists that women are *'naturally'* different, evoking the *reproductive body* − constructed as the kernel of difference within the shell of equality − as the ultimate justification for women's lower pay, status and opportunities. In this way we see how an organisational politics of the body ultimately evokes the 'woman in the body' (Martin, 1987) as the bottom line of gender inequality and male privilege in organisations. Aside from acquiring discursive significance, the womanly body, the reproductive body, is also literally ruled out of place in organisations that make few provisions enabling women to deal more easily with bodily processes such as menstruation, lactation or the premenstrual tension that many women experience (Martin, 1987; Cockburn, 1991).

Thus the notion of a politics of the body also encompasses the complex rules and activities that organisational actors engage with in presenting and comporting their bodies in everyday organisational life. Body size and shape, clothing and style, as well as manner and demeanour, clearly shape the ways in which people are seen at work, as well as being linked to the kinds of job that they do ('attractive' young women in receptionist posts or six-foot, 20-stone men in security work). Managing self-presentation is part of the on-going daily work that many organisational members engage in, involving considerable internal mental work, as well as physical effort and (often) expense. Finally, a notion of a politics of the body is also a productive way of thinking about forms of sexual harassment in the workplace, which invokes embodiment through verbal reference and/or physical actions.

Conclusions

In this chapter we have critiqued contingent and essentialist accounts of gender and organisation and provided an extended introduction to the 'embedded' perspective on gender and organisation which informs our analysis of gender, careers and organisational change in this book. The issues we have raised here will be developed and exemplified using empirical material from our case study organisations in banking, nursing and local government. In doing so, we intend to develop further some of the introductory analytical and theoretical points made in this chapter. However, before we proceed to our analysis, it is first important to introduce our case study organisations and to explain how we adopted certain research methods.

2 Researching Organisations

Introduction

This book is structured thematically around core analytical and theoretical debates on gender and organisation, each chapter using material from organisations across the three sectors of banking, health and local government. No one chapter specifically provides background contextual information on any of these organisations. Before proceeding to our analytical chapters we provide some descriptive information in order to paint a broad picture of the nature of gender relations in our case studies. Here we can provide information on sex segregation by grade and type of job, and, in some cases, statistics on recent patterns of change. This is also the only place where we can paint a full picture of the particular histories and features of each of our organisations. Readers who are primarily interested in the conceptual themes of this book might prefer to pass over this chapter and refer to it for reference as appropriate, but in this case a considerable amount of contextual information will be missed. This chapter also explains the ways in which we carried out our research in these organisations, describing the methods used to explore the issues raised in Chapter 1, as well as commenting more generally on our methodology and research philosophy.

Comparative research design

Our research design was comparative along two dimensions. First, because we used a case study approach we needed to select organ- isations which allow theoretically pertinent comparisons to be made. The specific organisations in each of three sectors we exam- ined share similarities in that they are all large bureaucracies oper- ating in the 'service' sector.[1] All employed substantial numbers of women in routine white collar occupations, some women in professional posts (many, of course, in nursing) and a few in management positions. This makes them ideal sectors in which to pursue our interests. However, alongside this broad similarity there are also some important differences between the three sectors. Hospitals and local government offices are public sector organisations containing professional hierarchies with a strong emphasis upon vocational qualifications and specialisation of competence, whilst banking is private sector managerial hierarchy, demanding no pre-entry professional qualifications. Although there is an accelerated graduate–entry career track in banking, most employees still follow a single career trajectory that starts in clerical work and stretches up into senior management. By comparison, the career ladders in local government are far more fragmented and specialised, and nursing too offers a greater degree of occupational specialism (usually credentialised) following initial entry. So recruitment and promotion practices in the three sectors have historically been rather different, and throughout this book we explore the significance of this for the gendering of careers. Nursing is also different from banking and local government in having traditionally been a female-dominated occupation, and that allows us a further point of comparison.

The second comparative dimension of our research was the fact that we compared organisations in two different local areas.[2] Drawing on debates in economic and social geography (Massey, 1984; Cooke, 1989), it has been argued that local labour markets have rather different properties, and in particular that gender rela- tions vary significantly between areas (Walby and Bagguley, 1991). It is possible that the recruitment and promotion of women may be affected by the state of the local economy, so that organisations will boost women's career opportunities when labour supply is tight. One of our case study areas, Southtown, is a medium-sized new town in the South East of England, which had experienced rapid and diverse economic growth throughout the 1980s and, at the time we designed our research, had one of the lowest unemployment rates in the country. In 1990 the unemployment rate was 1.9 per cent and the average period of unemployment was just 6 weeks. In the 1980s employers in Southtown were facing severe recruitment problems and employers' organisations were recommending radical changes to employment practice – including new ways to facilitate the employment of women – as the only way forward. The second area, Midcity, is a much larger metropolitan area with a traditional manufacturing base, which has been severely hit by deindustrialisation but continues to be a major regional centre for producer services, as well as being a retail and administrative centre for the region. Unemployment in the city remained high throughout the 1980s, although, even here, some specific labour shortages were reported towards the end of the decade.

However, it became clear to us that local labour market factors were of relatively little importance in shaping gender and careers in our organisations. One reason for this may be the onset of economic recession in 1990, which brought a decisive end to most of the labour shortages, even in Southtown. Perhaps if we had carried out our study two years earlier we would have observed more differences. Certainly, plans for a bank crèche, which had been drawn up in Southtown in the late 1980s, were shelved during 1991, indicating that labour market circumstances might indeed be closely tied into employment policies regarding women – although this explanation was officially denied. Also, by 1991, local government employees in Southtown were aware that their relative job security was a considerable bonus compared with private sector workers, whereas several years previously they had seen themselves as the 'poor relations' in terms of pay and conditions. (In Midcity the security and comparatively good pay and conditions offered by the public sector appear to have been appreciated right throughout the 1980s.)

Therefore, by the time we carried out our research, it seemed that differences between the sectors and organisations in Midcity and Southtown had little to do with locally specific labour market factors. As we shall discuss in Chapter 4, most employees had worked for their current organisations for many years and felt isolated from the immediate effects of local labour market conditions. This may be another reason why local labour markets had a limited effect on our research. Had we studied occupational careers, and movement between different employers, the state of the local labour market may have proved more significant. As it was, our research revealed that the comparative *sizes* of organisations in the two towns – with those in Midcity tending to be significantly larger than those in Southtown – were the most important difference between the two areas. Linked to this, in both nursing and local government, the organisations in Midcity had a reputation and position of national importance. By comparison, the organisations in Southtown were extremely small and attached to a rural and suburban, rather than metropolitan, environment. For these reasons the labour market comparison is not discussed systematically during the course of this book. Only where significant differences appear do we refer to them in the text. Generally, where comparisons are made between Midcity and Southtown – and these are considerable – they concern the impact of size, history and (to a lesser extent) politics on organisational forms and consequently on gender and careers.

Having provided this general background, we now turn to examine in more detail some of the specific characteristics of the organisations we studied in our research. Our aim is to describe the basic features of the organisational structures, and to come to some preliminary conclusion about the changing nature of gender relations in each of them. Readers should bear in mind that respect for the anonymity of our organisations has constrained the level of detail we can provide.

Local government

In 1990 British local authorities employed nearly three million people, or one in eight of all employees in the country. Despite public sector cuts during the 1980s, local government employment fell by only 4 per cent from 1979 to 1990, and most of this was accounted for by wholesale privatisations such as those of bus companies. In housing and social services the numbers employed rose during the 1980s by 36 per cent and 22 per cent respectively. There are a number of reasons why we might expect local government to provide particularly good opportunities for women workers. For a start as many as 60 per cent of all local government employees are now women. Although many of these women work in part-time and manual jobs, the dominance of professional staff in local government hierarchies may offer women opportunities to use 'the qualifications lever' (Crompton and Sanderson, 1990.) Furthermore, the presence of welfare and education professions in local government may offer women particularly enhanced opportunities, given the stereotypical links between these 'caring professions' and femininity, and the greater presence of women in these areas. (We explore this question, through a comparison with a traditionally masculine area of work, throughout the book.) Finally, some have suggested that organisational cultures in local government may be more supportive to women than are those in other sectors (Crompton and Jones, 1984). Although at the time of Crompton and Jones' study there were no more women in senior positions in local government than in banking, they were optimistic that change was on the horizon. Since Crompton and Jones carried out their study, little research has been carried out on the careers of local government workers, but there are a number of reasons to suppose that their predictions may have been borne out. Perhaps the greatest of these is the rapid expansion of equal opportunities (EO) policies for women in local government during the 1980s. By 1988 63 per cent of all authorities had made some EO provisions (beyond statutory requirements) (Halford, 1991). Many of these concerned the local authority's role as employer and emphasised the importance of enhancing women's careers.

These observations clearly make local goverment an excellent arena for exploring the gendering of organisational life and employment careers. However, beyond these basic points we must be aware of the very great diversity both *within* authorities and *between* authorities. Internally, each authority contains a number of different occupational hierarchies. Each of the professional groups – from accountancy to architecture to planning and social work – tends to be arranged in its own autonomous way. In addition to these professional groups, local authorities employ a great number of clerical and administrative and manual staff as well as specialists in areas such as computing and policy analysis. This complex range of occupations is ordered into different but often overlapping hierarchies. These arrangements may vary from one authority to another, and this point leads us to the second axis of differentiation in the sector.

There are enormous variations in the size of local authorities, in terms of both the population covered (from 12,000 to 2,000,000) and the number of staff employed (from a few hundred to tens of thousands). In addition, larger metropolitan authorities have more statutory (legal) duties than smaller district councils. However, authorities are also allowed some leeway in the organisation and implementation of statutory services and this varies according to history and tradition, geography and local politics. Of course, unlike both banking and nursing, the executive decision-making body in local authorities is comprised (officially at least) of elected politicians, and this may on occasion result in dramatic changes of policy and priorities. This may also be connected to local variations in internal structure and management systems (Leach *et al.*, 1994). For example, different jobs may exist from one authority to another, and apparently similar jobs may be graded differently. Furthermore, local authorities are allowed some discretion in going beyond statutory provision, for example in the development of EO initiatives that go beyond the letter of the law.

In short, diversity both within and between local authorities makes it likely that gender is embedded in local authority organisations in differing ways, and that women's and men's work experiences and career opportunities will vary from one authority to another. In designing our research we wanted to recognise the diversity of local government employment, whilst not being overwhelmed by such variety. We therefore limited our study to white collar staff[3] in just two departments – Housing and Finance. This simplified the range of professions and occupations involved and allowed us to research the same departments in both authorities. Housing Departments manage and maintain the Council's housing stock, which involves housing officers as well as surveyors, maintenance workers and ancillary support workers. Finance Departments manage local authority budgets, dealing both with income from council tax, rents and other services, and monitoring or controlling outgoings such as the payroll, the purchase of supplies and benefit payments. These two particular departments were also chosen as a deliberate contrast to one another. Whereas finance is highly professionalised and has a conservative and masculine image (Silverstone, 1980), housing has been less fully professionalised and has a more progressive image. This is linked both to the welfare/caring nature of the work and to some involvement of housing professionals in the new urban left during the 1980s (Gyford, 1985). Although both Midcity Council and Southtown Council had Housing and Finance Departments, they were important differences in size and structure. In the following sections we briefly describe our two authorities, their structure and management and our general impressions of the two departments in each case in order to consider some of the broad features of gendered inequality involved.

Southtown District Council

Southtown District Council covers a medium-sized new town in South East England. The council is controlled by a traditional, moderate Labour Party. The local authority has an orthodox departmental structure, based on functional specialisms, and employs under 1,500 staff (1991). Two-thirds of staff are in white collar posts. Women comprise just under half the total workforce and just over half the white collar workforce. Women are heavily concentrated in the most junior white collar jobs (Table 2.1).

Table 2.1 indicates clearly the stark relationship between sex and position in the organisational hierarchy. Nearly all senior officers are male, whilst nearly all junior posts are filled by women. This having been said, the proportion of women employed in intermediate and senior clerical grades increased significantly over the five years to 1991. This has coincided with the adoption of an EO policy in the authority, which has resulted in changes to the recruitment and selection procedure, the introduction of a job-share policy and a subsidised workplace nursery for children aged two to five. It is certainly possible that these initiatives have had some impact on the appointment of women. However, within the authority, there remains considerable scepticism as to how far Chief Officers in each Department (who still have the main responsibility for recruitment and selection) are committed to EO. In the present economic climate it seems that EO is receiving less backing from elected councillors, and there is a widely perceived sense that EO was actually a response to past labour shortages and thus no longer 'necessary'. This might indicate that the recruitment of women from 1986–1991 was an outcome of labour shortages at the time and that the trend might not continue into the 1990s.

Table 2.1   **Distribution of white collar staff by grade and sex: Southtown District Council, February 1991 and March 1986**

Grade	Women (%)	
	1991	*1986*
Chief Officer	4.5	–
Principal Officer	10.2	1.9
Senior Officer	17.3	11.1
Clerical: Scale 5/6	38.4	16.8
Scale 3/4	55.4	56.0
Scale 1/2	89.3	87.3

Source: Internal statistics 1991

The Treasurer's Department: This department is divided into three sections: accountancy and audit (the 'professional' side), exchequer and computing. Overall, the Department employs under 200 staff (full-time equivalent), approximately 63 per cent of whom are women. Accountancy and audit is where most of the professionally qualified staff – CIPFA[4] staff – are located, and this section has the most senior posts and most male employees. By contrast, most women here are in support and administrative work. Women employees are most likely to be found in the 'Exchequer', which deals mainly with community charge and benefits, where 85 per cent of staff in this section are women. The career ladder is short, stopping at Senior Officer level and offering no possibility of progression beyond this point. The computing section employs a combination of analysts, program-mers and data entry staff. Half the women employed in this section are in data entry posts, and the programming/analysis side is almost exclusively male. The computing manager post is graded higher than benefits management, but promotion beyond this point would not happen in this authority.

A senior officer in the authority described the Treasurer's Department to us as 'authoritarian, top-down, unparticipative and *ad hoc*'. Communication within the Department was described as poor, and there was thought to be little sense of team spirit. Nonetheless, the Department fulfilled its functions faultlessly and it was difficult to challenge its authority within the organisation.

Housing and Estates: The Housing and Estates Department also has three divisions: housing management, technical services and valuation, each headed up by second-tier managers who report to the Chief Housing and Estates Officer. The Department employs over 100 staff (full-time equivalent), of whom 50 per cent are women. The predominantly male housing management division accounts for over half of all staff, and is split into two, each section with responsibility for a geographically defined area of the town. The only female Chief Officer in the authority was in this department. Housing management contains the most senior posts and the professional housing staff, but valuation also has senior posts and qualified surveyors. Within the authority the Department is seen as more communicative and better managed than Borough Treasurers, although the Chief Officer has a repu-tation for being 'tough' and having a tendency to invoke disciplinary procedures over relatively minor incidents, causing departmental resentment.

Even in a relatively small authority such as Southtown, there is clear evidence that employment is clearly fragmented by department as well as by specialisms within it. There is preliminary evidence that men and women continue to be divided along these axes, and later chapters will consider this issue in more detail. Let us now turn to the larger authority of Midcity.

Midcity Council

Midcity Council covers a large metropolitan area in the Midlands. It is controlled by the Labour Party, which contains a substantial left grouping, able to exert some influence on policy and practice, although overall local politics remain to the centre-right of the political spectrum. The majority of the authority's departments are based on functional specialisms, but during the mid-1980s the service departments have been decentralised into multi-function neighbourhood offices across the city.

In 1991 the authority employed over 50,000 staff, including 17,500 part-time workers, making a full-time equivalent worforce of nearly 41,000 staff. Women make up 49 per cent of this workforce but over 85 per cent of the part-time staff. Over 86 per cent of part-time workers are on manual grades.

Table 2.2 suggests that, as with Southtown, Midcity is characterised by a clear gender hierarchy. However, compared with Southtown there are far more women in senior posts (nearly three times as many in Principal Officer and Chief Officer posts), and there is a slightly higher proportion of men in junior posts. EO initiatives relating to women workers are more developed than in Southtown, developed primarily by a central Directorate of Management and Personnel. At the time of our research, the 'city-wide' (cross-authority) initiatives especially relevant to the employment and career development of women were flexi- time, job-share possibilities for most jobs, extended maternity leave, adoptive parents leave and family-related leave provisions, and positive action training for career progression. In addition, all those involved in recruitment were required to undertake EO recruitment and selection training. All departments are offically obliged to implement these initiatives, although it is not clear that they all do, and were encouraged to develop their own enhanced policies.

Table 2.2 **Proportion of workers in different grades who are women: Midcity Council 1991**

Grade	Women (%)
Chief Officer	14
Principal Officer	
PO 4–8	28
PO 1–3	26
Senior Officer	31
Clerical: Scale 6	54
Scale 4/5	55
Scale 2/3	67
Scale 1	80

Source: Internal statistics

Treasurer's Department: With over 1,500 staff this department employs more people than the total workforce of Southtown District Council! The departmental structure is more complex than is the case at Southtown, reflecting both the relative sizes of the two authorities and the broader range of activities in a metropolitan authority. All the staff in City Treasurers are in white collar posts and there are fewer than 7 per cent part-time workers. Women make up 58 per cent of the Departmental workforce. As many as 90 per cent of women are in clerical and administrative posts at grade 6 or lower, and there are fewer women in senior posts (principal officer and above) than is average in the authority. Thus the Treasurer's Department appears to be something of a male bastion.

There are six subsections: accounting services, exchequer services and technical services, supplies, revenues, management and audit, each with its own internal hierarchy reaching up to management team level. Qualified accountants run the first three sections whilst the other three are run by non-CIPFA staff. The Chief Officer is always a CIPFA accountant. The whole management team is white and male. At the time of our research the City Treasurer's Department had made no additions to the city-wide EO package, although extended efforts were made to implement the policies on time off for sick dependants and EO advertising.

The size as well as the decentralisation of some staff to service departments (housing, social services, etc.) makes it difficult to derive an overall 'sense' of the Department, and this is compounded by the recent influx of 700 staff into a new benefits section in the Department as well as recent efforts from senior management to 'change the culture' of the Department (an issue which we discuss at length in Chapter 3). However, through interviews and observation it seems that the Department is a conservative one, in comparison with others across the authority, and that it holds a position of considerable power, as is common for finance departments in local government.

The Housing Department: Midcity's Housing Department employs over 4,000 staff across four main directorates: housing management, housing services, housing improvement and building services. Almost all the staff in housing management are on white collar grades, whilst in building services the majority of staff are in manual grades. Each directorate has its own internal management hierarchy, headed by an Assistant Director of Housing. The size of this Department, compared with that of Southtown, offers more opportunities because of staff turnover and because there is a broader range of posts, graded to relatively senior levels.

Women make up 45 per cent of full-time workers and 98 per cent of the part-time workforce.

The Housing Department has the best representation of women in senior posts of all the four departments we researched – although with no female chief officers and only 10 per cent of senior principal officers posts held by women, this is still a limited achievement. The Department has extended the city-wide package of EO measures by transferring all part-time Administrative, Professional, Technical and Clerical (APT&C) staff onto job-share contracts and was considering introducing a career break scheme. Key informants placed emphasis on the fact that Housing *did actually* implement the city-wide measures – implying that this was not the case in all departments.

Table 2.3   **Full-time APT&C staff by grade and sex: Housing Department, Midcity Council**

Grade	Women (%)
Chief Officers	–
Principal Officers	
PO 4–8	10
PO 1–3	27
Senior Officers	27
Clerical: Scale 6	No staff in this grade
Scale 4/5	52
Scale 2/3	82
Scale 1	61

Source: Internal statistics

Summary

In broad terms the position of women continues to be one in which they are under-represented in senior positions, although there is evidence that women are making inroads into Senior Officer posts. We have also noted that broad lines of differentiation, between more masculine Treasurers Departments and less masculine Housing Departments, are modified in the context of specific authorities. The size and associated diversity of both Departments in Midcity offers a greater range and volume of opportunity, and possibly more chance to build an organisational career within the authority. Midcity has also been involved in more innovative management and policy initiatives than Southtown, a function certainly of local politics and of a commitment to make initiatives worthy of a city of this size and national importance, something we explore in depth in the next chapter. Midcity also has more women workers in senior positions than is the case in Southtown, and elaborating the links between this pattern and specific organisational features and processes will be one of the concerns of the following chapters. Southtown is a small and mainly traditional authority, although some steps have been taken – such as the EO policies – which distinguish it from most other comparable authorities in the South East. Despite this, size and a low turnover restricts organisational opportunities. The number of women in senior positions is very small, and the only woman in a Chief Officer's post has left the authority since the time of our research.

Banking

'Sellbank' has been one of the major British clearing banks since the early 20th century and, in common with the entire financial services sector, was undergoing major restructuring in the period of our research (see Chapter 3 for a fuller discussion of this). Our decision to use a major clearing bank as a case study continues a long research tradition of studying gender relations in banking. This tradition has been stimulated partly by the fact that banks are known to offer one of the most dramatic and clearest examples of patriarchal exclusion of women (until the First World war women were hardly ever employed in this sector), and subsequently by the demarcation of women employees, where women were employed on specific 'women–only' grades and conditions of services until the later 1960s (see generally Crompton and Jones, 1984; Crompton, 1989; Llewellyn, 1981; Savage, 1992, 1993). Thus, although women came to comprise the majority of bank employees by the 1960s, they were employed on separate grades from men (in which their salary increments were not permitted to increase to the level which men could expect), usually performed specifically 'female' tasks (such as typing, bookkeeping and, from the 1950s, cashiering work), were expected to leave work on marriage and had virtually no chance of promotion to managerial rank. For these reasons banking has, historically, been an illuminating sector in which to examine how women have been incorporated into forms of paid employment in ways that ensured that they were subordinate to men.

Recent research has focused on developments that appear to suggest a major redefinition of gender relations in the banking industry. Following the formal outlawing of gender discrimination by EO legislation in the early 1970s, all the banks were forced to restructure their grading systems and most began to introduce EO policies (see Crompton, 1989). Sellbank became a particularly prominent advocate of EO policies. During the course of the 1980s the proportion of women achieving management positions in Sellbank increased remarkably quickly, and by the time of our research 18 per cent of managerial posts were filled by women (for a further discussion of these trends, see Savage, 1992). This development has opened up debate concerning the future prospects of women in the banking sector. Crompton and Jones (1984) and Crompton (1989) tend to draw a relatively optimistic picture in which the growing career-mindedness of women, and the potential for such women to use the 'qualification lever' (in this case, by obtaining Institute of Bankers credentials), will over time lead to a significant improvement in the position of women in banking. Other researchers, however (e.g. Knights and Morgan, 1991; O'Reilly, 1992a,b; Kerfoot, 1993), present a more pessimistic view and have pointed to the way in which women are being concentrated in employment 'ghettoes'.

Compared with local government, the banking labour market is much more internally cohesive. Although (as we shall explore in Chapter 3) there are various occupational specialisms within banking, there is not the same type of departmentalism as in local government, and hence no need for us to concentrate our research on specific departments. The banking labour market is often thought of as being a classic case of a 'firm internal labour market' (Althauser and Kalleberg, 1981), a hierarchical structure with senior jobs being filled by promotion from below. The main divide is that between managerial and clerical employees. This distinction is both an occupational and status one. Traditionally, nearly all managers were placed in charge of specific

branches, with only a relatively small number of managers in
Head and Regional Office functions (see Savage, 1993). In
recent years the managerial grading has changed so that some
people without managerial responsibility, but nonetheless
carrying out highly expert work (for example, in merchant
banking), are appointed to managerial grades. The proportion of
managers in the total workforce has also increased from around
10 per cent to around 25 per cent in recent years.

It is also important to bear in mind that our fieldwork took
place at a time when Sellbank was experiencing a severe downturn in its economic fortunes after a perod of considerable pros-
perity and expansion. This marks it out from local government
and nursing, which had been subject to more economic
constraints during the earlier 1980s and which had not been so
immediately affected by the economic downturn. At the time of
our research Sellbank was reacting to changed economic conditions with a major job-cutting and branch-closing exercise,
which involved job cuts at all levels of the bank, including the
managerial level. One of the most striking results of these job
cuts was the elimination of workers aged over 50 from Sellbank
and a much more pronounced concentration of younger
workers than was found in the other two sectors. This retrench-
ment was very important in marking the end of the security
typically associated with the banking career, and its impact needs
to be borne in mind as we discuss our research findings.

It is also important to note that Sellbank differed significantly
from the local government and nursing components of our
research since both these latter organisations were spatially
congruent with the local areas we studied. Sellbank, however,
was a national (indeed, international) organisation that carried
out many activities and operations outside Southtown and
Midcity. In particular, all Head Office functions, and most
merchant banking activities, were centred in London. Certain
servicing operations (such as credit card operations) were also
located outside the case study areas. The result is that – unlike
local government and nursing – we did not have access to all
levels and activities of the organisation in our research, and in
particular the most senior parts of Sellbank were excluded from

our study. Thus the proportion of staff who were employed in managerial capacities was around 17 per cent in the branch banking network, but in many of specialist and Head Office units they exceeded 50 per cent.

However, although this may suggest that our research is limited by not being able to stretch 'up' to the top of the organisational hierarchy, it should be pointed out that in practice the branch network is run largely autonomously from the other units of the bank and there is, for example, very little job movement between it and other parts of the bank's activities. The important exception is the small number of senior managers who may be moved between the branch network into other of the bank's units, but these form only a very small proportion even of the managerial workforce.

From the point of view of our research perhaps the most important implication of this spatial separation of functions concerns the fact that Sellbank's extremely active Equal Opportunities unit was based in Head Office and had no specifically local presence. Personnel officers and regional management were expected to respond to central initiatives, but in general the spatial separation of EO from the regions, as well as individual branches themselves, encouraged the possibility of there being no straightforward translation of EO into practice.

Midcity banking

Because Midcity is a large urban area, Sellbank had a major presence, with over 70 retail branches, a number of specialist units carrying out activities such as securities (legal and estate work) and specialist lending work (to small and large businesses), and a regional management centre. This having been said, around 90 per cent of staff worked in the branches themselves. Altogether nearly 1,000 staff were employed.[5] These included senior regional managers whose grading and position ranked very highly in Sellbank as a whole. Within Midcity around 15 per cent of employees were employed on managerial grades. Of these managerial grades, over one quarter were employed in regional and city-wide management centres, and a further handful were employed in specialist units, leaving well over half the managerial staff working in the branches. Of the 85 per cent of employees who were employed as clerical workers, it is important to distinguish senior clerical staff from the rest. Senior clerical staff, comprising about 13 per cent of the workforce, carried out responsible, skilled jobs, and promotion into such jobs could not be regarded as automatic. Many senior clerks have had expanded work duties as a result of restructuring (for more detail see Chapter 3), and the senior clerical post itself is frequently regarded as a gateway to management. Below these ranks lie the majority of employees, well over two-thirds of the total, who work in junior clerical employment, in areas such as cashiering, routine book-keeping, etc. Although there is a grading system within junior clerical employment, promotion to more senior grades is usually fairly routine given experience and training. It is therefore clear that banking is a relatively proletarianised occupation, with a considerable majority of bank employees working in routine jobs.

Table 2.4   Gender and grades: Midcity Sellbank 1991

Grade	Women (%)
Managerial grades	10.9
Senior clerical grades	70.4
Junior clerical grades	81.2

Source: Internal statistics

Table 2.4 indicates the gender composition of these different grades in this region, and indicates clearly a very skewed gender distribution according to seniority in Midcity Sellbank. Nearly 90 per cent of managerial posts are composed of men, but women form the vast majority of junior and senior clerical positions. Looking at these figures from another perspective, nearly one third of all men are working in managerial posts, whilst less than 2 per cent of women do so. In fact nearly all men aged over 40 are working in management positions, compared with only 10 per cent of women. At the time of our research, and despite the considerable efforts to introduce EO policies, it was still apparently the case that long-serving men could routinely expect promotion, whilst only a very few women could. This having been said, it is notable that the senior clerical grade, from which promotion into management is certainly possible, has now become an overwhelmingly female preserve. These are issues which we examine in greater depth in Chapter 4.

There were a number of important EO initiatives in Midcity. There was a workplace nursery, which was, however, not widely used, a series of seminars encouraging women employees to gain skills for career development, and also a small support network for women staff. The most widely used EO measure, however, was the maternity break scheme, which allowed women to leave work for up to five years but be reappointed to a post equivalent to that which they had left. Over 100 women in Midcity, over 10 per cent of the entire staff, were on such a scheme at the time of our research.

Southtown banking

Sellbank only had one (large) branch in Southtown itself, and we therefore decided also to include other branches within a 20-mile radius of Southtown in order to increase our sample size for the research. This reflected the fact that the Southtown branch was itself linked into a regional network and had relatively little autonomy of its own. In the end we included eight other branches and the local regional management centre in charge of the Southtown branch, giving a total of around 300 employees. Table 2.5 indicates the gender distribution of the workers in this area.

There is a slightly higher proportion of men at all grade levels than in Midcity, especially at the managerial level. This is interesting because one of the expectations we had when we began our research was that the 'tighter' labour market in Southtown might permit greater career opportunities for women, since employers might be forced to resolve labour shortages by promoting women. In fact, if anything, women appear to be

slightly more advantaged in Midcity, where double the proportion of managers are female. In fact it may well be that the
crucial factor is not the geographical location but the fact that
Midcity is a conurbation with a more diversified labour market
and possibly somewhat more liberal attitudes towards women's
employment. It should also be noted that EO policies were
considerably less visible in Southtown than in Midcity. There
was no workplace nursery and little evidence of women's
support groups, for example. However, in any event, it would
appear that the differences between Southtown and Midcity are
in no way marked, which suggests that local variation is not
especially significant.

Table 2.5 **Gender and grades: Southtown Sellbank 1991**

Grade	Women (%)
Managerial grades	5.0
Senior clerical workers	69.4
Junior clerical workers	79.4

Source: Internal statistics

Summary

In general, the background information from banking suggests
that only a few women have currently moved into senior positions in the Midcity and Southtown parts of Sellbank. Indeed,
there is a striking similarity between the position of men and
women in Sellbank and the two local authorities. Around 80 per
cent of low-graded workers were female, whilst around 10 per
cent of those with senior grades were female. Furthermore, in all
these cases women have moved into more senior positions in
clerical and support ranks. There are two ways of interpreting this
development. One optimistic explanation is that although
women have not yet made a significant breakthrough into
management, they may be about to make such a move and the
next few years will see a decisive breakthrough. Alternatively, it

might be argued that senior clerical and support positions are being constructed as alternative 'career positions' for ambitious women who are not expected to move into the management grades themselves (see Knights and Morgan, 1991, for the case of banking). We discuss these points further in Chapters 3 and 4.

Hospitals and nursing

Nursing offers an obvious contrast to the other two sectors we examined in that it has historically been constituted as a predominantly female profession (Witz, 1992). However, there are recent suggestions that this feminisation may be undergoing some current changes as a result of the massive restructuring that took place in the National Health Service during the 1980s. In addition to organisational changes in the context of nursing work, there have also been considerable occupational changes in nursing since the mid-1980s (Walby *et al.*, 1994; Witz, 1994; Davies, 1995). Furthermore, what nurses themselves define and understand as 'nursing' has been undergoing considerable redefinition in Britain since the early 1980s (and earlier in the USA and Canada).

We looked at two hospitals, one in each of the local areas. Southtown Hospital was a general hospital, and Midcity Hospital was a large teaching hospital and centre of national excellence. We focused on Registered General Nurses[6], ranging from newly qualified staff nurses (grades D and E) to nurses in various managerial posts (grades H and I). Midcity Hospital was one of the 68 units[7] located within the 20 District Health Authorities that made up the large Regional Health Authority. Southtown Hospital was located in one of the 13 District Health Authorities that was part of a much smaller Regional Health Authority. Southtown Hospital was one of two hospitals in a 'Unit' that provided fully integrated hospital and community services. 'Units' are now the 'providers' of health care, whilst District Health Authorities basically operate as market regulators, strategic planners and 'purchasers' of health care (see Chapter 3 for a more detailed discussion of these changes). Each District has different patterns of health care provision, which in turn means that patterns of demand and supply for nursing labour vary between Districts, and so career structures will vary between Districts.

Midcity Hospital was a centre of specialist forms of health care provision. Nurses came from all over the country to work here, often to gain experience in a particular specialism (for example, the renal unit), possibly for short periods of time. Nursing staff turnover was therefore fairly high, at just under 30 per cent per annum, and considerable experience was needed in order to become a Sister. By contrast, Southtown Hospital was not a major centre and recruited its nursing staff locally, although a few nurses might come from further afield to gain experience in the infectious diseases service. The main pool of nursing labour in Southtown had traditionally been women moving to the area with their husbands, remaining for a while and then moving on as and when their husbands' jobs dictated. However, in the recessionary 1990s nursing turnover in South-town Hospital slowed down considerably, partly because of less male job mobility, so that:

> The effect that the recession has had on us is that it has made our recruiting easier. And the calibre of staff that we have to choose from is astonishing and it's very satisfying to us. [Personnel Officer, Southtown Hospital]

In addition, nursing turnover had slowed down because of the impact of male unemployment, which means that it is less likely that nurses will leave nursing or opt for part-time work if their husbands are unemployed. So, whereas in the 1980s there was a fear that nursing vacancies would not be filled (fuelled by projections about the 'demographic timebomb' lowering recruitment into nursing), the picture had changed dramatically by the early 1990s when we did our research. For example, Southtown had made plans to introduce the new Health Care Assistant grade in order to attract older women into nursing, but had then found that it was easily able to recruit qualified staff into nursing for the same cost. On the other hand Southtown Hospital has always been in close competition with other major employers in the town, who were able to offer better salaries and who had tempted many nurses away, at least until recruitment slowed down in the late 1980s.

Neither Midcity Hospital nor Southtown Hospital had fully operational EO policies. Organisational restructuring had placed EO low on the agenda of priorities. One of the effects of health service restructuring in Southtown had been to devolve personnel functions to Unit level, replacing a District-wide function – including EO – with independent and *ad hoc* arrangements. At the time we did our interviews (1991–92) there was still only a draft EO policy, although unwritten practices continued from earlier times, particularly around the encouragement of part-time working, but the hospital did not advertise itself as an EO employer. The relatively low priority given to EO issues was evidenced by the lack of money available to expand childcare places at the hospital crèche to include the under-twos. There had been a top-down initiative from the District level – a 'family and domestic commitments policy' introduced in October 1990 – which provided opportunities for job-sharing, career breaks, shared maternity leave, paternity leave and sabbaticals. This was designed explicitly as a measure to retain staff, particularly women, but was still in the process of being 're-jigged' at Southtown, so not fully operational.

At Midcity Hospital, there was no operational EO policy because the recent amalgamation of districts had disrupted personnel policies, which were, in any case, extremely dated and were in the process of being updated. There was an on-site nursery, taking babies from six months, but there was an 18-month waiting list for places and, even though priority status was given to nurses, the opening hours (7am–6pm) did not correspond well with nursing shifts. Indeed, none of the respondents to our survey used the crèches at either of our case study hospitals, relying instead on family, kin and friends for childcare.

Organisational restructuring was implemented much more quickly and smoothly in Southtown than in Midcity, probably owing to the smaller size of and the absence of strong Consultant 'fiefdoms' within the former. Southtown had already introduced a new corporate structure (see Figure 2.1) and a new clinical directorate structure (see Figure 2.2).

Figure 2.1 Southtown Hospital: corporate structure

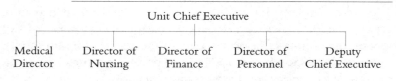

Figure 2.2 Southtown Hospital: clinical directorate structure

From the point of view of nursing careers, it is important to note that each clinical directorate had a Senior Nurse Manager, who headed the nursing team, but who was accountable to the Clinical Director. It is rare for a nurse to be a Clinical Director, although in Southtown the Clinical Director for Accident and Emergency was a nurse. Of course all nurses are ultimately accountable to the Unit Chief Executive. In Units where clinical directorates have been introduced, the clinical directorate level is increasingly becoming the ceiling to nursing careers, so the nursing career structure within Southtown Hospital has only three major steps: Staff Nurse, Ward Sister and Senior Nurse Manager. There are only two posts above this level (Director of Nursing Services and District Nursing Advisor), a far cry from the nursing career structure up until the mid-1980s, when all nurses in the District were managed by a District Nursing Officer, who controlled over half of the District Authority's revenue! Furthermore, it is difficult to jump up from a Sister's to a Senior Nurse Manager's post, so the ceiling of the nursing career in Southtown is effectively a G graded Ward Sister. This is partly because higher Sisters grades were created with the intention of encouraging the creation of clinical specialisation, and there is clearly limited scope for such developments in a small general hospital.

The organisational picture and shape of the nursing career at the much larger and more complex Midcity Hospital was in a state of flux. Reorganisation into a clinical directorate structure similar to that in Southtown was underway, but at the time of our research clinical directorates co-existed within a more traditional, functional management structure (Figure 2.3).

Figure 2.3 Midcity Hospital: organisational structure

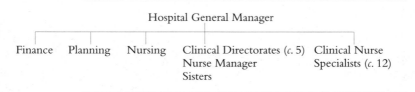

At Midcity, the major difference compared with Southtown was the much more widespread introduction of H and I graded Clinical Nurse Specialists alongside the creation of new Clinical Nurse Manager posts within clinical directorates, because of the greater range of specialist services in Midcity. Clinical Nurse Specialists occupied a position somewhere between Sisters and Clinical Nurse Managers, and were found in highly specialised units in the hospital, such as the renal unit. The role of the Clinical Nurse Manager, on the other hand, was to mediate *between* clinical specialisation and managerial demands.

At Southtown Hospital, 27 per cent of nursing and midwifery staff were part time and 3 per cent were on the 'bank' – a pool of casual nursing labour to be called on as and when needed. Only 2 per cent of the total nursing and midwifery staff were men, and all were on full-time contracts. Excluding midwives, the distribution of men and women across the 6 grades was as shown in Table 2.6.

Table 2.6   Nursing workforce by grade and gender: Southtown 1991

Title	Grade	Women (%)
Senior Nurse Managers	H & I	71.4
Sister/Charge Nurse	F & G	92.3
Staff Nurse	D & E	99.3

In Midcity nurses were distributed through the grading system as outlined in Table 2.7.

Table 2.7 Nursing workforce by grade and gender: Midcity 1991

Title	Grade	Women (%)
Senior Nurse Manager	H & I	85.7
Sister/Charge Nurse	F & G	94.2
Staff Nurse	D & E	92.5

There was a slightly higher proportion of male nursing staff at Midcity (7 per cent). All worked full time. There is some evidence here that women's position was rather better in Midcity than in Southtown, a point which is in fact common to all the sectors we have examined. All grades of nursing are nonetheless dominated by women. This makes nursing an obvious point of comparison with the other sectors, and we will take up the various points of contrast in later chapters.

Research methods and methodology

The objective of our research was to explore the gendering of contemporary careers and organisations. We adopted a variety of research methods to pursue this, including interviews with key informants, documentary research, a workplace survey and in–depth interviews. We did not see research as a neutral process of observation or in any way an objective 'test' of the sorts of theoretical account we have discussed in Chapter 1. Like many other social scientists we believe in the usefulness and importance of empirical research without any blind faith in positivist–empiricist approaches to knowledge. To simplify, positivism can be said to be concerned with forms of association between measurable 'variables', from which it deduces causality and makes claims to objective, scientific and universal theories. Positivism is widely criticised for the exclusive focus on pattern rather than process, as well as the assumptions surrounding the neutrality and completeness of knowledge derived through observation, and the privileging of 'science' as knowledge (see for example Sayer, 1984; Gunew, 1991). However, whilst supporting these general points, we wish also to avoid the relativist view that 'anything goes'. In our view grounded research remains essential (cf. Strauss, 1989; Layder, 1993).

One way of spelling out the differences between positivist methods and those we adopted is to note that positivists emphasise that (amongst other things) research needs to be *reliable* in order for it to be scientific. Reliability refers to the fact that if the research is repeated, it should produce the same results. However, it is doubtful that this is a particularly useful formulation for social scientific research. Social scientists differ from natural scientists in that they deal with 'open systems' in which people are constantly monitoring their activities and changing them, rather than with 'closed systems' where patterns and processes are invariant. Some sociologists, such as Giddens (1990) and Beck (1992), have argued that such processes of reflexivity have reached a new peak in recent times. Certainly, the people we spoke to worked in organisations that conduct regular monitoring of their staff, in the form of appraisals, training courses, and so forth. As we fed back some of our research to people working in our organisations they would endorse our interpretation but often point out that 'things are different now'. As we go on to examine in Chapters 5 and 6, people themselves were also highly reflexive about the relationship between their own lives and their employing organisations (see more generally Pahl, 1995). In short, the goal of reliability is of dubious value.

However, this does not mean that we should not be concerned with the question of *validity*. Validity refers to the need for the

research techniques to be appropriate to their purpose and therefore to produce data that are not an artefact of the research design
itself but a valid index of social processes occurring in the field. A
common way to establish validity is through 'triangulation',
whereby a variety of methods is used. We cannot, of course, claim
that this reveals undisputed or complete versions of social events
or processes, but at least it provides different approaches to these.

We approached our research in the following ways. First, we
approached key informants in each of our organisations. Usually
informants gave us their view on gender and careers in their
organisations, as well as providing documentary information,
including EO policies, internal reports, job specifications,
personnel policy, and so forth. We were also given a comprehen-
sive breakdown of employees by sex, grade, organisational location and age (some of this material has been used in the
preceding discussions). This allowed us to derive a sample for a
postal questionnaire of employees and also provided a range of
relevant material in its own right. In the course of our research
a number of other documents were also made available to us by
some of the people we interviewed, some of a remarkably confi-
dential nature, such as specimen appraisal forms. We have used
these as appropriate.

Second, we carried out a workplace survey, approaching 300
employees in nursing and local government and 400 in
banking.[8] The survey achieved a response rate of slightly over 50
per cent, producing 150–200 completed questionnaires from
each sector. The same questionnaire was used in all cases and was
designed to provide broad descriptive information about
employees, careers, and their attitudes to their organisation and
to opportunities for women in particular. Questionnaires were
distributed through the internal mail of the organisations, with
replies being posted directly to us. We also used the survey as a
filter for choosing people to interview in depth. These in-depth
interviews, the third research method we used, were carried out
with between 25 and 35 workers in each sector. The interviews
were semi-structured, and (with a few necessary modifications)
the same schedule was used in all organisations. Interviews were
usually carried out in the place of work, in a private office, and

lasted between one and three hours, although on two occasions the interview was conducted at a person's home. Because the organisations gave their approval to our research, line managers were instructed to allow their staff to spend as much time with us as we wished. Nonetheless, it was clear that whilst managers would usually talk for as long as we wished (an interesting fact in its own right, incidentally, since these same workers often took this time constantly to complain of being overworked!), junior staff given time to attend the interviews were often expected to make up the work lost, and often began looking nervously at their watches if the interview seemed to stretch to over an hour.

The sampling strategy for the workplace survey was as follows. Because we wanted to compare the responses of both men and women across the hierarchy, we had to ensure we obtained enough responses from those employees (notably senior female staff and junior male staff) who were numerically under-represented. Therefore we adopted a form of stratified sampling, since random sampling would not have thrown up enough of these cases for analysis. We first divided the sample between Midcity, which because of its larger size comprised two-thirds of the sample, and Southtown, which comprised one third. Subsequently, we divided workers in each organisation into three groups by their broad grading. Twenty per cent of the sample was composed of senior staff, managerial grades in banking and nursing, and Principal Officer or Chief Officer status in local authorities. Forty per cent of the sample was of intermediate graded staff, such as senior clerical workers or nursing Sisters. The final 40 per cent of the sample were junior graded staff, clerical staff in banking and local government, and qualified nurses in the most junior post of Staff Nurse. Within each of these broad groupings we attempted to interview 50 per cent of men and women. In practice this was not possible, since even though we tried to interview every senior woman within the sampling frame, this did not add up to 50 per cent, and there were similar, although not quite so pronounced, problems in interviewing junior men. There was a particular problem in nursing, where it proved impossible to find enough men at any grade level to push up their proportion to 50 per cent, and although we finally surveyed every male nurse on the sampling frame, we still only had 13 responses.

We should make clear that this form of stratified sampling led to certain limitations in data analysis. Primarily, it meant that we could not use our questionnaires to ask questions such as what proportion of the workers of a particular grade were men. In practice, however, this limitation was not especially serious since this type of information could be collected from other sources, such as the documentary material provided by the organisations (some of which is shown earlier in this chapter).

The initial reasoning for carrying out both questionnaire and in-depth interviewing was based upon our adoption of the distinction between intensive and extensive research (Sayer, 1984). Extensive research, based on our workplace survey, is designed to reveal common patterns, the typicality of certain events or actions. Intensive research, based on our in-depth inter-views, is designed to analyse the causal mechanisms operating in a particular context. Our questionnaire was designed to elicit information on respondents' employment histories and their domestic circumstances, and to gain some indication of attitudes towards their employing organisation, and their lives and careers. Material gathered from the questionnaire was not designed to explain what was found but to describe broad patterns of response across a range of areas, such as occupational mobility, for different subgroups of the sample (for example, junior men compared with junior women), or attitudes to the organisation. Such findings are then treated as in need of explanation. In Pawson's (1993: 31) words this involves taking 'a pattern of data... and regard[ing] it, not as the end of the research process, but as a configuration to be explained'. We might add that such an expla-nation might be the causal processes at work in the organisations, in a person's home life or elsewhere, or it might simply be the product of possible problems with the design of the question-naire itself. In other words the fact that the patterns revealed by the postal questionnaire present us with patterns to be explained does not commit us to the view that an explanation must lie in social processes taking place within the organisations rather than in the artifice of the research method itself. To ascertain which of these is operating further analysis is needed.

Our prejudice against over-reliance on the survey was confirmed by many of the comments we received from respondents during the intensive interviews. Several needed no guidance from us in pointing to weaknesses in survey methods!

> I went on a course once and they gave us, I don't know if you have seen these, these questionnaires, I bet you have; it's the sort of thing they dream up in a university, there were about 20–30 reasons for working, what are your main reasons for working, you know remuneration, status, you know 'I am a bank manager', all that sort of thing. I was ever so surprised, I think that a lot of people answered it with the questions they felt they were supposed to put down... a lot of my contemporaries were putting at the top job satisfaction, doing a good job, making profit for the Sellbank and sort of salary was coming about eighth or tenth and I thought that was bloody nonsense. I mean if they said to me you are not getting paid this month I would say well I ain't coming... . [John][9]

> I find it very difficult when you are asked these questions [ranking the importance of work as opposed to family, leisure and other interests] to rate them in importance because quite frankly I think they are so interlinked that I could have rated them all at 'one'. [Doug]

> I think the men are liars and they're trying to create an image for themselves. Even in the questionaire, they can't be honest, basically. That's all I can say about that. They know damn well that women haven't got a chance... they're just trying to create the impression that they think that women are equal and they're just lying. [Claire]

We frequently found the information provided by in-depth interviews more revealing. In-depth interviews allow dialogue between researchers and respondents to provide much more detail on context and process. We chose respondents for the in-depth interviews from those who had indicated on their surveys that they would be prepared to participate in this second stage of research. They were chosen to allow roughly equal numbers of men and women to be interviewed, with equal numbers chosen across the three grade bands applied in the survey sample. In practice this was impossible in nursing, where men made up less than 5 per cent of the nursing workforce overall. The purpose of these in-depth interviews was to allow respondents to trace though the way their employment histories, personal lives and experience of the organisation related together, so that causal relationships might be distinguished from contingent, accidental ones. We should make it clear that these workers we interviewed were not necessarily typical of the wider sample.

In-depth interviews do not, by themselves, secure 'authentic' responses from respondents. It is important to make this point since there is a current of thought that attaches a rather overly romantic view to such interviews. Sayer (1989), for example, has argued that:

> with a less formal, less standardized, and more interactive type of interview, the researcher has a much better chance of learning from the respondents what the different significances of circumstances are for them. The respondents are not forced into an artificial one-way mode of communication in which they can only answer in terms of the conceptual grid given to them by the researcher (1989: 245).

The idea that the semi-structured interview can allow the respondents to lead the discussion and set their own agenda is an attractive one, yet it cannot be sustained. In the later 1970s the use of oral history techniques seemed revolutionary, in that they appeared to reverse the usual relationship between professional researchers and the researched by putting the professional in the humble position of listening to his or her subject (Thompson, 1978). In fact, as Foucault's (1977) work suggests, there is nothing innocent about the in-depth interview. Modern forms of power constantly call upon us to confess our feelings, thoughts or beliefs to those in authority, whether the situation is a doctor's consulting room, the classroom, a job interview or an appraisal interview. In-depth interviews do not allow any privileged or unmediated access to people's thoughts and feelings, but rather produce specific accounts designed to meet the particular situation. In our case the problem did not seem to be that respondents might police what they told us because the interview situation might remind them of appraisal situations, or because they were afraid that the information they revealed might go back to the organisation. Rather, the problem seemed to be that many respondents treated the interviews as an opportunity to 'let off steam' in a 'safe' encounter that they knew would not get back to anyone in the organisation. The interviews seemed akin to the 'liminal' situation discussed by social anthropologists in which people step outside their normal routines and actions, allowing them to put these normal routines into question (Turner, 1969). A striking number of respondents told us that they were confiding information that they had not told anyone else in the organisation, and the majority of respondents took the opportunity to 'sound off' against particular people, policies or situations in the organisation for which they were working.

Now it might be supposed that such material is exactly what might be of interest to us, and in many ways it was. It certainly made the interviews full of interest and provided some fascinating incidents and anecdotes, not all of which can be used in this book since it might reveal the identities of specific people. The problem, however, is that it is not clear that such material is entirely valid since, as we have explained above, the interview material was constructed in a particular setting and may not reflect people's feelings and attitudes in other arenas. Here, however, we were helped by being able to return to the postal survey to see if this contained any other evidence in support of particular ideas. We could select material from the in-depth survey when it helped us to address the problems posed by the data and discount information elicited that did not bear upon them. For this reason we believe strongly that using the two methods alongside each other helps to reduce – if not entirely eliminate – problems that might be encountered by using one method alone.

Given that we are mainly interested in gender and careers, our data have one major limitation that must be mentioned. We only surveyed men and women who were working. This means that when we analyse career strategies and the meanings that career has for men and women, our data are biased towards those men and (particularly) women who, because they are in work, may have a stronger commitment to the work they are doing or to their 'careers'. Obviously, we can say very little about those men and, especially, women who – for whatever reason – are not in paid work. However, across the sectors we encountered many women who had taken time out of paid work to care for children and who were able to comment on the relationship between time-out and careers. In nursing there is a high level of labour turnover, and nurses especially move jobs and organisations for all sorts of reasons – to do further training, to get the experience necessary for promotion, because they are pregnant, to look after their children or to take non-nursing jobs (Mackay, 1989).

During the course of our analysis of the interview data, we increasingly came to recognise these data as a form of narrative. Indeed, by asking our respondents to reflect upon their past lives and think about what they had achieved in their careers, we were inviting them to construct 'career narratives' by reflecting upon their work life trajectories and tell us their occupational stories. We came to see these stories as 'stories of the self' and felt that those survey respondents who indicated they were willing to be interviewed wanted or needed to be able to tell their story – possibly because they had reached a particular turning point, or were undergoing some kind of 'career crisis' and welcomed the opportunity to think this through or, as we mentioned above, 'let off steam' about injustices they perceived or simply talk through their hopes and plans with a stranger. These career narratives are analysed in Chapter 5, where we present them in the form of 'case studies', selected not necessarily on the grounds of their typicality, but because they reveal the richness and diversity of work-life histories as stories of the self.

Conclusions

In this chapter we have provided a basic introduction to each of the sectors in our study and begun to explore the nature of gender relations in each of them using simple descriptive material. Clearly, there is considerable change going on in local government, nursing and banking. In the two local authorities and Sellbank it was clear that some women were moving into senior positions. However, it is equally clear that there remains a huge gender 'gradient', as the proportion of women rises in more junior jobs. Indeed, one of the striking features revealed by our discussion is the extent to which junior grades are overwhelmingly feminised. Over 80 per cent of junior jobs in all sectors were composed of female workers, which in the case of banking and local government raises the important question of the relationships between an overwhelmingly male management grouping and a generally female hierarchy. Nursing clearly offers a contrast, in the degree to which it is a female-dominated occupation, although there is evidence here of some degree of masculinisation at the top. In Chapter 3 we now begin to examine in greater detail the types of change that have taken place in the various organisations and attempt to consider how restructuring itself is directly tied up with the redefinition of gender.

3 Restructuring Organisations, Changing People

Introduction

One of the strongest impressions conveyed to us during the course of our research was that all employees felt they were living through a period of major restructuring and organisational change. This restructuring, we came to realise, is of fundamental importance for exploring the changing relationship between gender and organisation, and in this chapter we consider the ways in which restructuring itself is a gendered process.

In order to situate our study we begin with a conceptual analysis of the 'restructuring paradigm' that developed in economic geography during the early 1980s (see Bagguley *et al.*, 1990). Although the initial focus of this literature was the transformation of British manufacturing, insights gained from this work had, by the mid-1980s onwards, been applied to the service sector (Urry, 1987; Pinch, 1989). Whilst it was certainly the case that many of the 'restructuring strategies' delineated in this body of work existed within our case study organisations, a number of problems in the restructuring paradigm limit its usefulness for thinking about gender and organisational restructuring and, indeed, about organisational change more generally.

Our main concern is to demonstrate the centrality of organisational processes to restructuring, and also to explore how gender is embedded within these organisational processes. Within the restructuring paradigm organisations tend to be characterised as rational instruments in the implementation of economically driven strategies for change. Since these strategies are defined in abstracted and gender-neutral economic terms, specific configurations of gender relations tend to be considered as an *outcome* of restructuring strategies. Taking a gendered organisational perspective, we will argue that it is not possible just to 'add on' gender to an otherwise gender-neutral theoretical account of how organisations change or restructure. Rather, paying attention to both organisation and gender entails reformulating our understanding of the origins, design and outcome of restructuring strategies.

The first part of this chapter elaborates our critique of the restructuring paradigm and, developing some of insights from this literature, builds an alternative framework for thinking about gender and organisational change. Here our aim is to find a way of going beyond dualistic accounts that routinely separate out 'demand' from 'supply' factors, or 'restructuring' from its 'impact'. Our approach emphasises that restructuring is tied to the people who comprise organisations since it is these people who define, implement and contest restructuring strategies (albeit not necessarily under conditions of their own making). Simultaneously, we emphasise that, far from simply changing *structures,* which then impacts on employees, restructuring is tied up with redefining and contesting the sorts of personal *identities* and *qualities* which are seen as desirable or undesirable for organisational members to possess. People themselves are not simply passive recipients of such organisational changes and may be able to contest and reinterpret them. We introduce the concept of 'embedded restructuring' in order to explore current changes in the three sectors of banking, local authorities and health.

The restructuring paradigm

From the mid-1970s onwards it became apparent that some major changes were taking place in the organisation of both the private and public sectors in Britain. As well as a general shift in the economy from manufacturing to services, organisations were restructuring to introduce new technologies, new production systems and new management systems, and to find ways of accommodating themselves to the rapidly changing economic, social and political environment at the start of the 1980s. Neo-Marxist analyses were central to academic examination of these changes, offering a new sensitivity to the importance of labour in the process of restructuring. This was especially true of the perspective pioneered by radical geographers, which came to be known as the 'restructuring' paradigm (see Cooke, 1989; Baguley *et al.*, 1990). This was largely concerned with the geographical dimensions of economic change, especially in explaining why the economies of the traditional industrial areas had collapsed whilst the economic fortunes of medium-sized town and greenfield sites (especially in the South East) had improved (Massey, 1984). Explanations focused on employers' changing demands for particular sorts of labour. Thus Massey and Meegan (1982) and Massey (1984) emphasised how various restructuring strategies all involved changing the sorts of labour employed, in particular moving from more skilled and unionised labour to less skilled and non-unionised labour. It was argued that firms located specific processes and forms of production in areas to draw upon 'appropriate' labour, be this software companies searching for scarce (male) professional workers in the South East, or multi-national manufacturing firms searching for (female) semi-skilled, part-time workers on assembly lines in old industrial regions. This framework therefore explored the way in which restructuring was intrinsically tied to changing labour demand, and how labour market supply factors (i.e. the presence or absence of particular types of labour in specific labour markets) affected geographical patterns of restructuring (Cooke, 1983, 1989; Massey, 1984; Murgatroyd *et al.*, 1985; Warde, 1985). Thus, whilst making a subtle attempt to consider the interrelationship between labour demand and supply, the restructuring paradigm maintained their analytical distinction.

The restructuring paradigm, important though it has been in focusing attention on the nature of contemporary change, has a series of interlinked flaws. First, an instrumental view of restructuring was accepted. Restructuring was seen as primarily concerned with economically rational ways of reducing costs and raising productivity, and the consequent effects these objectives had on firms' demand for particular types of labour. Of course, firms usually *presented* restructuring strategies in this way, but this does not itself constitute a satisfactory explanation of them. Whilst the claim of economic rationality may place a given restructuring strategy in a privileged discursive position 'the claim and the ability to enforce the claim should not be mistaken for the reality of rationality' (Morgan, 1990: 80). Rather, economic rationality needs to be placed in cultural context. Thus, it might be argued that many innovations – such as the adoption of Japanese styles of management or 'flexible' systems – have been adopted because of popularity in management cultures. Cultural factors may account for the adoption of particular innovations. Of course, these may also have had economic benefits for the enterprise, but to *explain* their introduction purely in these terms is to commit the functionalist fallacy of explaining causes by effects. Rather, the adoption of restructuring strategies should be understood in terms of the internal political and cultural dynamics of organisations; the external environment in which organisations are located; and, more widely still, the recognition that 'organisation' is not a constant or abstract condition but is variable and contested, both at the level of theory and at the level of social practice.

Linked to this problem, the restructuring approach tended to ignore the sorts of social process internal or external to organisations, which revised, modified or even undermined various restructuring strategies. Admittedly, there was some interest in explicit conflict, for example negotiations with trade unions, resistance to redundancies, wage cuts and increased pace of work (for example, Bagguley *et al.*, 1990: 32ff; Beynon *et al.*, 1989), but these conflicts all took place within the formal organisational hierarchy. There was little consideration of how the informal politics and culture of organisations might affect the implementation of change.

This leads on to the central theoretical weakness. The restructuring literature drew upon a series of dualisms such as that between demand and supply, and that between organisational structures and the people employed in such structures, which we feel are difficult to sustain. Use of these dualisms meant that the process of restructuring is conceptualised as changing structures rather than changing the people who animate those structures. One example is found in Bagguley *et al.* (1990), who examined restructuring in Lancaster in the 1980s. Whilst wishing to avoid an economically determinist view of such restructuring (see for example Bagguley *et al.*, 1990: 211), their endorsement of the structures/agents dualism gave them no real alternative to it. Thus their chapters on restructuring in manufacturing and services did not refer to the activities of specific people inside the various organisations they studied. It is only in a later chapter that they study the changing positions of different types of employee, which they present as a study of the 'experience of restructuring'. They therefore take the process of restructuring as 'given' and only then proceed to examine how people's work life mobility is affected by it. By putting it in these terms restructuring is seen as something which happens to people, rather than as something which happens because some people choose (not necessarily in conditions of their own choosing) to make it happen.

These limitations mean that although many researchers within the restructuring paradigm were interested in the relationship between restructuring and gender relations, against their own inclinations they could only conceive this in a rather narrow way. Because restructuring was conceived instrumentally, in terms of a drive for profitability, it was difficult for writers within the restructuring perspective to show how organisations changed in other ways. Thus, whilst Bagguley *et al.* (1990) critique the existing research on gender and restructuring, their main sugges-tion is to develop and refine analyses of the spatial specificity of gender relations in local labour markets (Walby and Bagguley, 1991). Thus their stress on gender relations as central to an under-standing of what they term 'social restructuring' is investigated at the level of the labour market rather than the organisation. Whilst such a development is welcome, it demonstrates the persistent tendency to treat organisational restructuring separately from gendering processes, with the result that restructuring can only 'impact' on gender relations. This makes it difficult to register the way in which gender relations embedded within organisations may themselves contribute to organisational change.

This leads us to question how far 'demand' for labour can really be separated from the 'supply' of labour, and in turn how far we can separate organisational 'structures' from the 'people' who inhabit those structures. It is as an alternative to these dualisms that we regard the notion of 'embedded restructuring' as useful. This draws upon and develops a number of emerging currents in recent work on restructuring. One influence is Urry's considerations of how the restructuring paradigm can be extended to the service sector, where no 'material' product exists (see also Massey, 1984; Pinch, 1989). Urry showed that restructuring in services was more complex and multifold than in manufacturing, and argued that restructuring services entailed transforming the product (service) delivered as well as finding more efficient ways to produce that product (service) (Urry, 1987). More recently, Urry (1990; Lash and Urry, 1994) has emphasised the difficulties in disengaging the restructuring of service work from the restructuring of people who do the work. The quality of service provision is intimately related to the characteristics of the service providers. Thus it is not that restructuring has an impact on people but that the very process of restructuring is bound up with redefining the workforce. In developing these arguments Lash and Urry draw on Hochschild's (1983) work on 'emotional labour' in service employment, indicating the extent to which service sector work is directly constituted by the personal qualities and social skills of its workers. Adkins (1992, 1995) has also extended this analysis by examining the 'sexual labour' performed by women in service environments. However, these insights have not been extended to management or to other work where there is little or no direct contact with a consumer. In this book we attempt to show how the labour embedded in the production of services may be crucially linked to the gender of the producer, and how other forms of work, especially management, are also defined in terms of the personal, often gendered, qualities of workers (see also McDowell and Court, 1994).

One recent exploration of the cultural construction of managerial work is that of Massey, Quintas and Wield (1992) on the growth of science parks in Britain. Here a more explicitly culturalist approach is adopted which denies that the expansion of science parks can be understood purely in terms of economic effectiveness – since in fact, by most economic criteria, they have failed. Instead, Massey *et al.* show that the character of science parks needs to be understood in terms of the dominant social and cultural values that inform these developments, such as the particularly British concern with keeping manufacturing and intellectual work split and the resulting desire of firms to cluster near universities. The authors indicate some of the gender, class and status assumptions that govern such developments. However, they are largely silent on the issue which we wish to take up in this book: internal organisational cultures and practices.

This critique can be extended, with further insights being drawn from radical organisational theory. Within organisational theory, instrumental and rationalist notions (for example, those associated with Weber's well-known ideal type of bureaucracy) have been under severe attack in recent years, and writers such as Morgan (1986) and Clegg (1990) have emphasised that organisations construct their own meanings, activities and cultures rather than simply responding to an external environment. One particularly important rendering of this point is that organisational inequalities are at least in part the result of organisational processes and not simply derived from the wider economic and social environment. Writers on social class have also begun to acknowledge and discuss the nature of 'organisation assets' (Wright, 1985; Savage *et al.*, 1992) and to explore the links between gender inequalities within organisations and access to such assets.

Once the actions of organisational members are emphasised a rather different approach to the study of organisational restructuring suggests itself. Rather than restructuring simply being concerned with implementing rational strategies for profitability or efficiency, it might also be seen as being concerned with reforming the values and characteristics that people bring to organisations and which organisations themselves might try to influence. Furthermore, restructuring is not passively 'experienced' but is fought over and contested within organisations by various groups of people, often with very different agendas and assumptions about what changes should occur and how. Our term 'embedded' restructuring is designed to convey these dynamics, emphasising that restructuring takes place through daily routines and interactions in organisations. As such the origins, implementation and outcomes of restructuring are never solely economic, nor are they predictable in advance.

In the following sections we outline the restructuring that has taken place in our organisations, emphasising both the embedded and the specifically gendered dimensions of organisational restructuring. We show that restructuring has been as much about changing the culture of the organisation as about changing organisational structures, and that this has significantly redefined the qualities that workers are expected to bring to their organisation. This in turn alters people's behaviour and self-presentation.

Banking

Throughout the 1980s British banking was in a state of turmoil as it attempted to respond to an environment dramatically changed by the globalisation of financial markets and legal dereg-ulation of financial services. These changes forced intense competition between financial service providers and a major shake-up of the whole sector. Branch banking, traditionally dominated by the 'big four', has been opened up to new compe-tition from building societies (which had 15 per cent of accounts in 1939 but 44 per cent by 1984), who are much more efficient at routine activities. In the mid-1980s the account:employee ratio was 764:1 at the Halifax Building Society compared with 76:1 at Barclays. The challenge from building societies also threatened the easy money that banks had made by not paying interest on current accounts. By the late 1980s banking entered full-scale recession, due partly to concurrent economic recession, but also to these longer-term changes.

In response to these problems Cressey and Scott (1992) and Leyshon and Thrift (1993) have argued, in the tradition of the restructuring paradigm, that banks have responded by changing their demand for labour, in particular by segmenting their work-forces (especially by tiered recruitment) in order to develop more specialised activities better able to provide a wider range of services and products. The workforce has increasingly been divided between those employed on 'career lines' and a growing number of casual, often part-time employees (O'Reilly, 1992a). Leyshon and Thrift emphasise that these developments will accentuate the distinction between core and peripheral workers, whilst Cressey and Scott point to a developing crisis in employment relations, owing to loss of jobs and the breakdown of traditional career structures. Sellbank has experienced many of these changes, especially through the growing employment of (primarily) women in newly opened service centres that carry out routine processing tasks (see O'Reilly, 1992a,b; Leyshon and Thrift, 1993). The branches also employ a growing number of women cashiers on a part-time basis, whose hours are determined weekly and who have no certainty about how regular their employment will be. They tend to be older and are considerably more likely to have had children than are other women workers (Kerfoot, 1993).

However, changing gender relations within Sellbank are considerably more complex than is suggested simply by reference to new forms of gendered labour demand. As Crompton and Jones (1984), Crompton (1989) and Crompton and Sanderson (1990) have emphasised, the growing supply of credentialed women workers in the labour market is reflected in the movement of women into more senior jobs on career ladders. We have already seen in Chapter 2 that the majority of senior clerks and a significant minority of junior managers are women.

'Top-down' attempts to restructure labour demand *and* the qualitatively changing supply of female labour both clearly affect gender relations and careers in banking. It is also essential to recognise the broader cultural shifts in banking itself. By exploring these changes we can see that restructuring is far more complex than simply changing organisational structures in economically rational ways or exploiting new labour supplies. Rather, we can see that restructuring has been about changing the *personal characteristics* that people deploy in the workplace and altering the organisational worth of particular personal characteristics. Furthermore, these changes are gendered, with consequences for women's and men's positions in the bank. However, the implementation of the new culture has been a contested process, and thus the precise outcome, in terms of gendered careers, is uncertain.

Traditionally, banks have been rather authoritarian, austere and formidable institutions. In the words of Steven[2], a manager who had worked for Sellbank over 20 years, 'you entered that temple in awe'. This had great appeal when the main imperative was to encourage a shift from keeping money 'under the mattress' to opening a bank account (until the late 1970s the expansion of retail banking was largely from people opening their first accounts). In this context banks had to project a respectable and trustworthy image. This traditional image and culture was strongly linked to masculine images and to men as responsible and trust-worthy. Bank staff had to cultivate a sober, reliable image, which drew upon masculine and paternalistic imagery. Some of our interviewees explicitly referred to the familial qualities of older male managers. Jane, a long-serving bank secretary, stated that:

> the managers used to be real gentlemen, most of them, some of them were jumped up... but the older ones in their forties, they had got families, because they weren't appointed managers until they were married, and had probably got children, because they thought they couldn't manage a branch if they hadn't got children.

> **Q:** And how did they treat their workforce?

> Like fathers. The secretary who retired when I took her job at 24, she used to say to me, well when you are secretary the men were like fathers, and they become brothers, and then like sons...

John, now a branch manager, added his impression of the traditional, 'paternalistic' role that managers used to have in local areas:

> I always remember an old manager, this was in Corden, and Corden being a market town the manager was still someone who walked along the High Street, a Captain Mainwaring type, raising his hat to everybody, and they would all say 'Good morning Mr Jerome'... everybody knew him, he was a character in a fairly small market town.

Stuart, a long-serving senior clerk also noted that this concern with employing the right sort of bank staff also had traditionally had significant class implications:

> If you came from that sort of background, you know the right sort of
> background for want of a better expression, then you were going to be
> okay in the bank. I mean that seemed at that time to be more important
> than qualifications, I mean if you could come in and your parents were
> professional, and you went to a grammar school, and you came from a
> middle class background you were in, you passed your probation and
> you had got a job for life...

This 'ascriptive' culture became less attractive by the 1980s,
when nearly everyone had a bank account. From simply reacting
to customer demand for services, offered on a take–it–or–leave–it
basis, Sellbank had to become more proactive, competing with
other banks for existing accounts and diversifying into a range
of new services such as mortgages, insurance and extended
credit facilities. Customers had to be persuaded to take out more
'products' from the financial services sector.

In an effort to improve its competitiveness Sellbank tried to
introduce a 'sales culture' to the bank. Embedded within this is a
rethinking of the types of staff quality valued by the bank. In
part this has involved re-evaluating the traditional masculine
ethos of banking, including downgrading the branch manager
who was previously the (literal) embodiment of all that was
valued in traditional banking (the remote, austere and judge-
mental father figure). Several of our respondents emphasised that
whereas in the past the manager had a great deal of power and
respect, this was now restricted by area offices and regional
corporate divisions. As Karen, a junior manager stated:

> The branch managers in fact are not very senior in the bank, they used
> to be, and some of them still are in a sense because they have been
> there so long, but when they eventually retire, it's junior management, it's
> management of my sort of level that will be in charge of the branches.

As Sellbank has restructured, there has been a specialisation of
managerial functions and roles. In place of the branch manager
with general jurisdiction and control over all branch activities
has come a much more variegated set of managerial responsibil-

ities, mapped unevenly onto the traditional branch structure. Steven put it in the following way:

> The old bank manager had got respect, you could talk to him about anything... and he would be able to give you a decision, if not straight away – and more than likely straight away – after consulting with Head Office and going through certain formalities... what has happened is that they have taken what were the old senior management jobs and inserted in that chair a manager who has less experience, etc., and put certain restrictions on him; he can only lend up to a certain amount without having to go to area office. If it's above that amount he has not to go there; he has got to go to corporate division... so the branch manager has lots of restrictions.

Branch managers have effectively had their autonomy and authority reduced both from above *and* from below. From above the development of specialist function units has taken some of the branch manager's responsibilities away. In the later 1980s Sellbank split their lending activities into three sections: corporate, enterprise and personal. Where once branches had responsibility for all forms of lending, restructuring has removed the business of the largest and most prestigious customers away from the branches, which are left with more routine personal lending.

The new corporate managers working at regional level embody the new organisational values and are in many ways now the '*crème de la crème*' of managerial staff, working in plush offices and each with a small portfolio of large customers. Virtually all these corporate managers are male, and the relative lack of any clerically graded staff (more likely to be women) means that the office has a distinctly masculine atmosphere. Lesley, one of the few female (clerical) workers in this division, commented:

> there are so few women up here... the elder chaps... when I first arrived the[ir] shock was amazing.

> **Q:** What happened when you arrived?

they didn't mind if you were doing the jobs they don't want to be doing; when they realise that you actually want to, you have got ambitions, they don't like it very much.

Enterprise managers, who are responsible for dealing with small businesses, are based in the larger branches. They have less prestige than corporate managers but more specialised work than branch managers. Like managers in corporate lending they are also predominantly men. One of the ways in which this superiority is marked is linked to the fact that they visit clients off site. This allows staff to replace the corporate uniform with a smart (anonymous) suit. Branch managers, by contrast, have less excuse to avoid uniforms, which identify them as staff.

The hostility of branch managers to their loss of the more prestigious staff and status is understandable. As John put it:

the best staff are being creamed off into corporate. I guess if there had been corporate in my day I would have gone through corporate rather than retail.

Q: Do you see yourself as being lower status than corporate?

I think they perceive us as low status. I don't because I know some of the wallies that work there, and that is a fact. Some of them 10 and 15 years ago as senior clerks I wouldn't give them house room... The lads who are in corporate at the moment, they would be absolutely lost if you sat them in front of a customer in a branch.

From below, the main change has been a functional split between operations and lending managment. Operations managers are effectively in control of administration and systems within the branches and, although answerable to the branch manager, usually operate with a considerable degree of day-to-day autonomy:

he [sic] is like a production manager... we have to make sure that we provide the services that the customer requires and produce the goods if you like. [Steven]

I run the office, I supervise the staff, supervise their training, their rotation of jobs, their personal, if they ever have any, problems I am the first port of call. [Amanda]

The job of operations manager originally evolved from that of the 'accountant', who was an appointed officer but not a manager and was clearly subordinate to the branch manager. Whilst this hierarchy formally continues, it seems that the operations manager has now taken on greater autonomy and in some cases is not answerable to the branch manager at all but to a regional operations manager.

This leaves personal lending as branch managers' main responsibility, and much of this has been automated through computer scoring, removing any need for significant discretion or judgement. Those branch managers who are determined to retain some influence emphasise their lending skills and attempt to retain a large degree of customer contact through interviews. John did just this:

Yes I have quite a heavy interviewing commitment, probably out of a working day an average of three interviews, say, which will last anything from, I would guess anything from half an hour to an hour.

This method of lending is acquiring renewed status amid criticisms of lax lending policies in the 1980s. However, even here specialist account managers (formally responsible to the branch manager) may have greater expertise and ability than the branch manager, whose role may ultimately be undermined by them. Some branch managers delegate most interviewing to juniors, and when their account manager is independent and has high expertise, the branch manager effectively loses any role. Karen, a 'high-flying' woman manager, put it in these terms:

the branch manager is just, I just walk all over him...he actually refers to me now, he will say I am not sure about this, do you want to come and have a look at it... he has been in the bank a long time... and he is just one of those people that should have been left a little, you know, far back somewhere really... he is not really sure about these new-fangled

things that are going in, and he will say, Karen can you come and
explain them to me.

This attack on the traditional (male) branch manager in Sellbank represents a rather different pattern from that found by
Knights and Morgan (1991). In their case study they found that
male branch managers were relatively untouched by the 'sales
culture' and were, in fact, able to use it to their advantage by
encouraging ambitious women to move into senior clerical sales
jobs, geared to selling new financial services, rather than management itself. This allowed them to insulate themselves from the
main effects of change. In the case of Sellbank the situation is not
so clear. Two particular trends appear to have rather different
implications for patterns of gender relations in Sellbank.

First is the new emphasis on accessibility and the gendered
concomitants of this. Some of the general features of this new
banking culture are well known. Bank architecture has changed,
from relying on dour, austere buildings ('it was so dark, everything was dark wood, dark carpet, dark walls, no light' [Suzanne])
to designing well-illuminated buildings with an easily recognisable logo and bright colours. Larger branches have been
redesigned with a large reception hall, which is supposed to draw
in customers who can then be directed to more specialised
service staff. Sellbank also introduced uniforms in the later 1980s
to make their employees easily identifiable. Since they no longer
always worked behind a counter, but moved through the branch
talking to customers, they had to be distinguished from the
public. Television advertising for banks stressed the 'human' face
of bank employees, showing clerical staff relaxing and dating each
other. Managers were supposed to be more accessible and have
often been moved out of their own private offices. Sellbank even
conducted an advertising campaign around one manager.

These developments highlight the qualities of accessibility,
culturally linked to femininity, in place of the distant authoritarian image associated with the male branch manager. The bank
has tried to put women in visible positions in the bank (see also
Knights and Morgan (1991) and Kerfoot (1993) on this point)
to encourage people into the bank and sell services to the

customers. It is these 'front stage' rather than 'back stage' personnel who are now seen as crucial to the success of Sellbank. Indeed, one of the most important new jobs created in the large, revamped branches is that of receptionist. A number of women clerks felt that 'attractive' women were given special preference in being placed in this spot. Sara noted that:

> when I first came all the really nice girls were on there and that was what everybody was saying, it's because they were sexy, they were front line people, and they had to look nice and smart.

This trend appears to give women a more visible role in the bank and might explain the rise of women in senior clerical jobs, although it has its limitations (see below).

A second important dimension of restructuring is the way in which Sellbank has tried to construct new types of managerial qualities. Managers are now set annual targets, given performance-related pay and expected to apply for jobs rather than be promoted to them unasked. This redefinition of management is an attempt to undermine the 'time-served', reliable but unadventurous manager in order to cultivate the new managerial virtues of being 'proactive', forward-looking and 'change masters' (Kanter, 1989). One possible implication, however, is the way in which the new managerial culture endorses the attributes of 'competitive masculinity'. Kerfoot and Knights (1993) have argued that this new management style encourages a form of competitive masculinity that encourages:

> a way of relating to the world wherein everything becomes an object of, and for, control… [which] generates and sustains a hierarchy imbued with instrumentalism, careerism, and the language of 'success'; emulates competition linked to decisive action, 'productivism' and risk taking (p. 671).

The result has been that whilst an older form of male dominance has been undermined in the bank, a newly emergent form of organisational masculinity can also be detected. This applies especially to managers involved in corporate lending, where the continued masculine culture in an area of management with particularly high status was remarked on by a number of respondents (Savage, 1992). On the other hand women tend to be concentrated in those areas of management, especially operations management, which are junior, reflect women's responsibility for 'domestic' affairs within branches and are not so 'risky' or 'challenging'. Nonetheless, women are not barred from the new management culture, as they were historically from the old paternalistic one, and it is possible for women to adopt the sorts of competitive trait valued in the new management culture, although this may be very difficult to reconcile with childcare responsibilities and other commitments (see Chapter 6). Some of the contradictions and tensions in the new gender-neutral discourse of management are amply revealed by the views of Doug, a senior male manager:

> They are one of the team, and I do try and treat them as one of the lads, and I don't mean one of the lads in terms of male–female, but look if you want equality we are going to have equality.

It is not clear how else to define 'lads' except in terms of 'male–female', and the defensiveness in the rest of the quote indicates all too well the ambiguities that remain. Indeed, this manager went on to add that since 'we' (i.e. men and women) 'are not actually equal, we are made different', it seems that he did actually entertain doubts as to whether women could be fully committed to the new competitive culture.

In sum the nature of bank management itself is being redefined as social groups within Sellbank contest to use the changing culture of the bank to their advantage. Since we completed our fieldwork the very branch managers whose position has been undermined by the specialisation of management functions have been successful in pressing for the revival of branch activities. Sellbank has qualified its drive towards managerial specialisation by introducing a 'networking' system that allows the managers of large branches to take control over smaller branches within their area. Branch managers have also gained by taking greater control over the appraisal of staff, as the system in place in the early 1980s whereby specialist personnel managers used to visit branches and carry out appraisals has been replaced by a system in which staff are appraised by their line managers. In short, restructuring has opened up tensions between older forms of banking culture, based on the branch, and a new form of banking sales culture. These tensions are not simply between abstract business ideas but are bound up with images of who bankers 'should' be, in terms of the qualities and values they bring to their work. It is partly for these reasons that restructuring itself is so emotive to people and bears on the identity of workers. It is also this fact which explains why many employees seek to change, modify or oppose various restructuring ideas.

Local government

Local government in Britain has been continuously restructured throughout its history but change has been particularly rapid and extensive in the past decade. Public sector restructuring has rarely been explained solely in terms of securing profitability through the search for new labour supplies (cf. the restructuring paradigm). Rather, restructuring is seen as the result of a political and ideological reshaping of local state institutions in the context of Thatcherism or, more widely, the collapse of consensus around the Keynesian welfare state or, more widely still, as linked to a shift from Fordism to post-Fordism whereby new social and political relations are forged round a new regime of capital accumulation (Stoker, 1990; Hoggett, 1991; Cochrane, 1993; Goodwin *et al.*, 1993). Nonetheless, however the imperative for change is defined, it seems that many of the restructuring strategies delineated in the private sector are also present in the public sector (Urry, 1987; Pinch, 1989). Pinch (1989) suggests public sector examples of all 11 of Urry's restructuring strategies, including investment and technical change (for example, the use of information technology), enhancement of quality (retraining) and subcontracting (compulsory competitive tendering and privatisation).

These strategies may well have consequences for labour demand in local government but this remains relatively unexplored. Service subcontracting has been given most attention in this context since the rationale has often been interpreted as a search for cheaper, more tractable labour, but other restructuring strategies may also change demand for labour, for example by creating new types of job, by emphasising new skills or by substituting women, non-white and part-time workers for full-time, male, white workers. Furthermore, Stoker (1990) and Hoggett (1991) suggest that macro-level shifts towards post-Fordism, especially a new imperative for flexible organisation, are restructuring the local state, which, in turn, demands new forms of management. However, this literature has said remarkably little about *gendered* employment relations within local government. Some subcontracting has affected traditionally female occupations such as cleaning and catering (although other stereotypically male occupations such as refuse collection have also been privatised), and Pinch (1989) suggests that gendered strategies of labour substitution may be taking place. Certainly, the proportion of part-time workers in local government has grown enormously since the 1960s, and most of these workers (91 per cent according to Stone, 1988) are women. However, as in banking, the gendered dynamics of employment relations in local government are far more complex than this and cannot be explained solely by reference to top-down restructuring strategies or changing labour demands. As in banking, the changing *supply* of female labour has also been important, with more credentialed women entering local government and some of those rising to senior positions. However, we will argue below that neither changing labour demand nor the changing labour supply explain shifting gender relations in local government organisations. We begin by outlining the traditional forms of local government organisation and argue that specific forms of masculinity have been embedded in these organisational designs and cultures. We then consider recent organisational changes, illustrating our argument that restructuring has privileged new identities and forms of behaviour amongst employees, and that these too are gendered.

Traditionally, local authorities have been divided into functionally based departments managed by a core profession (e.g. accountants in finance departments, social workers in social services, etc.). Typically, faith has been placed in professional knowledge as an adequate foundation for management, each department tending to believe in the superiority of its own knowledge base (Elcock, 1982; see Chapter 4 for a further discussion of these points). The relationship between local authorities and their service users has been based upon a culture of authority and distance, whereby bureaucratic judgements were made about individuals' access to standardised services and users were given little say in the design of those services. Harry, a Senior Housing Manager who had worked in local government for over 30 years, claimed that the attitude used to be that 'this job would be all right if it wasn't for the punters'.

This form of organisation in local authorities has been intimately connected to the staff characteristics valued by local authority organisations. Johns (1973) suggests that organisations noted for their security and stability of work functions (which includes the traditional local authority) attracted employees themselves motivated by security and stability, which in turn were 'clearly associated with personal rigidity and resistance to innovation' (1973: 68). Certainly, one key attribute traditionally valued in our authorities was the need to be seen to 'toe the line', to ensure the smooth reproduction of existing organisational norms. Harry reminisced:

> When I was 16... we had to remember two golden rules... you don't need to have initiative and you don't enter politics... it was a requirement not to rock the boat.

In practice, there was little room for initiative, especially from junior members of the organisation, since a small oligarchy of senior managers controlled most departments:

> you only needed to know eight people to know where the power lay. Once you'd sorted out those eight people there were no problems. [Harry]

And this was in a department with thousands of staff!

Linked to this a high value has also been placed on 'time-serving', length of service being a major factor in promotion decisions. Keith, a senior finance manager, revealed:

> I found with men, some are very committed, fine, but others... my experience has shown me that some of them just expect to get promoted because that's just 'what happens'... it was always Buggins's turn. I mean a lot of people weren't promoted on merit.

Although less explicit than in banking, management in local government has in the past clearly been linked to masculinity both literally, in that most managers were male, and in terms of the masculine qualities linked to constructions of management. In Midcity a photograph of one departmental management team showed eight white men, with some striking physical similarities, all in their forties and fifties. Claire, a junior clerk in the department, was clear about the reasons for this:

> [It's] to attract people. They'd probably feel more secure with someone like that. More confident in their abilities because they've got the secure family life and they're level headed and they know their wife is at home waiting for them so they're more relaxed, that sort of thing.

Furthermore, although local authority staff have never been subject to the explicit gender controls exercised over bank workers – in terms of recruitment practices and the monitoring of personal life – they have been expected to 'order their lives with such circumspection that there can be no cause for adverse comment about their way of life' (Jackson, 1958: 128). It is clear that homosocial reproduction has taken place at management level and that this is connected to qualities of stability, loyalty, rationality and 'fit', which are in turn linked to white, heterosexual masculinity (Pringle, 1989a; Cockburn, 1991). (See the discussion of Kanter in Chapter 1, and Chapters 6 and 7 for discussion of the organisational construction of bodies, emotions and sexualities.) Stability and loyalty are also linked to length of service, which, given actual or predicted career breaks for childcare, is also more likely to be seen as a feature of the male worker.

Also, as in banking, the traditional local government image rested upon a culture of authority and distance from the public. This has recently become difficult to defend. Largely under the guise of economic rationality and improving service quality, successive Conservative governments mounted a sustained ideological attack on local government, drawing heavily on a critique of the nature of local authority organisation. Central government was not the only place where such criticisms were mounted. Service consumers, and indeed many local government staff themselves, endorsed criticisms of weak management and user-unfriendly 'bureaucratic paternalism' (Hoggett and Hambleton, 1987) contributing to the impetus for organisational change.

Local authorities have responded in different ways to these developments. Although some have embraced the ideals of Thatcherism, most have rejected 'market forces' as the means to quality service provision, preferring instead to introduce other changes. The degree of change varies, but two general trends are evident. First, as in banking, there have been attempts to develop more accessible and democratic relationships with the public. Second, attempts have been made to introduce new forms of corporate and generic management. Strategies to improve local authority relationships with consumers include greater provision of information, improved accessibility to council services, the democratisation of service design and delivery, and recognition of the diverse needs of different sexes, ages and ethnicities. This new approach has been referred to as 'public service orientation', and its implementation is seen to require far-reaching changes to the culture of local government organisations. The segmented, top-down nature of local government authority management and the rigid demarcation of job boundaries might be acceptable in a stable environment, where departments determine standard service provision, but they are seen as increasingly inappropriate for local government in the 1990s (Passmore, 1990). Also, long-running injunctions to 'modernise' local government organisations, and enhance corporate and generic managment, finally appear to have taken hold during the current period of restructuring (Leach *et al.*, 1994). Across the sector there is now an emphasis on the need for innovative organisation. Gone are the days when 'for many officers the responsibility of making decisions under delegated powers [was] a fearful one' (Knowles, 1971: 79). Today there is demand for 'change masters' (Kanter, 1989), with the vision to move beyond established patterns of practice.

Both these trends were identifiable in our two authorities, although more changes had taken place in Midcity than South-town. This is perhaps not surprising given the size and national prominence of Midcity and the relatively greater influence of the new-left on local politics there. In 1984 Midcity began a decentralisation initiative, which by 1994 had resulted in a network of neighbourhood offices, each representing the major service departments in the authority. Front-line staff were decentralised to these locations, where consumers can carry out all their business with the authority. The Council has also improved the flow of information to citizens and extended its complaints procedure, and makes frequent public commitments to quality service provision (Figure 3.1).

Figure 3.1 Extract from Midcity's Annual Report

QUEST FOR QUALITY

Quality. It's hard to define, even harder to measure… but obvious to service users when it's not delivered. Midcity recognises that the people who know best what a quality service should be are the people of the city. That's why the City council is serious about listening to its citizens and learning from them the value they place on the wide range of services offered.

Decentralisation has altered the structure of departments with the multi-service nature of the neighbourhood offices, breaking down departmentalism, and managerial responsibility is being devolved down the hierarchy and linked to defined geographical areas. In addition at the time of our research, finance staff had recently been redeployed from a central department to each of the budget-holding centres across the authority (ie. the Finance Department was being broken up and staff distributed across other departments). The authority now has a Department of Strategic Management, and across the authority far greater emphasis is now placed on the need for managerial competence.

The smaller size of Southtown makes this kind of decentralisation less feasible, and the persistence of a more traditional organisational culture and local politics has also limited restructuring. However, there has been a drive to change the public face of the authority. The volume of public information has increased, and in 1993 a post was advertised which would specifically entail managing the image of the authority to the 'outside world'. The Town Hall has been enlarged and refurbished, making it more accessible, and staff now wear uniforms so that the public can readily identify them. The structure of the authority has actually changed little, with departments still self-contained and tending towards departmentalism, but even here an early shift towards managerialism, rather than professionalism, is recognised by many workers.

The changes described above challenge the traditional structure and culture of local government organisations and also redefine the qualities privileged in workers. With greater emphasis being placed on generic and corporate management skills and on the capacity for innovation, the older qualities of technical competence, stability and fit with tradition are becoming less serviceable (Elcock, 1991; Cochrane, 1993). Linking management style to the new emphasis on decentralising authority, the ability to empower staff and respond flexibly to user demands replaces the ability to impose fixed bureaucratic rules (Hoggett, 1991). It is the gendered implications of these changes which we particularly wish to explore here. In what follows we concentrate on Midcity, where restructuring has been further-reaching.

In Midcity the qualities of openness, innovation, flexibility, participatory management and awareness of EO have been highlighted in recent years. Considering the question 'Who gets ahead here and why?', Elaine, a senior manager working in a personnel function, said:

> Innovators, at the moment. ... The people we get here are the general management and they get the credit and get recognised and get taken

seriously... the problem-solving innovators are the people who get ahead at the moment.

> **Q:**   And that's a change from the past?

Very much so, yes.

And Harry said that in the past:

> what you learnt to do was to get yourself out of big holes... and you prided yourself on this sort of macho environment that was very much about 'we can get out of any mess that we're in' rather than 'how did we get into the mess in the first place and how do we stop getting into the mess?' And that's where we [are starting] to focus now.

Similarly, Christoper – a junior finance manager – told us that when he started with the authority:

> It was more, like you know, old guard. The idea of single top bosses. There was a certain way to do things and that was the proper way. [Now] the overall management style has changed. It's much more relaxed, more approachable.

Like banking, these trends appear to undermine traditional male bastions of power. Emphasis upon new skills, a move from established managerial practices, empowerment of those further down the ladder (predominantly women) and greater emphasis upon customer care (linked to 'feminine' qualities of accessibility and caring) all potentially offer greater opportunities for women. Indeed, in several cases it was suggested that women were benefiting from the changes (see also Maddock, 1993). Keith, the manager who talked about the 'Buggins syndrome', linked this specifically to men (see above) and contrasted women, who, he felt, had never assumed that long services equalled promotion. Elaine argued that:

> Women are much more comfortable with what's going on. I mean this organisation is making enormous demands on its managers at all levels to change, to adapt, to improve, you know. To be more efficient, more

effective, to manage better in every kind of way and… the women have responded to that challenge I think more forcefully, much more constructively and with much less personal grief than the men have.

Neil, a junior clerical worker, contrasted the old and new styles of management:

You've still got managers that were under the old management regime, still trying to implement old management ways, but because the majority of them are now new managers there's been like a new wave of enthusiasm. But there are still one or two [living in the past] when things were done properly. I suppose it's like your parents always thinking old fashioned values, it's exactly like that in [my] office. You've got Mr. Hitler sitting there who still wants the section run the same and you've also got Ms Flexible who's like 'well, we'll change what we used to do and we'll get a better way out'.

He went on to describe the styles of his two bosses, one male and the other female:

For one half of the week it's completely unbearable because you've got the guy bringing down his forceful image of male management, and on the other hand you've got the more sympathetic, subtle approach from the female manager.

This evidence indicates that Midcity is placing enhanced value on qualities that have been culturally identified as 'feminine', at the expense of those culturally linked to masculinity. However, as in banking, there are some significant qualifications to this point. First, we should be wary of the dubious essentialism entailed in suggestions that women 'are' more open, friendly and accessible or that men 'are' rigid, inflexible or unapproachable, however widely these notions are now represented in both texts and popular discourses on women and management (Leonard, 1995). Underscoring this point our second qualification concerns the apparent emergence of a new form of organisational masculinity in local government management, qualitatively distinct from more traditional qualities and marked by virtues of competitiveness, dynamism and innovation similar to those we saw in banking. Coyle (1988: 47) describes a 'workaholic "macho" ethos taking over local government management'. Whilst the old, time-served patriarch 'town clerk' model of management is under threat, Coyle suggests that rather than the new managerialism improving women's opportunities 'we are witnessing a creeping "hard" managerialism... which increasingly associates managerial competence with masculinity' (1988: 48). Furthermore, extremely long hours are expected of the new managers and, just as in the past, home life continues to be subsumed to careers, and male sociability continues to shape careers and working life. Our third and final qualification concerns the resilience of established professional groups in the face of these recent challenges to their privilege. Whilst new non-professional skills have been increasingly emphasised and the older currency of technical competence has been undermined, it appears that professional groups may be adapting to accommodate these new skills and qualities rather than being sidelined by them. We discuss this at length in Chapter 4.

Nursing in the National Health Service

The National Health Service (NHS), too, has been subject to constant changes in organisation, management and funding throughout its history, but especially in the past decade. In addition to intense pressure from central government to reduce costs, two major national programmes of organisational change have been introduced during this period. The 1983 Griffiths Report introduced new NHS management structures, whilst the 1990 NHS and Community Care Act imposed an 'internal market' in the service. This created a clear organisational distinction between 'providers' (i.e. hospitals) and 'purchasers' (e.g. fund-holding GPs and Health Authorities), giving purchasers budgets and the right to choose which services to buy.

Government discourse linked both programmes of reform with cutting public expenditure, but they were also clearly concerned with changing the culture of the NHS. Common themes addressed how the NHS should be managed, by whom and with what guiding principles. The Griffiths reforms not only required new management structures (principally new general managers with overall responsibility for particular services or 'Units'), but also attempted to instill a managerialist culture throughout the NHS, right down to the 'shop-floor' level of care delivery. Allied to the Griffiths Report, visible budgeting was introduced, marking a shift towards financial/ business management, a transformation consolidated by the introduction of the 1990 Act shifting power from professional and clinical judgement towards financial, managerial and consumer (purchaser) demands.

Several writers have used the restructuring paradigm to examine recent changes in the NHS (e.g. Mohan, 1988a, b; Pinch, 1989). However, more academic attention has focused on how both reforms are reshaping the articulation of 'professional clinical values' with 'managerial values' (Owens and Glennester, 1989; Strong and Robinson, 1990; Flynn, 1992; Hunter, 1994; Walby *et al.*, 1994). In his enquiry into NHS management Griffiths claimed that the 1974 reform of the NHS had failed to introduce effective management. This was mainly because there was no single hierarchy of authority, but separate professional hierarchies working collectively, and because professional interests blurred good management. The Griffiths Report represented a determined attempt to settle once and for all the question of 'professional' versus 'managerial' values and culture in the management and provision of health care. A new cadre of general managers was introduced, with clear lines of accountability and a set of financially driven objectives that were to be polluted as little as possible by the 'noise' of clinical interest groups.

To date these issues have been debated and assessed almost exclusively in terms of managerial encroachment on medical, that is *doctors'*, autonomy. Nursing has been largely ignored in academic evaluations of restructuring, reflecting and indeed reinforcing the lesser influence and power of nurses as an occupational group. In this section we will consider the ways in which the shift towards managerialism has impacted on the location of nurses in the NHS, and the ways in which nurses themselves interpret the shifting interface of 'managerial' and 'professional' qualities in nursing work and in NHS organisations.

We begin with the small body of work that explores changes in nursing today, and contextualises these within analyses of restructuring and gender relations more generally. Mackay's study (1989) of nurses in one Health Authority in the late 1980s offers a rich and informative account of nurses' current experiences. However, analytically, Mackay 'holds apart' nurses and restructuring, presenting a highly partisan analysis of 'how awful it is to be a nurse' in the context of a changing health service. This is not to say that Mackay's analysis is incorrect. Undoubtedly, Mackay vividly conveys what it means to be a nurse in a climate of rationalisation, cost-cutting and chronic understaffing, and indeed many of the nurses we interviewed echoed many of these same sentiments and views. However, in Mackay's analysis nurses come across as hapless victims of restructuring: as somehow set apart from it. Restructuring is presented as something that 'happens to' nurses, who are described as 'suffering from the present economic policies of the Health Service' (1989: 178). There is little appreciation of what we term 'embedded restructuring'. Decision-making and change are not being carried out 'to order' by passive employees of the NHS, as a result of political directives from above (which is very much the flavour of Mackay's account). Rather, the work of nursing is being conducted within a changing organisational context and nurses are *part* of this change. Listening to what nurses say tells us more than what nurses are doing and how they feel; it can also reveal something about the complex process of change and resistance to change currently going on within NHS organisations.

Walby and Greenwell's study (1994, with Mackay and Soothill) of doctors and nurses in the NHS firmly locates both groups' experiences within an analysis of restructuring. From the outset it is recognised that any study of doctors and nurses in today's NHS will confront the paradox that, in both cases, work practices are highly traditional yet placed in the middle of an ambitious restructuring programme, driven by attempts to impose 'new wave management' on previously autonomous teams of professionals. The analytical stage in Walby *et al.*'s account is thus set for conflict and change, whereas Mackay's analysis sometimes verges towards representing nurses as dinosaurs in a modern world which is changing all around them. The crux of Walby *et al.*'s analysis is that of a current uneasy co-existence between Fordist and post-Fordist styles of management and working practices in the NHS, where Fordism is characterised by specialised divisions of labour, rigid bureaucratic hierarchy and centralised control, whilst post-Fordism is characterised by flexibility, decentralisation, devolution of decision-making and the flattening out of work organisations, as well as the notion of more responsiveness to consumer-led demand. Walby *et al.*'s diagnosis of change in the NHS is that:

> A general move towards Fordist practices characterised the post-war period in health until the early 1980s, and has since been replaced by an attempt to shift health work in a post-Fordist direction (1994: 162).

However, there is no question of a wholesale shift or clean break with Fordism. Rather the two uneasily co-exist:

> The NHS changes represent a form of post-Fordism in so far as there has been devolution of budgetary control and decision-making to GP budget holders, and to the Trusts and their clinical directorates, but this is contradicted by the way that the market mechanism operates, compelling professional staff to make decisions within a tight contractual framework that is budget limited, and controlled finally by Treasury decisions. Within hospitals, the apparently contradictory principles of devolving authority to autonomous teams, and management through controlled sub-division of tasks are both evident (Walby *et al.*, 1994: 173).

In relation to our argument about 'embedded restructuring', Walby *et al.*'s analysis succeeds in conveying the flavour of contestation and change in interprofessional relations between nurses and doctors, as well as in those between managers and professionals. Restructuring, interpreted as a historic shift towards post-Fordist structures of control and organisation within the NHS (albeit with some Taylorist undertones), is understood as a complex process reaching from government policy-making down through the layers of health service organisation, from the Treasury to the hospital ward, but animated by people and interests at each level.

Unlike local government, where changes to management systems have been largely a matter of organisational choice, much NHS management restructuring has been highly prescriptive, with central government imposing new national systems and hierarchies. In this respect it has more in common with banking. However, without underestimating these imposed changes, it is clear that restructuring in the NHS is not simply *determined* by them. Implementation of the general framework set by Griffiths (and other top-down reforms) varies from one Health Authority to another. This highlights the way in which actual restructuring is an embedded process. In order for restructuring to take place, Health Authority and hospital staff have to implement change, but, as we have shown in banking and local government, implementation is never predictable or certain. Second, and connected to the previous point, hospitals are composed of individuals and groups with interests that colour the interpretation and implementation of any proposals for change. These individuals and groups have their own agendas for change – organisationally and/or professionally – which articulate with changes imposed from outside the organisation or individual professions. In this, hospitals are like any other organisation.

In both the hospitals we studied there were instances of the three restructuring strategies delineated by Massey and Meegan (1982) from their study of manufacturing (cf. Mohan, 1988a; Pinch, 1989). The introduction of the internal market has given greater prominence to *rationalisation*. In Midcity, for example, a women's hospital was shut down, and maternity services were relocated within Midcity Hospital. *Intensification* was in evidence, for example at Southtown, where the decade from 1982 to 1992 had seen an increase of 20 per cent in real money, a decrease of 20 per cent in beds, but an increased throughput of *43 per cent* in patients. Clearly, this means that nurses are now carrying heavier workloads. As Anne, a nurse at Southtown, said:

> The whole structure has changed and it's been very turbulent. I mean... at times it has been abysmal with all the changes going on at once... The

actual number of patients that have come in, like on the medical side, which I work a lot on, has been up 25 per cent but they've tried to treat them and the turnover has been huge. They've not employed more staff.

In Midcity there were also moves to introduce *new ward-based technology* – linked mainly to financial management systems – and a new nursing post had been created specifically in order to facilitate this.

A Sister, Janet, described the changes to nursing work thus:

When I first started the amount of patients we had was relatively small in comparison to what it is today, and the manager who ran the unit was a very different manager. It was very friendly and there was time to talk to one another and to the patients, and everybody knew each other and the patients, whereas now I think the whole structure of it has changed because the amount of patients that we have has doubled, if not trebled, and therefore the amount of work that's involved has doubled, if not trebled.

This illustrates well how NHS restructuring has combined quantitative change (in this case intensification of work) with more qualititative changes in the nature of organisational management. We found pervasive evidence of a shift towards a managerialist culture in both hospitals, although this was less marked in Midcity than in Southtown, an interesting reversal of the situation in local government. This difference was connected both to the relative sizes of the two hospitals (Southtown was far smaller and change seemed a simpler process) and to the presence of particularly powerful medical interests at Midcity, not all of whom were in favour of the proposed changes. The size difference also meant that nurses in Midcity usually placed their descriptions of change in the context of their particular specialism or department, whilst nurses in Southtown had a far stronger sense of the overall organisation, sometimes stretching beyond the hospital to regional management. Despite these differences there are some clear similarities in the accounts from both hospitals.

In particular, nurses articulated a strong sense of the organisational rationale shifting from a 'service' to a 'business' ethic. Diane at Southtown Hospital put it in the following way:

the problem is that the higher management coming in now are just not nursing orientated, and how you can have somebody coming in from industry to sit on the board of a hospital and dictate about the policies of nursing when basically they've got no idea what nursing's about – I don't agree with that... The whole atmosphere of the hospital is changing no end. It's much more business oriented now. That's going down even to basic ward level, ...even there they are having to look at the resources they've got, and staff that they've got, ...if not, why not. We are looking at running the units as a business... We're now more accountable for our funding. We are budgeting and working out the costs of everything that we use, and the ordering of things, and looking more at getting a better service from the supplier.

Nurses felt an increasing distance between themselves and senior managers. In Southtown this was expressed by Susan at the level of regional organisation:

We're always being told that the authority care for us, they're a caring authority, but there's very little evidence, from our side, as to how much they care for us because some people... I don't know, there's a gulf. We don't seem to be able to communicate. We're supposed to have channels of communications to them and we should be able to put in suggestions of what can be done and what can't be done. But people generally feel that nobody cares at top level.

Marginalisation was more commonly felt at hospital level. Nurses felt it was difficult to get their views heard by senior management and that managers appointed from industry had a different, more money-oriented approach. The motivations of people entering the NHS were perceived as shifting, suggesting that people were bringing different qualities into health work. Janet at Midcity commented:

I suspect that in my generation people came into whatever field in the health service because they wanted to serve and they thought as a way of contributing to the community. But now they come in because they see it as a business. I mean, OK, health is important, but they don't come in for that. And other people are not attracted in the way they were because it was a steady job. We got a lot of people recruited into nursing at one time because they thought that it was a steady job. They may have been dedicated or they may not have been dedicated. I think those times have now gone and people working in the health service is not necessarily for life.

At Southtown there was an even stronger sense of 'them' and 'us', counterposing a hospital management tier, who were introducing the changes, and a tier of health workers on the receiving end. Brenda contextualised this through comparison with the 'old days':

At the moment with all the NHS reforms I can't really identify the structures of management. I feel they can't identify with me and I can't identify with them. I feel more frustrated now having been in the old school of nursing, with the Matron and the Deputy Matron, and now there's nurse managers and directorates. In the olden days, and I mean the olden days – I'm going back to perhaps 20 years ago – the Matron and the Deputy Matron would liaise with you and listen to you. Management now doesn't seem to me to be a two-way thing. They talk, but they don't take anything on board. They're there and we're here.

At one level this could be taken simply as nostalgia for the days when nurses managed nurses, and when nursing was characterised by a Fordist mode of governance or control with a rigid, bureaucratic internal hierarchy (Walby *et al.*, 1994). But there is also a strong sense of 'two cultures' conveyed here – one managerialist, the other professional – with a gulf in between. The new managerialism was generating a lot of distrust about all the changes amongst nurses. Anne experienced it as:

[Those] up there telling you to save money... a them and us situation, which it shouldn't be really. ...They're more concerned with the budget. It's got to balance.

The uneasy co-existence of these two cultures was consistently articulated by the vast majority of the nurses we interviewed. The new managerialism was counterposed with the culture of nurse professionalism in terms of financial constraints versus patients' needs, of being a ward manager rather than a bedside nurse, of managing resources rather than caring for patients, and of financial management versus people management. The gendered subtext of nurses' negative evaluations of this new managerialism is complex. Some nurses clearly associated the new managerialism with the ascendancy of a 'macho' culture. Although there were still a lot of senior women in nursing, more and more men were seen to be coming in at the new managerial levels, and running through many of the interviews was the sense, if not explicit association, that the values of the new managerialism were fundamentally masculinist ones, literally embodied in the new breed of male managers. In this type of account managerialism was linked to a preoccupation with masculinist values centering on the rational, quantitative, decision-making criteria of budgets. Nurse professionalism was contrasted to this through reference to more feminised values centring on the intangible, qualitative and relational criteria of a job well done by a nurse for a patient.

Perhaps the main ways in which nurses were being confronted on a daily level with the reality of the new managerialism in health care was through their experiences of working within clinical directorates (CDs). CDs operate as separate business divisions within the hospital, combining managerial and service functions at a sub-Unit level and with their own financial and patient targets. Whereas the relationship between higher and lower levels of the organisation was often described in terms of a gulf between these two managerialist and service cultures, the CD structure was described as the location where these cultures meet. It is here that we can best see the impact of current restructuring on nursing and explore the tensions, conflicts, reconciliations and compromises between managerial and professional or clinical cultures.

CDs had been introduced across the board at Southtown and at great speed 'without people that were actually getting into post knowing exactly where they were going or how they were going to handle it' (Susan). At Midcity, where CDs were being introduced during the course of our research, one Nurse Manager, Beth, decribed being caught in the crossfire between the rapidly shifting demands in the early 1990s emanating from the regrading of nursing staff, new managerialist directives around budgets and the introduction of a new CD structure. Told that she could regrade her professional and technical staff without regard for monetary implications (cost approximately £120,000), she then received only a fraction of this in extra funding and had to find £100,000 out of the following year's budget. As a consequence she was getting flack both from nursing staff and from the new clinical director. She also described how during this same period she was passed over for the post of clinical director after having been virtually promised it:

> politically it wasn't acceptable within the organisation because I was the only non-doctor offered a director's role and a certain group of medical staff were most uncomfortable with that. I felt I'd had an opportunity snatched away from me, and really felt aggrieved by it for a long time, although I tried not to let that get in the way of me doing the work and moving into a triumvirate situation [i.e. Clinical Director, Business Manager and Nurse Manager] for managing the department... Ultimately I felt squeezed out. Once I'd given them [the Clinical Director and Business Manager] the information that they needed to function, it was almost as though I was no longer necessary... and the department very much veered towards the financial management of the department and away from the people management, which I felt very uncomfortable with. [Beth]

Although there have been widespread claims that the new managerialism in the NHS will rob doctors of power, there is little evidence of this in our hospitals. Certainly, in Midcity there was little evidence of the CD curtailing consultant power through the shackling of clinical to budgetary criteria in decision-making. This is quite simply because, comparing the prestigious teaching hospital with a general hospital, consultant 'fiefdoms' exist in the former to a greater extent than in the latter. The 'old boy network', as Beth described it, was much more in evidence at Midcity and, in her view, where CDs had been introduced, it encouraged consultants to compete for *even more* power than before:

I think the health service reforms have put too much power with the medical staff... [In theory the reforms were intended to] put the management responsibility on the shoulders of the people who are using the resources in the hope of controlling that use of resource. To a certain extent that works, but what happens is that they [consultants] pick each other off and if they feel that they should have a greater slice of the cake, then they're not beyond jeopardising the future of one of their colleague's specialities. [Beth]

In fact there was also some evidence that CDs were *increasing* the inter-professional power of consultants over nurses. In one case, a (consultant) Clinical Director was determining nurses' training needs in terms of 'his' directorate rather than taking into account the professional development needs of the nurses, as has more usually been the case. CDs may also extend the accountability of nurses to medical staff, who are gaining most Clinical Director posts and to whom they are now responsible (instead of a senior nurse). These observations substantiate Levitt and Wall's (1992) suggestion that:

At a lower level of the organisation, the development of clinical directorates are seen by some nurses as a threat to their professional status because ward nurses are obliged to be much more accountable to the clinical directors, who are invariably doctors (1992: 232).

At Southtown, nurses were generally rather less pessimistic about the introduction of CDs. One described good working relationships in her CD. Another CD in community care was composed of three out of the four former nurse managers of Health Visiting and District Nursing. In addition, the decentralisation of decision-making that is part and parcel of the philosophy of CDs was sometimes seen as a positive move, particularly:

If directorates are going to have more control over their unit... it's more individual care – because a general surgical ward is completely different from an orthopaedic ward, and a paediatric ward is different to whatever... [Veronica]

In other words, CDs might enable clinical staff to be responsive to patient needs and allocate care accordingly (see also Walby *et al.,* 1994, who claim this to be part and parcel of a shift towards post-Fordism and the associated recentering of the patient).

In short, restructuring in the NHS is widely perceived as a renegotiation of the accommodation between professional and managerial interests in the health service. As far as nurses are concerned, these dynamics are often couched in terms that link managerialism to masculinised qualities, and professionalism to nurses and feminised qualities. On the other hand there is ample evidence of a widespread belief that nurses – as an occupational group – simply cannot, and indeed should not, manage (Owens and Glennester, 1989; Strong and Robinson, 1990) since (it is alleged) they are unable to escape from an inward-looking and narrow professional culture – or, in the words of one District Finance Director, 'drivelling endlessly about the profession' (Strong and Robinson, 1990: 55). There is also a gendered sub-text because the perception that nurses cannot manage is often linked to the perception that *women* cannot manage (Carpenter, 1977). More specifically, the denigration of nursing management styles as *ad hoc* and unsystematic has been accompanied by an association between such styles of 'coping management' and the fact that most nurses are women (Davies, 1992, 1995). Yet, as Davies so powerfully argues, a simple appeal to the gender of managers does not explain nurses' management style. Instead, we have to look at gender relations within the NHS to recognise that coping management styles are more the outcome of the neglect of nursing within the organisation of the NHS and not an intrinsically female mode of managing.

Whatever the situation in the current rhetoric of nurse professionalisation, as well as in the minds of most nurses, privileged nursing qualities are defined in terms of clinical, rather than managerial, skills. This distancing of nursing qualities from managerial competencies may not bode well for the position of nurses in the managerialist culture of the 1990s NHS. However, the dynamics of managerialism and professionalism and the future place of nursing in the NHS are more complex and indeterminate than this. First, current restructuring is clearly increasing nurses' managerial responsibility at the level of the ward. Despite the rhetoric of nurses' managerial incompetence, the recent introduction of visible budgeting, coupled with the pressure to decentralise the management of the delivery of care, are creating pressures on Ward Sisters to develop new kinds of managerial competencies. Ward Sisters are now primarily responsible for 'managing' care delivery by a team of staff and are themselves involved in very little bedside care. Various scenarios were painted by nurses from both hospitals. One scenario, with negative connotations was that:

> You're not coming in to be a bedside nurse. You're going to be a ward manager rather than a bedside nurse. It's going to be the care assistants who are going to be the basic nurses. Nurses will be doing the ward management. [Sarah]

But not all nurses regard these developments negatively. Another scenario highlights the multiple skills that a Ward Sister will develop, and links this positively to new moves to make all nurses more autonomous, including Staff Nurses. Judith stated that:

> A Ward Sister is doing much less patient care. ...there's a lot more managerial skill to it now, a lot of assessing [of trainee nurses], ... evaluating the whole care that a patient gets. ...I think the whole ethos of most sisters is to manage the workload of the patients in general, to make sure that all the staff are trained in order to do all those jobs that they have, to act as a mentor and resource for her staff ...although you manage the workload as a whole, I think it's much more about managing the staff than it ever was, because before you just dictated to your staff, and now your staff are going to be much more autonomous so you're there as a resource.

Despite this, nurses are not recognised as managers within the NHS, and many nurses themselves are critical of the changes – defining themselves as professionals first, who are having managerial responsiblities foisted upon them. Clearly, the position of nursing within discourses of managerialism and professionalism is not only driven by groups outside nursing (cf. Walby *et al.*, 1994; Witz, 1994). Nurses *themselves* endorse professional competencies over managerial ones:

> I would put my money on clinical nurse specialists where they put their expertise into their clinical areas and leave someone else to manage, as long as the managers will listen to those clinical nurses. Anyone can manage! [Andrea]

Indeed, the general drift of nurses' own occupational strategies over the past decade has been towards the deepening and specialisation of clinical skills. 'Clinical Nurse Specialist', 'Nurse Consultant' and 'Advanced Nurse Practitioner' are all terms recently or currently in vogue within nursing's professional and educational bodies. Precisely how the changes set in train by the nursing profession itself, around education, practice and the nursing career, are intersecting with the more general trajectory of health service restructuring is a fluid and rather indeterminate matter at present.[2] However, what our data consistently revealed was a definition of the content and meaning of nursing which was, for the most part, radically out of kilter with the ways in which the content and meaning of 'professional' labour are being reformulated in the context of restructuring. It is clear that notions of 'caring' and 'managing' can no longer be counterposed as incompatible activities, particularly for Ward Sisters whose evolving role demands that they 'do' management, and for Nurse Managers who, as part of a CD team, are no longer simply 'managing the nursing' but increasingly managing the delivery of packages of care *and* the budgets.

Our final point in this section concerns the clear parallels between the newly enhanced professional role of nursing and the new rhetoric of consumerism in the NHS, epitomised by the 'Patient's Charter', and the expressed aim of much current restructuring to transform the NHS from a provider-driven service to a user-driven one more responsive to the needs and wants of patients. One of the core notions in nurses' current attempts to reshape or enhance their professional identity is that of the nurse as 'patient advocate', translating patient-identified needs into practices of care. This may offer nurses a new source of authority within the NHS, although the outcome is as yet far from certain. On this point it is worth noting the similarities between what is happening in the NHS and the 'sales culture' in banking, and the increased emphasis on user accountability in local authorities. However, there are also important differences, for it is by no means clear that the 'patient' is a 'consumer', especially as it is Health Authorities that are charged with the task of 'purchasing' health services and assessing the needs of their local populations in order to secure services appropriate to the nature and amount of 'demand'. In addition, the dominant discourses of professionalism in health care have always placed the patient's needs at the centre – albeit if, in the case of medicine, this sometimes took the form of 'doctor knows best what patient needs'.

The main point to emerge from our discussion of nursing in a changing NHS is the perceived conflict between professionalism and managerialism, which is seen to be at the heart of organisational restructuring and very much on the minds of organisational participants. In other words nurses are clearly struggling to come to terms with new organisational perceptions of the kinds of qualities they are increasingly being called upon to possess. Nurses are living through a time of change. Some of these changes are emanating from within the profession of nursing itself; others are taking place within the organisational context of nursing work. It is important to stress, however, that we have not documented nurses' articulation of professional, service values simply with a view to legitimating and defending them. This is not our role as researchers. We have documented these in order to reveal how organisational participants articulate one set of values, whilst at the same time perceiving conflicts and tensions between these values and the changing expectations of others in a period of restructuring. Many of the new managers are cognisant of these values and of the gulf between the motivations for their own actions and those of other staff in the NHS. Indeed, the General Manager at Southtown Hospital, who had been a key 'change agent' introducing a new corporate structure and CD system, reflected on the subtle shifts over the past decade in the qualities that managers themselves felt were

needed. He reflected upon how, in the early years of the Griffiths reforms, there *was* a culture of 'macho management',
because that was what they thought was wanted, together with a
disdain for professionals. Since the introduction of the internal
market, which really does shift power away from the centre,
there has to be a new, less macho, culture of management, which
rebuilds bridges with doctors and nurses in order to delegate
and share power. This, then, is clearly a time when *all* key organisational players are being forced to reflect upon what they do
and, in the process, begin to do things a bit differently.

Conclusions

In this chapter we have outlined some of the far-reaching
changes that are transforming the nature of organisation in each
of our three sectors. We have argued that whilst existing
accounts in the restructuring paradigm are useful in that they
draw attention to the significance of labour, they are less than
adequate for exploring the gendering of organisational restructuring. Using examples from all three sectors we have shown
that restructuring cannot be understood simply as a top-down
economic imperative to change organisational structures.
Instead, we have argued that restructuring is centrally concerned
with changing the qualities of organisational members and that
restructuring is an on-going and human process open to contestation and manipulation. We have also highlighted processes of
cultural restructuring in organisations. In the case of banking
this was based around a tension between a traditional branch
banking ethos and a new sales culture. In local government and
nursing tensions between 'professional' and 'managerial' cultures,
discourses and practices were more apparent. In particular, we
have argued that restructuring at the level of the organisation as
it is lived entails shifting identities of organisational participants,
who find themselves simultaneously embroiled within and
alienated from new ways of doing things, new ways of seeing
things and new ways of understanding the intersection between
the personal and the organisational. Our term 'embedded'

restructuring is designed to do justice to the way in which restructuring is bound up with the redefinition of the personal identities and performative aspects of employees; it thereby draws attention to the way in which restructuring is grounded in everyday routines and tensions in the workplace, and also opens up the potential for forms of tension and conflict between organisational members.

Clearly, changes in the qualities that are organisationally privileged have implications for the careers of organisational members. We have alluded to this throughout the chapter but we go on to concentrate on careers in the next two chapters. Chapter 4 considers explicitly the employment careers of those currently working in our three sectors, examining in detail the ways in which organisational change have altered career routes. Chapter 5 will move on to consider how individuals relate to paid work, to 'careers' and to the work life relationship, in an organisational context. The notions of 'strategy' and 'narrative' become central for initiating our investigation of the subjective dimensions of organisational restructuring.

4 Organisational Change and Career Restructuring

Introduction

In Chapter 3 we explored how restructuring was an embedded process which, amongst other things, involved changing the personal qualities valued by our organisations, and we discussed some of the tensions this gave rise to. The next two chapters turn to look directly at how restructuring is related to the gendering of careers. The present chapter concentrates on broad structural changes and aims to show how the nature of career mobility, specifically the gendered nature of career mobility, is changing in each of our three sectors. We examine how restructuring has impacted on the established trajectories of organisational positions through which people have carved out careers over time. Then, in Chapter 5 we concentrate directly on people's attitudes, focusing on individual career narratives that illuminate the reflexive ways in which people engage with their workplace organisations.

It is important to begin this chapter by examining the concept of 'career', a term used in diverse ways. As we have already argued with reference to 'organisation' and 'restructuring', we will show that it is not possible simply to 'add on' gender to an otherwise gender–neutral account of 'career'. In this chapter we bring these points together by paying particular attention to the ways in which gender imbues career processes. Career pathways should not simply be seen as movements between positions in abstract organisational charts, but must be seen as literally fleshed out by real, embodied, gendered persons possessing varying amounts of authority, influence, skills and expertise relative to one another.

The concept of career

The concept of career is highly contested within social science (Evetts, 1992, 1994). Conventionally, it describes hierarchical, linear, upward mobility by employees through predefined organisational or occupational job slots. It carries strong connotations of security, of incremental progress as rewards for jobs well done and length of service to the organisation, and of continuous, possibly life-time, employment punctuated by ordered hops up a promotional ladder of opportunities. The emphasis is on *objective career structures* through which individuals move. Evetts (1992) criticises this model for reifying the career, by presenting careers as structurally over-determined by the systemic properties of organisations and assuming a reality over and above the individuals who track through them.

Evetts (1992) is similarly critical of the alternative 'subjective' approach to career. Within symbolic interactionist work, for example, the focus in on how individuals confront, negotiate and manage formal opportunity structures, and understand and interpret their passage through these. Thus there is a much stronger sense that the meaning of 'career' is actively constructed by individuals. However, this too reifies organisational career structures as 'already there' to be negotiated and managed by individuals, leaving intact the distinction between objective structures and forms of subjectivity. Evetts' (1992) own solution for overcoming this action/structure dilemma is to concentrate on 'career process', meaning the *process of change in career patterns,* and to avoid any notion of preexisting career ladders or structures. This can be done:

> by considering routine work place interactions, the work cultures that develop in offices, practices, firms and organizations, and out of which internal bureaucratic practices develop which are used to reach decisions about promotion potential (1992: 17).

This usefully emphasises how 'career' should focus on dynamic processes. However, there is a danger that in this formulation career processes come to be seen as entirely 'open' to pressures and influences, and there is underestimation of how certain types of career process are fixed and stabilised, making them difficult to change. As Layder (1993) emphasises, *individual* employees have relatively little power *vis-à-vis* their employing organisations because specific individuals can usually be substituted by others. Evetts suggests use of the term 'career pattern' to denote more fluidity than that implied by the term 'career structure'. Whilst we have considerable sympathy with Evetts' conceptual intent, surely the term 'structure' is designed precisely to capture the storing up of such 'patterns' of social action over time? One of the key points here is the way in which the bureaucratic, hierarchical career has been remarkably *resilient* to change. This particular meaning and pattern of the orthodox career has been socially sanctioned and constructed to convey material rewards, power and status to those who pursue it, as well as marginalising and disempowering those who do not, or cannot. In sum, we use the term career 'structure' to denote historically sustained patterns of occupational mobility, where multiple individual actions maintain a dominant pattern, which becomes highly resilient to any challenge.

The second point we want to make here concerns the need to understand the *gendering* of career in theory and in practice. In theory the concept of career has been typically androcentric – based on male work life patterns but presented as a gender-neutral concept – whilst, in practice, the accomplishment of this type of career has been more open to men than women. In short, our starting point for analysis should be the hegemonic status of the linear, hierarchical, *male* career, from which we can examine possible challenges to this associated with current rounds of restructuring. In this context it is clearly the case that the prevailing androcentric model of careers as linear occupational advancement is rapidly becoming too limited for understanding men's, let alone women's, careers.

Women's careers are no longer novelties that can be ignored by career theory, yet those currently engaged in the rethinking of career concepts generally pay only scant attention to engendering the *concept* of career (although they might recognise that gender has an effect on the structuring of opportunity in organisations) (cf. Arthur *et al.*, 1989; Pfeffer, 1989). At the same time much research on women's careers lacks a coherent framework into which incremental pieces of empirical analysis can be fitted (Gallos, 1989). Yet, as Marshall (1989) argues, rethinking career theory must entail a deconstruction of its androcentric underpinnings. Questioning the central notions of a self-asserting individual, linear time, and objective measures of success in career theory, Marshall suggests that 'New theories of career must give equal value to male and female aspects of being' (1989: 281).

Certainly, traditional career theory is imbued with essentialist assumptions about men. There is, for example, the 'naturalist' model of career man, which has been advanced by developmental psychologists (Super, 1957; Levinson, 1978). Here, the linear career is seen as central to men's search for meaning and identity. Indeed, the construction of a hierarchical career is presented as a psychological necessity in order that men can pass through adult development successfully. Levinson's views are implicitly endorsed by some feminist writers such as Marshall (1989) and Gallos (1989), who appear to accept his view of male psychology but are critical of its application to women. Drawing on writers such as Gilligan and Chodorow, Gallos argues that because women's development is tied to understanding and strengthening the self in relation to others, women do not pursue the same goal-centred instrumental careers as men, who put occupational progress first. Marshall (1989) develops a similar argument that whilst male careers are based around 'agentic, goal oriented behaviour', women's careers are best seen as organised around the notion of 'communion', which is more concerned to make contacts and relationships. Marshall also urges us to move away from an exclusive focus on the linear career as a series of sequential changes in a person's life and, instead, embrace the notion of cyclic phases, to capture notions of ebb and flow, and a dual appreciation of movement *and* stillness. Staying still, remaining in the same job, can also be a deliberate decision relating to development. In a similar vein, Gutek and Larwood (1987) propose the concept of a 'dual development' model of careers in order to capture ways in which women's careers cannot be entirely understood by reference to the stereotypical patterns of men's careers.

Thus Marshall re-visions career theory by supplementing the notion of the goal-oriented career (male) with one of communion (female). Developing this, Marshall is working with a number of dualisms resonant with (what she perceives as) gendered qualities. The 'agentic career' of forward-looking, goal-dominated individuals resonates with masculinist modes of social action, typified as rational and instrumental, whilst the very term 'communion' denotes a way of being rather than of acting purposefully, and thus resonates with feminine qualities, typically seen by difference theorists (e.g. Gilligan, 1982; Chodorow, 1978,1989) as relational and interdependent.

Whilst Marshall usefully problematises masculinist conceptions of career, her enterprise simply assumes typically gendered modes of engagement and detachment with workplace organisations. For example, she takes for granted that the male career is constructed around rational, agentic processes, although it can be argued that the male career has also been based around forms of 'communion', notably the sort of camaraderie and homosociality explored by Kanter (1977). Roper's (1992) history of male managers in post-war Britain indicates how many men saw their careers in familial and emotional, rather than rational and instrumental, terms. Becoming a manager was not simply about the pursuit of material self-interest but involved complex emotional issues such as winning the acceptance and approval of male father figures and gaining recognition. In short, Marshall's analysis lacks two important features: first, an analysis of gender as relational, and in particular a recognition of the fact that gender relations are institutionalised within job hierarchies that are, literally, fleshed out by embodied participants; and second, a refusal to reify 'career', whether 'agentic' or 'communion' oriented, as this tends to conceal the diversity of career strategies used by both men and women. The conventional paradigm of orderly career and planful, agentic development has limited applicability (Nicholson and West, 1989) for both women *and* men.

It would, however, be a mistake to leap to the opposite conclusion, supported by Evetts, of a 'gender-neutral' concept of career.

Fundamentally, various types of career processes have been constructed as a vehicle for the reproduction of dominant groups, and forms of masculinity are inscribed in career practices and cultures. What we seek to show in this chapter, using material from our case studies, is how the masculinities and femininities inscribed in careers are historically mutable and are indeed undergoing a period of significant change. In particular, we seek to explore how current shifts away from the familial idiom of the traditional bureaucratic career to current concerns have led to important new divisions between 'encumbered' and 'unencumbered' workers, in which an individual's family responsibilities play a key role in defining an employee's 'career worthiness' (see Chapter 6 for an extended discussion of this).

Thus far we have argued that it is vital to abandon both 'naturalist/masculinist' and 'essentialist/feminist' accounts of careers. By implication we are suggesting that the dominance of the linear hierarchical career should not be seen simply as the inevitable reflex of gender. Instead, it is better understood as the outcome of historically specific organisational processes that have played a critical role in defining careers. It is our view that closer attention to organisational processes, and the ways in which these are constitutive of both class and gender relations, is vital in understanding career patterns. Career ladders have become an important device in managing the social relations of organisation and in constructing particular forms of dominance (see generally Pfeffer, 1989). Careers are geared towards the reproduction of dominant groups in the organisation and are also used to secure the consent of subordinates. In what follows we describe how traditionally gendered careers in each of our sectors are being redefined by recent organisational changes.

The banking career

Historically, banking has offered a paradigmatic example of the linear organisational career. All entrants began at the bottom, working their way up through a series of well-defined jobs, in strict order. However, as a consequence of dramatic restructuring in the 1980s, it has been argued that the idea of an organisational career has become unrealistic:

> In theory at least, banking has traditionally held out the prospect of a life-long full-time career, with set hours and conditions that are in several respects superior to many areas within the wider finance sector. In practice, of course, this career path has been largely reserved for males... overall however, the bureaucratic organisational culture and its associated belief system for staff of appropriate behaviour being rewarded by steady promotion through the ranks has benefited banks... *however this happy scenario has been finally shattered as the banks enter the nineties – for good, we would argue.* (Cressey and Scott, 1992: 84; emphasis added).

Certainly career paths in banking are undergoing major upheaval but, in analysing these changes in Sellbank, it is important to both avoid romanticising the past and to place current changes in context. Let us demonstrate this by comparing the 'traditional' career with more recent developments.

Figure 4.1 offers a schematic illustration of the 'traditional' banking career. All jobs in banking were arranged hierarchically, occupying a specific role in the 'job ladder'. As an individual 'climbed the ladder' it was impossible to 'miss out' a particular stage. The most which could be hoped for was a very short posting to some of the jobs.

This type of career structure emphasised the hierarchical character of jobs. This was reflected in many of the accounts of older workers concerning their early careers. John put it as follows:

> I moaned a little bit because I felt I started with 'A' levels and I thought I was the bees knees and I moaned a little bit that *I was not getting on quick enough*, I was not on the counter quick enough, *I hadn't had an upgrade*, and I was told that I had to be patient... then I came back to another... very small branch, and *by then I was in middle clerical grades*... and I was at Kensington Street for five years in total, *moving through* the senior clerical grades [emphasis added].

These references to jobs are always hierarchical, referring to their *level* in the grading system rather than their *intrinsic* characteristics. This type of career was fundamentally about movement and measured success in terms of the speed of certain job transitions. As Figure 4.1 indicates, the traditional banking career rested on a pyramidal job structure, with more jobs at the bottom than at the top. This obviously had the potential to create promotion blockages, as workers at lower levels queued for more senior jobs. In fact this problem was resolved – for men – by employing large numbers of 'non-promotable' women in junior posts, thereby permitting men to have accelerated promotion prospects through the lower levels of the hierarchy, and by indicating to male entrants early on in their careers whether they had good prospects, thereby encouraging those deemed to be without prospects to leave. The resulting good chances of men earning promotion were in no way hidden from male recruits. John reported that:

> I was told, I mean in the days before there was quite so much equality, I can always remember an old manager, this was in Corden... I always remember him saying to me 'any young men joining the bank, two-thirds of them make manager'. Nothing about young women joining the bank in those days.

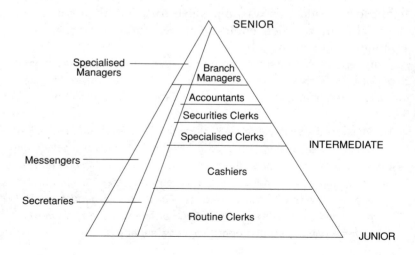

Figure 4.1 The traditional banking career

There was a high degree of predictability about male promotion prospects built into this career. With this emphasis on upward movement, particular significance was attached to the transition into management as a marker of 'success'. Until the mid-1980s, this transition involved being promoted from a senior clerical position to an accountant's grade, and then after a year or two into management itself. Accountants were traditionally the managers' deputies, and promotion to this grade marked the symbolic casting off of a clerical identity before the acquisition of a management one.

The acquisition of managerial status was linked to the taking on of manly responsibility and the shedding of youthful 'laddishness'. John noted that new managers were expected to move to a different branch:

> It was explained to me that you can't go from being one of the lads, and I was definitely one of the lads in those days, to being a manager in the same branch, it was felt it was a hurdle to get over in terms of being one of the boys to being accountable, making decisions, giving instructions and so forth...

Being a manager did not involve so much the acquisition of specialist skills as the taking on of responsibility. These characteristics defined the culture of the banking career as male, as based on climbing a job ladder that took in all the menial jobs within branches along its way, and that was concerned with imparting 'all-round' training and knowledge.

Figure 4.2 explores the changed career structure of the 1990s. In place of the traditional pyramid there has been an diversification of employment into various senior clerical and management positions, an expansion of cashiering posts, but a decline in routine clerical employment (within the branches). Let us explore how this has changed the banking career and the ways in which it is gendered.

The traditional exclusion of women from promotion has now been outlawed, but a new form of demarcation has developed in its place, involving the use of part-time workers in low-graded employment (see generally O'Reilly, 1992 a,b; Leyshon and Thrift, 1993). Although a relatively new development in banking, by 1991 24 per cent of women workers (but not a single man) in those parts of Sellbank which we studied were on part-time contracts (cf. 21 per cent in the banking industry as a whole; Cressey and Scott, 1992: 85). Sellbank has used growing numbers of part-time employees to staff branches during peak periods, and many part-time workers are also now employed in specialist units (for example, credit card departments, service centres for cheque processing, and telephone banking operations). These jobs and workers are outside the traditional job ladders on which job mobility has historically been organised.

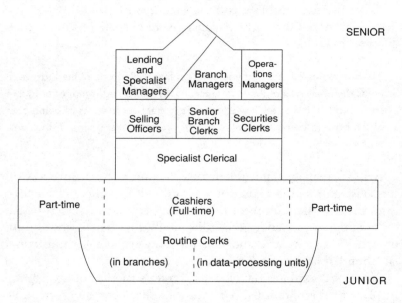

Figure 4.2 The restructured banking career

Contrary to Cressey and Scott's view this development appears to have accelerated the promotion opportunities for those working full time in the branches. Steven reported that:

> The first job when you came in was the junior's job, and that was people who paid the cheques and balanced it and put it all into the section in clearing... now it does not happen you see because what happens is

they pay it in and in fact... it goes to this factory and they process it, so we don't actually feed anything into our computer system, it's all done centrally. This has meant that the people who are doing the junior's job actually are seeing quite a few now on the enquiry counter and opening accounts so you could say that they are doing a more senior job now, although they are the junior people... When I joined the bank you were a remittance clerk and there was no way you could get onto the counter for at least five years... and you wouldn't dare say anything, I mean you just waited... But now of course they come in here and after six months they want to go onto the counter.

Indeed, in contrast to Cressey and Scott's apocalyptic vision, our survey suggests that most full-time male workers still enjoy good promotion prospects. Seventy-three per cent of men aged over 40 (although only 10 per cent of women) were in managerial positions, figures which are in line with earlier historical periods and continue to indicate that men have good prospects of reaching management (Savage, 1993).

As for the part-timers, it is important to note that although they fit many of the characteristics of the 'flexible' workforce, they are not entirely separate from other clerical workers. It is possible for full-time workers to become part time, and also for them to move back into full-time employment at a later stage. Sellbank encourages its female staff to transfer from full-time to part-time work, and our survey indicates that 4 per cent of full-time workers (7 per cent of women workers) had previously worked part-time for Sellbank. However, there is not a single case from our survey of any of these staff being promoted once back in full-time work. Part-time work is also novel in one other respect. Traditionally, Sellbank does not poach workers from other banks and indeed only very rarely takes on any staff from other employers. However 47 per cent of part-time workers in our sample had previously worked for a different employer, and Sellbank confirmed that it was less concerned that part-time workers should be internally recruited.

In short, it would appear that a new semi–permeable division between part-time and full-time workers has allowed the continuation of good promotion prospects for full-time male workers, even in the midst of restructuring. Good promotion prospects also seem to be enhanced by the elaboration of new management positions and specialisms, which create a certain amount of 'room at the top' for staff to be promoted into. It also needs to be noted that Sellbank's redundancy programme carried through in the early 1990s had affected workers aged over 50 and had, if anything, also created some 'room at the top' for younger staff to move into. The creation of new specialisms potentially allows for the diversification and specialisation of banking careers. Let us explore this issue in greater depth.

In theory at least there were no jobs in the traditional banking labour market from which mobility was not possible. People were not recruited to specific jobs. However, there have been recent suggestions that some jobs are becoming 'niches' from which promotion is very difficult and that branch staff in particular are becoming 'proletarianised' (Crompton and Sanderson, 1990; Cressey and Scott, 1992). Once again we are dubious about these generalisations. There is only limited evidence to support the idea that – in the branches – any full-time job has been removed from job ladders. In general, job mobility is extremely high, with 24 per cent of the bank workers in our sample having moved job in the previous year, 54 per cent in the previous four years, and 75 per cent in the previous seven years. The plethora of job titles and the small size of our sample makes it difficult to tell whether particular jobs have higher retention rates, possibly indicating marginalisation from internal labour markets. However, in-depth interviews and discussion with key informants suggest two types of job where respondents thought that workers may 'get stuck'. Cashiers, the largest category of staff, is an area where many (generally female) clerks may remain for a number of years. Cashiering is a job where aspiring young workers are 'rushed' through, often working there only a year or less, whilst (especially) women workers can spend a much longer time on the post. However, the situation is complicated by the fact that (especially in smaller branches) cashiering is often integrated into job rotation systems so that many clerks will work on the counter as one of a number of clerical jobs. There is a perception in the bank that it is the sort of mundane but stressful job that full-time workers cannot do for more than a few years. This is one reason why part-time workers have been recruited as cashiers.

Another candidate for niche status is the job of securities clerk. This is an interesting development since the post was traditionally an important staging post for senior clerks on their way to management (see Figure 4.1). Historically, its importance lay in the responsible nature of the job since it dealt with wills, property and stocks and shares. Today this sort of business has become more routinised. Securities work is increasingly concentrated in servicing units rather than in the branches, with the result that it can be dislocated from the traditional career routes based in the branches. Interestingly, a number of senior, male, clerks who did not seem interested in (or were not marked out for) managerial careers ended up here and expressed no interest in future career development.

The only job from which mobility was almost impossible was secretarial work. Several secretaries claimed it was impossible to move to managerial grades, a fact about which they expressed considerable discontent. This partly reflects the historical separation of clerical grades from secretarial grades (until the later 1980s secretaries being employed on different grades from clerical staff, which were specifically not designed to rise into management) and the continued tendency for secretarial duties to be defined in relation to a manager or group of managers. The case of secretaries is also revealing, however, since it throws clerical workers more clearly into relief – none of the clerical workers expressed anything like the same degree of dissatisfaction with their promotion prospects.

With these three partial reservations we can say that no full-time clerical job within Sellbank has been isolated from the promotion ladder. Having said this, the newer, specialist jobs associated with the 'sales culture' now seem to offer a better, more speedy route to management. Table 4.1 provides some descriptive information from our postal survey, which addresses this point.

Table 4.1 suggests that some streaming of personnel does take place within 'traditional' and 'specialist' clerical jobs. Specialist clerical workers are somewhat more likely to be male (although women comprise a majority), are considerably more likely to be composed of 'A' level entrants and appear somewhat more 'career oriented' in their attitudes towards promotion. It is still striking, nonetheless, that two-thirds of them previously worked in a 'traditional' job, implying that it is unlikely that the ambitious clerk can specialise only in the newer types of job and that 'all round' expertise remains necessary. However, it is clear that the contrary does not hold and that most of those in the traditional fields have not previously worked in specialist work.

Table 4.1   Career routes in banking

	'Traditional' clerks		'Specialist' clerks	
	All grades	Senior grades	All grades	Senior grades
% female	75	75.8	58.1	63.3
% 'A' level or above	25.9	24.2	41.9	33.4
% previous job in other field	4.3	8.1	62.8	66.7
% white	90.5	93.5	94	93.3
mean age		28.8		34.3
% hoping for promotion	35.3	37.1	41.9	33
% expecting promotion	12.9	8.1	16.3	8.1
N =	116	62	43	30

Notes: 'traditional' clerks = cashiers, securities clerks, remittance clerks
           'specialist' clerks = lending clerks, clerks involved in foreign exchange, stocks and shares etc. and
           other specialised work

We suggest, then, that a form of partial segmentation is taking place in banking labour markets, whereby women appear to be concentrated in cashiering and routine clerical work, and may be isolated from more dynamic areas of the bank's activities. Table 4.2 explores the nature of gender segregation further by indicating whether the respondents in our sample are currently working in jobs previously carried out by members of the same or opposite sex.

Table 4.2 indicates that gender segregation is now rather fluid in clerical employment, even though there is still evidence of its persistence. For example, male junior clerks are more likely to be occupying a job previously carried out by a woman than by a man. It should be pointed out that, given the distribution of the sexes, it is still true that at all levels it remains proportionately more likely for a man to be in a job previously performed by a man, and the same holds true for women. Nonetheless, it is still important to note, that given the fact that gender segregation is a nearly universal feature of patriarchal/capitalist labour markets (Hakim, 1979; Reskin and Roos 1990; Rubery and Fagan 1995), the figures from Table 4.2 actually indicate relatively fluid boundaries between men's and women's work.

Table 4.2   **Gender of previous job-holders, by seniority: Sellbank**

	Men	*Women*	*Total*
Junior clerical			
% in jobs previously done by men	32	12	17
% in jobs previously done by women	40	60	55
% not knowing gender of previous job holder	28	21	22
N =	25	87	112
Senior clerical			
% in jobs previously done by men	63	42	50
% in jobs previously done by women	25	33	30
% not knowing gender of previous job holder	13	8	10
N =	16	24	40
Managerial			
% in jobs previously done by men	84	86	85
% in jobs previously done by women	0	0	0
% not knowing gender of previous job holder	5	14	8
N =	37	7	44

Note: percentages may not add up to 100% because of missing data

However, although gender segregation does appear to be loosening, a new form of division amongst women staff appears to be developing. This is the difference between women with children and women without children. Our survey data shows that although men are slightly more likely to earn promotion more rapidly than women, nonetheless nearly two-thirds of those who appear to be earning rapid promotion are actually female. Two-thirds of those being rapidly promoted do not have high qualifications ('A' levels or above). The crucial distinction between those earning rapid promotion and those not concerns whether the women concerned have dependent children. In short, women appear to have as much chance of men of moving rapidly through clerical grades, as long as they do not have children. If they do, their prospects immediately worsen.

Let us now consider in more detail management careers and the way in which specialisation of management is impacting on the traditional, male-defined, career. There is no doubt that as management has diversified from branch management alone, there is now a greater recognition amongst staff that they can make choices about the sort of management career they want. Lesley, a young female clerk stated that:

> I would like to go into lending… I find it more interesting. I don't fancy operations – it is such a stressful job… it would appear that lending does give you more opportunities because you can loan to personal customers, you can loan to small businesses, the enterprise sector or you can lend to corporate customers… there are a lot more jobs in lending as well.

The relative merit of the 'lending', as opposed to the 'office', route to management was much debated by our respondents. Most regarded the lending route as superior since it did not require experience of all the office jobs and it offered a greater range of management opportunities. Our survey clearly indicates that some form of streamlining is taking place, with a degree of specialisation amongst managers. Of the 15 branch managers or operations managers, the previous job of only one had been in a lending capacity. By contrast, seven out of 13 lending managers had previously worked in lending jobs. The extent of separation between 'traditional' managers, working as operations managers or branch managers, and newer lending or specialist managers does appear to be increasing.

The position of women in management is complex. At the time of our research there were no women senior managers in our study areas, and only a handful of women had reached even junior management status. Nonetheless, two distinctive types of women manager did appear to be emerging. One type was the long-serving woman, often promoted in her forties after 20 years or so service, who usually became an operations manager in a branch. A very different type was the high-flying management trainee who was more likely to be employed in a lending position. In the former case it is interesting that women are moving into a branch of management that appears to be becoming isolated from the main promotion channels into middle and senior management.

The culture of the managerial career has changed. The transition to management, as we have shown, was traditionally defined as progression to full manhood, with the acquisition of manly responsibilities. As management itself has become more specialised and routinised, the transition into management has also changed and is now defined as an opportunity to trade security for risk. Traditional managerial careers do still exist, but they are increasingly defined as linked to rather marginalised forms of branch work and away from the more specialist and prestigious areas of Sellbank's activities:

> yes, quite often there is a position advertised around the country where they will say, you know, a family man is far more suited to this.... I mean various branches around the country, if there is a branch that is in a nice family community and he is a middle-aged bloke they will say that you are more suited than some young man... I think on the other side, the sort of personal financial services of it, they want people to work weekends and what not, they don't really want someone who has got a family in that respect. [Neville]

In general, however, the new dynamic management career operates on principles rather different from the old. Sellbank has redefined its job ladders so that security is deemed primarily a senior clerical perquisite, whilst management is defined as risky and uncertain (see Chapter 3). In other words different parts of the internal labour market are organised to maximise contrasting amounts of security and risk, so that there are now two different types of internal labour market, one reaching into senior clerical work, which offers a route to a responsible post offering a reasonable degree of autonomy and a secure income, and one into managerial work, which offers a

more 'risky' but potentially more financially rewarding management career. Although these two different career systems
operate on the same job ladders, they have different meanings
and work in different ways.

The existence of these two routes became apparent when a
number of senior clerks spoke of how they did not wish to
become managers. Stuart, a senior male clerk in his forties, talked
of the favourable 'effort–wage' bargain possible for senior clerks
compared to managers:

> The way that I look at work it is only, as I say, a means to an end to me.
> ...it has always seemed to me that if you aspire to the management side
> of it you have to devote more of your own time and personality to the
> bank, which I am not prepared to do... the package I get, I think is
> good for what I do, I find it sort of adequate really for what I do; it
> could be quite easy to, I think, to give more to the bank for basically
> less reward.

Stuart found that the benefits of senior clerical work – no
compulsory overtime, payment for that overtime which he did
wish to take on, job autonomy and pay similar to that of junior
managers (1991/92) – offered a good package compared with
management. This was endorsed by Joe, another senior male clerk:

> Going round the branches it actually opens your eyes... I have actually
> seen managerial grades are working under a hell of a lot of pressure,
> they are working for probably less pay then senior clerks are getting...
> because they don't get paid overtime.

One female clerk, Vanessa, who had given up a managerial
appointment in order to resume her clerical employment,
confirmed that she had not suffered financially. In theory managers
were offered performance-related bonuses, enhancing their salaries.
In reality, the recession ended bonus payments. Only when workers
are promoted into the second grade of management do basic salary
levels rise significantly above senior clerical levels.

The main point here is that whereas only 10 years ago a move
into management would have entailed clearly greater financial

rewards and perks, with no loss to job security, that is no longer the case. The career ladder in Sellbank has been constructed in such a way as to make the transition into a management a 'risky' one, more associated with the 'yuppie' culture of the unattached than with the traditional image of the family man. It would make little economic sense for clerks to move into management if they intended to stay simply at lower management grades. Only if they saw junior management as a staging post onto a high-flying managerial career would there be a strong economic motivation for moving into management. Steven, who had been promoted into junior management late in his life, recalls that when he was given his managerial post:

> I went for an appraisal with one of the area managers and he said 'tell me how you see your career going in the next five years'... and I just laughed, and he said 'did I say something funny?'. I said, 'look John, I am 50 soon, I have just had my first managerial position, I am very happy about it, I am very excited about it, I have worked 30 years for this; how the devil can I tell you what I am going to be doing in the next five years, I haven't a clue, I hope I am still working for Sellbank... let me ask you a question, what do you think you will be doing in five years time?'. He said, 'hmm, I don't know'. That gentleman was in one of the top positions in Midcity and was made redundant six months later.

In summary, the meaning of the banking career has been redefined. In the past, it directly excluded women and constructed the managerial career around traditional masculinity. As direct sex discrimination has been removed, new ways of 'policing' promotion have had to be developed. One crucial device is the introduction of part-time work. More generally, women with children have poor prospects of promotion. The transition to management, however, has also been defined as one associated with risk. The imagery the banking career has therefore adopted is one which tends to define the career as at odds with domestic responsibilities but as appealing primarily to single people, men and women who can devote themselves single-mindedly to the bank. We explore some of the ramifications of this new career culture in later chapters.

The nursing career

In this section, we use data from the questionnaire and the in-depth interviews with nurses as well as senior health authority staff, in order to paint a picture of the nursing career in the current climate of organisational restructuring. All the male nurses and virtually all (87%) the female nurses in our sample saw themselves as having 'careers' rather than 'jobs', which was far higher than in either banking or local government. It could be that this strong perception of nursing as a career rather than a job derives rather more from the association between 'vocation' and 'career' rather than from the existence of linear, hierarchical, bureaucratic careers, as in the cases of banking and local government.

Table 4.3   **Respondents thinking they had a job or career by sex and sector**

	Men (%)			Women (%)		
	Banks	LG	Nursing	Banks	LG	Nursing
Job	29	39	0	46	36	10
Career	65	55	100	44	59	87
Don't know	6	6	0	10	5	3
N=	80	67	17	122	66	141

Indeed, in nursing the linear, hierarchical, bureaucratic career existed for little more than a decade from the mid-1970s until the late 1980s. Since then the 'nursing career' has been volatile and indeterminate in its meaning.

Our analysis of nursing requires a departure from the script so far, where the gendering of career has traditionally described its masculinisation, particularly in banking, but also in local government. Indeed, the masculinisation of the nursing career occurred relatively late, compared to banking and local authorities, and the current trajectory of change could de-masculinise the nursing career. The male career in nursing arose on the back of the creation of linkages between clinical nursing and managerial functions in the NHS in the reforms of the 1970s.

Its history, however, was to be brief, spanning only a decade, because in the mid–1980s another round of restructuring hit the NHS, effectively pruning back the nursing career by slicing off the middle and top layers of the career hierarchy.

Analysing nursing careers feels very much like trying to take a snapshot of a moving target. Not only have successive rounds of restructuring fundamentally altered the organisational structure of opportunities open to nurses, but these changes have also been closely associated with shifts in the gendering of the nursing career. Although nursing has historically been dominated by women, this gendered subtext confirms, rather than undermines, the arguments made so far in this chapter about the masculinisation of linear careers in organisations. Although the nursing career is currently in a period of considerable indeterminacy, we will describe in what follows the impact of recent restructurings and speculate on the outcome of current changes.

Historically, the nursing career has been exclusively female but, rather than being a linear, bureaucratic 'ladder' of opportuinty, it was a command hierarchy presided over by the Matron. The reform and development of modern hospital nursing, spearheaded by Florence Nightingale in the 19th century, can be seen as a process of constructing a female chain of command within male-dominated institutions, securing for the hospital Matron jurisdiction over her female staff (Witz, 1992). Indeed it could be argued that for the best part of the 20th century there was no 'nursing career' in the commonly accepted sense of the term, but rather a relatively flat, female 'hierarchy of command' consisting of Matron, Ward Sisters and Staff Nurses, where authority was literally embodied in the Matron, whose position derived often from ascribed characteristics of gender, race, class and age – she was inevitably older, white, middle class and single. It was not until the Salmon reforms of the mid–1970s, which integrated key professional groups into a functionally based NHS management hierarchy, that a linear, hierarchical, bureaucratic career was put in place in nursing. This new career hierarchy consisted of an extended range of posts stretching from ward level, through Unit level (e.g. the hospital) and right on up through the newly created administrative tiers of Districts, Areas and Regions (see Table 4.4).

Table 4.4   The post-Salmon bureaucratic career in nursing

Health Authority level	Posts
Region	Regional Nursing Officer
Area	Area Nursing Officer
District	District Nursing Officer
Unit	Director of Nursing Services
	Senior Nursing Officers
	Nursing Officers
Sub-Unit/ward	Senior Sister
	Sister
	Staff Nurses (State Registered)
	Staff Nurses (State Enrolled)
	Staff Nursing Assistants (Unqualified)

Each level of nursing was a rung on a typical career ladder, and there was a strict order of progression through these posts – it was not possible to skip any steps. The crucial point distinguishing the pre-Salmon structure is that moving up this ladder meant moving away from *clinical* into *managerial* posts. These reforms were accompanied by a 'male take-over' of the new nurse management hierarchy. By the early 1980s nearly half of senior nurse management posts were occupied by men, although men still made up less than 10 per cent of the nursing workforce (Davies and Rosser, 1986). Whereas in the pre-Salmon era, male dominance over nursing had been *external*, mainly by doctors and administrators, in the post-Salmon era women became increasingly subject to male authority *within* nursing (Carpenter, 1977). There had been a 'male takeover' of the new nursing hierarchy.

But why and how was this masculinist bias mobilised within the overwhelmingly female occupation of nursing? The main gendering process brought into play by the construction of the linear, hierarchical career was that, for women, career breaks to have children still led to real barriers to progression. The new bureaucratic 'length of service' career logic contained an inbuilt gender bias, as it mobilised masculine bias and mapped onto men's typical work life patterns whilst grating discordantly with women's. Male mobility through the expanded career hierarchy was particularly rapid. It took men eight years on average to reach Nursing Officer grade after initial qualification, but it took women on average 18 years. Women with no career breaks took 15 years, whilst those who had taken breaks took 23 years (Walby *et al.*, 1994). In other words the nursing career was stratified not only on the basis of gender, but also on the basis of motherhood. An interesting point here is that if male career routes in banking and local government are partly premised on the immobility of women, clustered in the lower grades of work, then both male and female careers in nursing are forged partly out of either the rapid turnover or downwards mobility of women with children. Some women get on because other women get out or are literally immobilised in the 'dead-zones' of part-time work, agency/bank work and night work:

> I think the only reason that I'm here is because of other women. I mean, as a woman you have to make a choice and you either have a career or you have a family. I think it's very difficult to have the two, and I've made the choice to have a career, and the reason I've been able to do that is because I've also made the choice to not have a family... when others move aside somebody's got to go forward. [Beth]

Night duty is one of the 'dead-zones' into which nurse-mothers are shunted. Most nurses we spoke to saw nights as a dead end as far as any future job movement or career progression was concerned. Not only is it difficult to move from nights to days, but Night Sisters are restricted to F rather than G grades.

We were particularly struck, at both the hospitals we studied, by the lack of any systematic, organisational level response to the needs of mothers, despite the overwhelmingly female composition of the nursing workforce. Indeed both men and women nurses believed that there was an irresolvable conflict, given existing organisational arrangements, between being a nurse and being a mother:

You've got to give up something else if you want the same opportunities, like me. ... Well, ... doing the shifts and things. You either work or be at home with the family. [Jennifer]

It was particularly difficult for women at senior levels to continue nursing with more flexible hours. Returning to part-time work usually meant dropping one or two grades since Sisters' posts and nurse management posts are generally only available on full-time and shift-work basis. (See Chapter 6 for an extended discussion of these issues.)

However, the masculinisation of the new linear nursing career of the 1970s was not simply the result of the mobilisation of bias in favour of men's typical work life trajectories. It is also vital to recognise that the Salmon Report itself contained a discourse of nursing competencies with a gendered subtext. Salmon's critique of the command hierarchy in nursing was a critique of a specifi-cally female authority structure, whilst his blue-print for its reform rested on an argument for the introduction of manageri-alist principles into nurse management. This can be read as the explicit injection of masculinist principles into nursing manage-ment (cf. Carpenter, 1977) or, at least, as an implicit critique of nurses' ability to manage, linked closely to the fact that most nurses are women (Davies, 1995). Certainly, some of the nurses we spoke to (male and female) described men as better at managing than at the actual nursing:

[Men] might be lousy at the bedside, but they may be quite good at actually managing a ward. I've met a very good Charge Nurse who was a lousy nurse. The ward was very organised, he had a good skill mix and the opportunity to get his voice heard at meetings, and did a lot of good for the Orthopaedic Unit, but was lousy at the bedside. [Veronica]

In fact we quite commonly encountered nurses using a female/caring, male/managerial dichotomy. There was also a strong sense amongst our nurses that men received more encour-agement to strive for managerial careers than did women. Forty per cent of women nurses felt that men were given more encouragement, and even 20 per cent of male nurses acknowledged this!

In short, we can see that the introduction of the Salmon reforms has had clearly gendered effects on nursing careers. However, this linear, hierarchical male career in nursing was short lived, swept away by the implementation of the Griffiths reforms in the 1980s. The Royal College of Nursing was quick to recognise the potential of Griffiths to destroy the relatively new nurse management structure and ran an advertising campaign in the mid-1980s questioning the ability of the new Griffiths breed of general managers to manage nurses (Owens and Glennerster, 1990).

Effectively, the Griffiths reforms have top-sliced the nursing career by completely dismantling the linear, bureaucratic managerial career above Unit (e.g. hospital) level and by hollowing out the management functions from nursing, at least above ward level. The point to emphasise here is that because of organisational restructuring, the ladder-type, hierarchical, bureaucratic career has disappeared. There is no organisational rationale for it to continue – and many Nursing Officer posts at Unit level and above have been abolished by the new General Managers. This almost total demolition of nurse management posts and functions above ward level in the immediate post-Griffiths phase of restructuring has been followed by the almost total exclusion of nurses from the newer 'purchaser' management function, which District Health Authorities have assumed since the introduction of the internal market in April 1991. In both the Districts we studied, Nursing Officers have been allocated a limited and tightly circumvented brief of 'quality', and whether or not they enjoy any executive powers at District or Regional levels is entirely at the discretion of the new Chief Executives. In the region where Midcity Hospital is located, the Regional Nursing Officer had no executive role. She could not speak unless spoken to at Regional Health Authority meetings, and had no voting rights.[1] Her brief was purely around nursing strategy for the Region, with a small input on operational issues, but only in an advisory capacity. However, in the Region where the other hospital, Southtown, was located the Regional Nursing Advisor did enjoy executive powers.

What then is left of the 'nursing career'? And how will these changes impact on the recent masculinisation of the nursing career? There are now five nursing grades (E to I) for State Registered Nurses, put in place as a result of the national regrading exercise carried out in the late 1980s. These are essentially clinical grades, but the management function has not altogether disappeared. Rather, it has been redefined as managing the *delivery* of care in hospital ward or community settings and much more explicitly incorporated into Sisters' roles. There are also qualifying time periods in each grade before movement up to the next one. The combined effect of the Griffiths reforms and the clinical regrading exercise has been to flatten out the nursing career, reducing eleven levels of nursing to a mere five, and to slow down movement between these new grades. Nursing had previously been a 'fast-track' career from Staff Nurse to Sister and it was possible to become a Sister within three to five years (Owens and Glennerster, 1989). Above the levels of Senior Sister and Sister, men in particular were able to move quickly into managerial posts at Nursing Officer level. Henry, a male Charge Nurse, described to us how, entering nursing in the mid-1970s:

> I expected that I would probably end up in a management post somewhere by the time I was 30 plus, which was reasonable in those days. When I was 21, I had nine years to go and I was already a Staff Nurse. Six months after that I was a Senior Staff Nurse.

Now, there are indications that because of qualifying periods in each grade, movement up through nursing grades is slowing down. Andrea, a Senior Sister, told us how the requirement for her high grade post was to have spent at least three years as a lower grade Sister, as well as acquiring post-experience training. Another nurse noted with approval the longer qualifying time periods to be spent in each post, ' so you're talking about a G grade Sister having at least four years experience before getting there, which is much, much better'.

It is highly probable that the rapid progress of male nurses set in train by the 1970s Salmon reforms may be impeded, especially as this so often depended on the rapid movement up through and *out* of clinical posts into managerial posts. First, as we have just noted, rapid movement through clinical grades has been slowed down. Second, the managerial nursing hierarchy is just not there any more. What managerial posts do remain depends upon the localised decisions of the new General Managers.

A further feature of clinical regrading has been to discourage 'experience gathering' by nurses moving between specialities, and instead to encourage 'skill deepening' within one speciality. It is no longer possible to move up a grade at the same time as shifting from one specialist area to another. Now, to switch between specialisms, movement has to be sideways or downwards. Regrading has therefore been designed to foreground clinical skills and specialisation, and to function as a mechanism of keeping experienced nurses in the clinical area. At Midcity the advocacy and introduction of Clinical Nurse Specialist posts, Professional Development Sisters, Rehabilitation Nurses, and Nurse Counsellors, all of whom will operate at high level H or I grades, is an attempt by the organisation to reward the accumulation of specialist experience and expertise, as well as to enable the organisation to benefit from these. This development could impact on the nursing career in two quite gender-specific ways.

Although the structural edifice of the 'fast-track' male career into nurse management has been toppled, there was nonetheless evidence that a new, less well-defined, fast track was emerging, linked to choice of speciality within nursing. In our survey, 35 per cent of male nurses, compared with only 16 per cent of female nurses, worked in specialist areas, such as intensive care, theatre, or renal units. Conversely, over half of female nurses, compared with only one quarter of male nurses, were working in general nursing on the wards. The speciality route may therefore be one way in which men can continue to mobilise masculine bias in the promotion and seniority stakes in nursing. Joseph, a male nurse we interviewed, articulated this well:

> Well, I went into nursing to go into theatre because there's a better career structure, as opposed to going as a technical assistant in theatre, where basically you qualify, become senior and the most you can go up to is co-ordinator. Whereas, being a theatre nurse, I can, with basic

training, go off into any area, into management, into teaching, ...I think
you'll find a lot of male nurses in technical areas as opposed to just the
routine slog on the wards. [Joseph]

On the other hand, the discouragement of speciality
switching, by permitting only sideways or downwards grading
when moving from one speciality to another, may adversely
affect women nurses by closing off one of the means whereby
nurse-mothers could continue in nursing after the birth of a
child, which was to move from a full-time to a part-time post,
often in a different speciality area. This was because:

It may well be that when you have children perhaps the place where the
part-time jobs are found may be in one of those other areas that you are
quite prepared to work in. [(Henry]

To summarise, then, the Griffiths reforms may impact in
gender-specific ways on nursing careers. For male nurses the top-
slicing of the nurse management hierarchy and enhancement of
clinical specialisation may work to both undermine and enhance
their career moves, linked to typical male work-life history, whilst
for women the discouragement of speciality switching restricts
movement from full-time to part-time posts during periods of
responsibility for childrearing.

Overall, masculine dominance of the nursing career seems
highly resilient. Men continue to occupy the senior posts in
nursing.[2] The majority of both male and female nurses we interviewed felt that it *was* easier for men than for women to get ahead
in nursing, despite the fact that nursing is a predominantly female
occupation. Indeed, some nurses felt that it was precisely because
men *were* in the minority that they got ahead more easily:

I do see more men rising quickly to the top. Perhaps it's because there's
only a few of them so it's more obvious that they're getting up there. But
there just seems a lot of men up there considering there's only a few of
them in general. [Samantha]

Oh yes, not just here, but other places I've worked it's clear that men find it easier to climb up the ladder just because they are men. [Anne]

We see so much of the promotion going to men. You see the male nurses being made up to Nursing Officer status, Clinical Specialist Director, or whatever you call these people, and it's always the male nurse that gets the post. [Veronica]

Women nurses also felt that men assumed they would get ahead, be promoted and move up the career ladder more quickly than women. A Senior Nurse with considerable experience of interviewing nurses for promotion observed that, comparing the applications of men and women, men going for senior posts were often less qualified and experienced than women, but this did not hold them back from putting themselves forward. It was interesting to note how women nurses felt that men seemed to put less effort into developing their careers than women felt they had to, but were simply more pushy and self-confident:

There may be many ways of discriminating against women which means they don't even apply for jobs for they're not encouraged to apply, and I think it's those perceptions and those difficulties that really have not been sorted out. I think women on the whole put a lot more barriers of their own in their own minds, and those are not ever challenged or contradicted, whereas men, on the whole, don't see any barriers and go for it, irrespective of whether they're suitable or not. I think they've got a different approach. [Gillian]

I think men can get on, even in nursing, better than women do. I think men almost expect it of themselves, to get on, going back to the old ideas about being the breadwinner and all that jazz. I think they assume that if they get there, it's because they're meant to get there, because that's what's meant to be. [Samantha]

The male nurses we interviewed also acknowledged the relative ease with which men climbed the career hierarchy in nursing compared with women, but attributed this rather more straightforwardly to attitudes and orientations to work which men are alleged to bring into the organisation, rather than to gender discriminatory processes operating within the organisation:

> they [men] may think slightly differently about their jobs or about their career or about what they do than some women do... [Henry]

> I mean, men are more ambitious, I find, in this profession. It's female dominated so you stand out, so if you're good, you're noticed above the many females that are around. But that also works against you. If you're bad, people don't have to identify you by name, but just say 'oh, the male nurse, that's it, so it stems from there'. But I mean, I know men. They're more ambitious. They push themselves. You do find some women like that, and I've read a few articles about it, but I mean although you cannot discriminate at interview if you're interviewing two people, everybody knows that the man is going to stay within post for a while without getting pregnant and leaving. I think because of their ambition they drive themselves harder. They will take a gamble in applying for jobs, whereas females think 'oh, I won't get that' so they don't apply. [Joseph]

So, although men might have a tough time when they first enter nursing, because their motivation and abilities are scrutinised more than women's, they generally find it easier to get ahead. Whilst both men and women recognised gender differences in the extent to which nurses wanted and expected to get ahead, some women nevertheless expressed surprise at how much easier it *was* for men to get ahead, even when they were not particularly good nurses. One drew explicit parallels between her own abilities and those of a former male colleague:

> I had worked with a male Charge Nurse who actually was quite a burk, and was held in high esteem. He's got quite a good command of language and was very self-assured and so on, and he was listened to. He wasn't knowledgeable. He wasn't good. But you had to be there working to see that. [Andrea]

In conclusion we have shown that gender and motherhood operate as the major axes of stratification in the nursing career. It is those for whom it is possible to think in terms of 'conventional careers' who make up the privileged occupational core, particularly childless women and men with or without children. Women with children constitute a periphery, for whom nursing becomes in effect much more of a 'job' than a 'career'. This stratification has been evident throughout both the Salmon and the Griffiths reforms, indicating the pervasiveness of negative assumptions about part-time work, career breaks and, more nebulously, the commitment of nurse-mothers (see Chapter 6 for detailed discussion), as well as the resilience of masculine domination of the nursing career. Typical male work life patterns, in the context of organisational opportunities – be they bureaucratic or more linked to speciality – ensure that male nurses continue to advance more rapidly than female nurses. Furthermore, in the new NHS it seems clear that assumptions of male managerial competence will only act to further enhance the opportunities for male nurses.

Local government

As we have discussed in Chapters 2 and 3, white collar careers in local government have never been formally segregated by sex, nor has there been the uniformity of grades and job hierarchies found in the other two sectors, largely because of the diversity of activity within local government but partly because of variations between local authorities. Whilst certain specific posts (for example, weights and measures inspectors) have been a statutory requirement, beyond this local authorities have had great independence in determining overall staffing levels, organisational structures, which posts to create and whom to appoint to those posts (Finer, 1945; Robson, 1954; Jackson, 1958; Knowles, 1971; Stanyer, 1976). Even after the advent of Whitleyism, which encouraged the national regularisation of grading and other terms and conditions, and the establishment in 1946 of a National Council that was supposed to govern recruitment, training and promotion practices, individual authorities in practice retained a great deal of flexibility (Warren, 1952).

However, despite considerable variations in detailed matters such as grading and the precise nature and number of posts present in different authorities, the hypothetical potential for radical differences between local authority organisations, and also between types of local government career, has not been realised. There has in practice been some remarkable uniformities across the sector (Leach *et al.*, 1994). Specifically, the professional career has enjoyed virtual hegemony, and this has been almost completely dominated by men. A clear distinction between professional and non-professional careers was built into the design and practice of local government as it developed throughout this century. Professional staff formed the core of most departments and usually had guaranteed access to hierarchical career ladders reaching to the top of their department and, in practice, virtually to the top of the authority since there was almost no hierarchy above senior departmental management. Clerical and administrative staff, by contrast, had only limited promotion opportunities and even the most successful non-professional staff were restricted to moving half or three-quarters of the way up a departmental ladder, whilst the newly qualified professional would *begin* a career half way up (Stanyer, 1976). Unlike banking, therefore, jobs were not all integrated into one ladder stretching across the hierarchy, and staff were never required to learn every job on the way up.

The professional paradigm in local government ensured that there was a hierarchy, commencing with the lowest graded 'general workers', moving up through clerical grades, and being capped by a professional and technical band. Traditionally there were only two entry points. Most new recruits to local government came straight from school. Sixteen year old 'O' level entrants were directed towards the most junior posts whilst 18-year-old 'A' level entrants were appointed to slightly more senior clerical posts and were the most likely to be given the opportunity to study for post-entry qualifications. If, and only if, they were able to acquire professional credentials (usually undertaken via day/block release arrangements whilst already in employment), individuals could construct extended linear careers stretching from this relatively lowly clerical work up to the most senior management positions at the top.

Well into the 1970s it remained unusual for local government to recruit graduates at all, especially generalists (Bains, 1972). Once in employment it was rare for staff to move between departments; this was particularly so for professional trainees whose careers depended on deepening their specialist knowledge and experience. In many cases careers were constructed within individual authorities and, at least up to the late 1950s, movement between authorities was frowned upon (Jackson, 1958). Staff could count on considerable security of tenure once they had gained access to local authority employment (Finer, 1945; Jackson, 1964). This was widely endorsed on the grounds that security insulated staff from the whims of councillors and would attract good staff into the sector. Paradoxically, the practice of life-long employment also resulted in close relationships between elected members and staff, often affecting careers as councillors intervened to promote particular officers (Jackson, 1958). Throughout the 1960s and 70s lifetime employment with one authority gave way to life-time employment in the local government sector, although too many moves were still viewed suspiciously.

It could be argued that the professional hierarchies that developed in local government allowed qualifications, and more generally professional competence, to be used to police career advancement, which therefore meant that gender did not need to be used in this way (as it was in banking). This is not to say that gender was not a *de facto* device for promoting workers. Descriptions of the classic professional career are infused with references to 'loyal men' (Jackson, 1964), 'local men' and 'young professional men' (Warren, 1952). Robson proves a rare exception to these accounts, adding a section on the employment of women into a list of 'ancillary points' at the end of his chapter on employment in local government (1954: 361). He confirms that women's employment in the sector was 'extensive' by the early 1950s, including teachers, assistant medical officers, sanitary inspectors, housing managers, nurses, health visitors, domestic workers, clerks and stenographers (ibid). Indeed, by this time, nearly one third of all local government staff were women (Warren, 1952). However, occupational segregation was already well established, in terms of both the type of work women performed and their location in the hierarchy. Whilst 43 per cent of the total work-force was to be found in the lowest 'general' grades, as many as 79 per cent of all women were located here (Warren, 1952). Prior to the Second World War these patterns would have been partly explained by the persistence of a marriage bar, which was only exempted where a husband was unable to work and then with discretion. However, although the marriage bar was lifted in 1939, and Whitley made provision for maternity leave after 1945, by 1967 women still only comprised 31.4 per cent of the work-force (Mallaby, 1967) and were still not gaining access to hierar-chical careers. At this time women were almost completely absent from the dominant professions of law, accountancy and engineering, and had only limited representation in the more feminised social services, education or 'cultural' departments (Stanyer, 1976: 127). At the end of the 1960s women in local government were still younger than their male colleagues, with shorter periods of service and few career moves between author-ities, indicating that the Whitley provisions had done little to enhance women's long-term careers.

This pattern of segregation and limited careers for women persisted well into the 1980s. The overall numbers of women working in local government almost doubled from the late 1960s to the mid-1980s, and this increase was in large part accounted for by a dramatic rise in the use of part-timers. In 1954 as few as 21 per cent of local government posts were part-time, but by 1984 this had risen to 38 per cent. Over the same period the gendering of part-time jobs became more pronounced. The proportion carried out by women rose from 81 per cent to 92 per cent (Stone, 1988). However, over the same period the number of women working full time in the sector also increased significantly, from 35 per cent to 43 per cent of the overall workforce. By the 1980s 61 per cent of the total local authority workforce was female, but women continued to be concentrated in the lowest grades, in 'women's services' such as education, social services and libraries and often in manual work, especially cleaning and catering (Webster, 1985). However, even in 'women's services' women do not dominate the senior grades. Indeed, Maddock (1993) claims that it is still harder for women to get senior promotions in any of the 'mainstream' service departments than in the new specialist units, for example strategic policy units or even equality units. Thus although women have never formally been recruited into women's grades or women's posts, the practical segregation of women into non-professional clerical and administrative posts has limited their careers, albeit through superficially meritocratic mechanisms.

Hitherto there has been no research on how the major wave of local government restructuring in the 1980s affected career patterns, and thus our research offers new findings. As we outlined in Chapter 3, the professional paradigm is facing some major challenges. In brief these include: a declining faith that professional models offer the only, or even the best, solution to given problems; criticism from the public about the narrowly technocratic approach of professionals; the rise of public sector consumerism and associated demands for 'representative bureaucracy' (Laffin and Young, 1990: 44); and an increased emphasis on corporate and generic forms of management (see Chapter 3). Calls for corporate and generic management in local government can be traced back at least to the 1920s (Laffin and Young, 1990) but until recently appear to have been stalled by arguments in favour of professionalism. However, some have suggested that this time the challenges are so fundamental that we really will see a decisive shift way from the established professional paradigm (Leach *et al.*, 1994). Laffin and Young (1994) cite the state's refusal to sanction an exclusive right to practise to a central housing training body as an example. This may well indeed mark a significant halt to the professionalisation process in local government and, in itself, has interesting consequences for the pattern of careers in housing, as we will show shortly. But if the professional paradigm is threatened more broadly, this may undermine the very foundations of local government careers and indeed local government organisation, as well as the gendering of both.

It should be noted immediately that the professional career paradigm has developed in rather different ways in housing and finance, and that there are also some differences between our two local authorities. Finance Departments are highly regulated around the accountancy profession, which itself has a highly conservative and masculine image (Knowles, 1971; Stanyer, 1976;

Silverstone, 1980). By contrast, despite attempts at professionalisation from the 1960s onwards, housing has only marginal status as a profession both within Housing Departments themselves and within the local government hierarchy of professions. Whereas local authority accountants must be members of the Chartered Institute of Public Finance Accountants (CIPFA), and senior posts in Finance Departments have been held almost exclusively by CIPFA members, local authorities have exercised far greater discretion over the Institute of Housing (IOH) qualification. It is not a legal requirement that housing workers should have IOH qualifications, and many senior managers are not professionally qualified. Furthermore, the image of housing work in local government is linked to the caring/welfare image, and this together with its shorter, professional history, means that it has a less masculinised image than finance. Indeed, Robson (1954) recommended housing management as one of the possible test-sites for part-time work and career breaks for women, indicating not only the gendering of the work, but also its marginal ranking in the local government hierarchy. Although both Midcity and Southtown local authorities had Finance and Housing Departments, there were also some significant differences in the organisation and gendering of careers in each place. We will return to these throughout this section. In what follows, we consider contemporary career paths in local government, paying particular attention to changes in the gendered patterning of these.

Let us begin by considering those workers who have been most successful in climbing the career ladder. Looking across the two local authorities, there have been some significant increases in the numbers of women in top posts. In Midcity 14 per cent of the very top posts are now held by women and as many as 26 per cent of those in the next band down (Principal Officers; POs) are women (Midcity statistics, 1991). Whilst in Southtown the numbers are rather lower — here women made up 15 per cent of all PO posts and above (Southtown statistics, 1991) — this proportion had risen from a mere 2 per cent only five years earlier, and women made up 17 per cent of the intermediate 'Senior Officer' grades in the band below PO, indicating increased movement into supervisory posts and into posts that may offer more career opportunities.

Women were however *under*-represented amongst the professionally qualified staff in top posts, offering counter-evidence to the idea that women would succeed by using the 'qualifications lever' (Crompton and Sanderson, 1990). Less than half of the women in senior posts in Finance Departments were CIPFA-qualified (compared with more than half of the men) and only two out of the seven IOH-qualified staff in housing were women. Thus women remain *less likely* than men to follow a professional career path. However, perhaps the most striking point here is that as many as 54 per cent of all officers in top posts had no professional qualifications. This marks a dramatic decline in professional dominance of the local government career hierarchy. Professional qualification is clearly no longer necessary for a successful linear career, even in finance where careers have historically been so thoroughly regulated by CIPFA.

There are other notable breaks from tradition, too. As many as 30 per cent of all senior officers in finance, and 44 per cent of senior officers in housing, were graduates, the vast majority from non-vocational degree courses. The non-graduate senior officers were mainly 'O' level entrants but 90 per cent had undertaken various post-entry qualifications, confirming that the more traditional pattern of career advancement in local government does still exist and endorsing credentialism, although not necessarily professional credentialism.

Turning to career patterns, although most of our senior officers had worked for up to five employers (a pattern that has become acceptable since the 1960s) a significant minority (32 per cent of men and 26 per cent of women) had worked for up to ten employers, indicating further decline in the organisational career. This is linked both to changes in employer/organisational values and to the stagnation of local government expansion from the 1970s onwards, which meant that staff could no longer rely on vacancies appearing in their own organisation. Amongst the senior officers there was also a minority whose careers had involved employment with private sector organisations, indicating some erosion of sector-specific careers. However, the majority of senior officers in local government (68 per cent of men and 79 per cent of women) had never moved house to change job.

This suggests that the traditional 'localness' (or parochialism) of local government managers persists into the 1990s.

There have clearly been some marked changes to the established gendering and general pattern of senior careers in local government. Can we conclude from this that male dominance and the professional career will become a thing of the past? In the Finance Departments, CIPFA is no longer absolutely necessary to achieve a senior post. However, although it is no longer the only possibility, CIPFA qualification remains a passport to a certain degree of linear advancement. All bar one of our CIPFA-qualified respondents were in senior posts. Furthermore, while non-CIPFA staff may move into some management posts, the most senior posts of all were totally dominated by CIPFA staff. Women made up just over half of the CIPFA staff – indicating some use of the 'qualifications lever' alongside non-professional career routes – although *none* of the most senior posts were held by women. Furthermore, the two lowest graded CIPFA staff were both women and, probably not coincidentally, these were the only two CIPFA staff to have taken career breaks for childcare during their working lives. None of the other CIPFA women had any children, and there were no part-time CIPFA staff.

The second important point to note here is that all the non-CIPFA senior officers were found in Midcity. There were none in Southtown, where CIPFA retained an even stronger hold on career advancement. A major explanation for this was a decentralisation initiative undertaken by Midcity council. The city is divided into 12 constituencies, each with its own team responsible for the registration and collection of community charge. Each team is headed by a Constituency Officer (CO). This effectively created a new layer of management not colonised by CIPFA, probably because CIPFA accountants have been less concerned with revenue collection than with expenditure and financial management. Nonetheless, these new posts appear to have offered new opportunities for non-CIPFA staff, for non-graduates (none of the COs has a degree) and for women. However, none of the female COs who replied to our survey had had a childcare break and none worked part-time. Furthermore, it is as yet unclear where these COs might progress to. Clearly, restructuring has opened new opportunities for non-professional staff, for whom a career path beyond intermediate grades was previously undefined. Christopher, who joined the council as an 'A' level school leaver and is now an constituency officer, explained:

> I'd been in the council so long, I didn't really know where I was going as far as a career was concerned... the last couple of years coincided with the poll-tax coming in... and the opportunities that brought that I've now got to the stage where I'm managing a section.

However, a new phase of restructuring might move the goalposts yet again, and even if the present structure remains there is only one post above CO that is not professionally based. Christopher was aware of this:

> Above that you're getting to the level of [the Deputy Assistant Treasurer] and I think that might be beyond me... gradually getting to know these people [above him] there does seem to be a lot of accountants.

The remaining non-CIPFA senior officers occupy miscellaneous accounting positions. However, although some of these staff are Institute of Ratings and Revenues Valuation (IRRV) qualified and two hold quite senior posts, the average age is 53, suggesting that they have reached the ceiling of their opportunities and are unlikely to progress any further in their careers. IRRV credentials have never challenged accountancy qualification and seem unlikely to do so in the future.

Turning to the Housing Departments we found some more major differences between careers in the two authorities. The first concerns the place of the IOH qualification in housing careers. As we have already discussed, professionalism is far less well established in housing than in finance. Efforts were made to professionalise through the IOH, and for some time these strategies appeared successful. Although the Institute never gained state sanction for the exclusive right to practise (as CIPFA has – for actual accountancy work), numbers taking the qualification rose throughout the 1970s and 80s and its career currency also appeared to be strengthening. However, it now appears that the credibility of professional qualification is waning. These changing fortunes are represented well in differences between Midcity and Southtown. As a smaller and more conservative authority, Southtown still places considerable emphasis on professional qualification, and all the top officers here hold professional qualification (either IOH or Royal Institute of Chartered Surveyors). Whilst Midcity might have approximated this pattern in the past, by 1991 only one out of nine senior managers in our survey was professionally qualified. Here, housing careers had become far less predictable:

> what happens is you… get some experience in one place and you transfer it to somewhere else, you work on the front-line for a little while; you might get seconded to do different things; you might get some training or you might not. I don't think there is one [a classic housing career] anymore. [Linda]

In Midcity, the most common career route for Senior Housing Managers had been through clerical work to housing advice, Housing Officer and up the management hierarchy. Women were rather less likely than men to take this route however. Whilst in Southtown equal numbers of women and had taken the professional route, housing management in Midcity was dominated by men, and senior women were in non-housing management posts (training, computing and support services). All these women were graduates. Thus whilst professionalism retains some currency in Southtown, it has become very weak indeed in Midcity, and whilst women's presence in housing is now strong this is linked to new types of work as well as to the feminised image of housing management itself.

Computing staff were found in both departments. Not surprisingly, this is an area of local government work which has grown substantially over the past decade, and there are now some senior posts linked to the establishment and maintenance of databases and management systems. Predicting this growth in 1984, Crompton and Jones suggested that the jobs which would emerge would be highly polarised – between highly graded programmers (male) and analysts and data entry staff (female). This prediction has been partly borne out in that the majority of the routine work is indeed done by women, on low grades and with few promotion prospects. However, we also found a reasonable number of women in analyst/programmer posts, and we found evidence of intermediate grades that may offer some potential for movement between clerical and more senior posts. However, of all the emergent specialist hierarchies, computing appeared the most insulated from the mainstream departmental hierarchies, with no evidence at all of sideways movements into core housing or finance activities.

Overall, then, the newly emergent hierarchies − for example those based on decentralisation and on new technology − are offering some new routes out of clerical work and into senior posts. This certainly seems to offer enhanced opportunities for those staff who would previously have been 'stuck' at an intermediate level to progress into PO grades.

However, the majority of clerical workers do not progress into these new areas. Post-entry qualification is one way of enhancing one's prospects in these circumstances, but this opportunity is rarely open to those staff in the most routine clerical posts, particularly benefits and cash desks, which still remain 'dead-zones' as far as career opportunities are concerned. Staff are not encouraged to pursue credentials, hierarchies are very short indeed (usually only two or three layers) with only a handful of posts above the most basic grades, and turnover is low. Claire, a benefits assessor, explained:

> The main structure of the work is that there's three [grade] fours and then there's, say, one supervisor to every ten or whatever and then there's an SO1 which is the team leader, and they're always there and they have worked here as long as I have [9 years]... It's very rare that, once they're in that position, they leave the job... There's only one that gets promoted once a year or something like that.

Furthermore, experience in these areas is rarely recognised as a suitable foundation for any other type of work. Neil, a front-line benefits worker, despaired of any career prospects:

It's to do with the set up of it, of the Council itself. It works in funny ways, you know? The job I've got now you'd think – because I have to have knowledge about everything, about community charge and collection and revenues – you'd think that would give you enough avenues to go into other jobs, higher up the grade, but it doesn't. It's sort of like a dead end job. You know bits and bobs about everything but you don't know about one particular subject. And so it blocks off avenues. I've been for a couple of interviews recently and it's like 'oh, you work on an inquiry counter, that's it, you're staying there, you're not moving'. And at the moment, after speaking to my boss last week about it, it's like my job/career has come to a standstill.

But benefits staff are also told that they are too specialised to move into career grade posts. Claire felt that her expertise was perceived too narrowly:

I've worked within housing benefits for nine years so I'm very experienced, but if you attempt any way to get out of that, within the Council, you've got no chance because they don't see you as having any other experience.

The vast majority of these structurally segregated workers are women; part-time work is more widespread, and it is only amongst these workers that career breaks for childcare have been commonly taken. This group is also distinguished by a lack of sectoral commitment: most of the mixed sector career histories are found here as women move between routine clerical posts with different employers. This was far more pronounced in Southtown, where the stronger local labour market in the late 1980s had encouraged such moves.

Overall, there were some important differences between our two authorities in terms of the gendering of careers and of organisation. We have already mentioned the uneven significance of professional qualification in housing, but more broadly than this we found that whilst internal organisational careers were common in both departments in Midcity, this pattern was almost non-existent in Southtown. This is not surprising given the relative sizes of the two organisations, with far more posts and therefore turnover and opportunities in Midcity than Southtown (see

Chapter 2 for further details). We have also seen the implementation of new organisational forms (decentralisation) in Midcity, whereas such a change would be less viable in a small authority like Southtown, where in any case the local politics and local management are less adventurous. We also found far more women in senior posts in Midcity than in Southtown, maybe again linked to the more progressive nature of the authority and to the size of the authority. However, despite these differences, we can see some sectoral features across the two authorities.

Clearly, women are doing better than in the past, especially in the new non-professional hierarchies that are emerging in local government (see Figure 4.3 for a summary of the patterning of career hierarchies in local government).

Women are also getting into PO and Chief Officer posts faster than men: the average age of women in our senior band of grades was 38 years old compared with an average age for men of 42. This age gap is especially wide in housing, with women averaging 35 compared with men's average age of 42. However, the characteristics of these women confirm a more typical pattern, with few children, no career breaks and no part-time work.

In conclusion, the nature of local government careers is undoubtedly changing and, as part of this, more women are successfully establishing linear careers. However, this is in part tied to newly emergent areas of work (computing, decentralised management, personnel and information systems), which, at the end of the day, remain subordinated to older professional hierarchies (Figure 4.3). More generally, predictions that this time managerialism really would triumph over professionalism have been unevenly borne out. In housing, especially in Midcity, this transformation is advanced. In Southtown Housing Department, and in both Finance Departments, we are still not finding 'pure' management staff at the most senior levels, although it is certainly the case that senior professional staff are taking on new generic managerial competencies. As Harry reflects:

> the last 10 or 11 years the screws have been tightened and tightened
> and so there has been a learning curve from that as to how it's survived,
> and all of a sudden it's interesting to see how the legal people, our

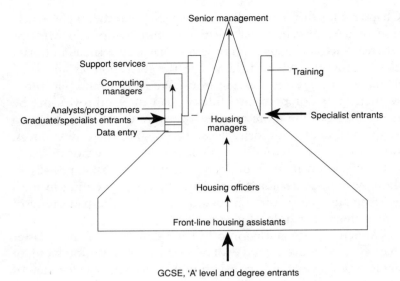

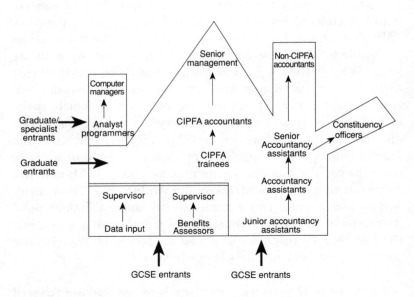

Figure 4.3 Career paths in local government finance and housing

finance people and our planners talk about service delivery agreements when, you know [in the past] it was a case of 'what's one of them?' ...and now they're talking about being more corporate.

Management may be being redefined but, especially in finance, those in senior posts bear a striking resemblance to their predecessors. The new managers may be younger than their predecessors, have worked for several employers and are endorsing new managerial performances, but the traditional mainstream route to the top remains male dominated.

Conclusions

Significant changes to career structures are taking place across our three sectors. In each case these are clearly intertwined with the restructuring that we discussed in Chapter 3. As Evetts (1992) claims, such changes allow us a valuable insight into the gendering of career processes. Looking backwards from the 1990s we can see only too clearly how gender was embedded in the old, linear career paths in each sector. In banking and local government it was not only that linear careers were the near-exclusive province of men, but also that managerial competencies were defined in masculine terms. This also came to be true in nursing, post-Salmon, where the traditionally female-embodied position of Matron was replaced by a new, ostensibly masculine, managerialism. Comparing the position of women 20 years ago with that today, the lack of opportunities and explicit discrimination then as compared to now is breathtaking. However, close attention to the gendering of certain 'deadzones' – cashiers' work in banking, night-work in nursing and benefits work in local government – reveals the persistence of structural segregation from linear careers that many women continue to experience into the 1990s. Thus our material and analysis do not endorse the essentialist career conceptions held by Marshall (1989) and Gallos (1989). These patterns are not an inevitable reflex of gender. Rather, our material illustrates the continuing ways in which organisational processes, and dominant groups within organisations, continue to generate gendered career paths.

There are some interesting patterns of convergence and diver-
gence between our three sectors. The two sectors with histories
of male dominance – banking and local government – appear to
be converging in their career patterns. In both sectors the 'traditional' career still exists but has been overlaid by new career paths
that have complicated the internal labour markets and offered a
variety of routes to senior posts. From having had rather different
histories, with banking being a managerial hierarchy and local
government a professional one, they are both developing into
something of a hybrid. This diversification of career routes appears
to allow women some potential for moving into senior positions
as the disruption of established, male-dominated conventions has
allowed greater potential for less conventional routes to senior
posts. Nonetheless, there is some evidence that women are clus-
tering in specific sorts of senior job that may still be removed
from the main power centres of the organisations concerned. The
situation in nursing is rather different. Whereas banking and local
government have seen piecemeal changes, so that newer career
routes exist alongside older, more traditional ones, the career
ladders in nursing have been fundamentally changed several times
in recent years. The result is to create a more uniform job ladder,
but one whose steps have been shortened.

In all three sectors one of the most common developments is
the growth of a major division amongst women. It is nearly
always women without children, and domestic responsibilities,
who are moving into jobs on career ladders. This division has a
close association with the distinction between part-time and full-
time worker, which has taken on a new significance, largely as
gender has stopped being deployed as a formal division. This point
is, of course, hardly an original one. We have also detected, at least
in the previously male areas of banking and local government, the
emergence of new forms of professional and managerial work
that do appear to be undergoing a degree of feminisation, in line
with Crompton and Sanderson (1990), Crompton (1995), Savage
(1992) and Devine's (1992) arguments. However, what is worth
emphasising is the way in which the sorts of 'niche' middle-class
jobs that Crompton and Sanderson (1990) claim are partly
adopted by women as a means of combining childrearing and

work are not, in fact, being filled by women with children but by 'high-flying' single women. Now it may of course be that these women are deliberately moving into fields of employment which they think will allow them in the future to have children, but this is by no means certain. In short, we would argue that the creation of niche forms of employment is probably not simply due to women choosing to move into certain forms of employment, but also to do with the way in which gender is embedded in the restructuring process itself (see Chapter 3).

Finally, we should emphasise that despite the apocalyptic comments of Crompton and Jones (1984), or Cressey and Scott (1992), the organisational career continues to operate and permits high levels of mobility from junior to senior positions. It might also be argued that the diversification of internal labour markets away from one conventional type has made it easier for those not conventionally qualified to earn promotion. What has changed is the idea that there is a normal career route that has been sanctioned by tradition ('this is the way to get on'). In all three sectors traditional career routes are changing. They have either been totally restructured, streamlined and flattened out (as in nursing) or overlain by more complex and variegated routes (as in banking and local government). This raises the question of how individuals make sense of these new complex career pathways. This is the subject of Chapter 5.

5 Gender, Strategy and Career Narratives

Introduction

So far we have emphasised that organisational change cannot simply be understood as the product of the impersonal working out of rational economic processes. We have demonstrated the embodied character of current changes, emphasising that individuals within organisations are not passive in the (re)making of their workplaces. In the remainder of this book we seek to extend this analysis by focusing on the *subjective* dimensions of organisational membership, in order to show how the sorts of identity, value, aspiration and attitude that respondents hold towards their participation in their organisation help to clarify their actions within the organisation itself.

The argument that people are active participants in their working lives is not, of course, a novel one, as a major theme of recent sociological theorising has been to emphasise the role of agency in social life. One common element in this work, found in writers such as Giddens and Bourdieu, is the way in which individual agency is linked to the *strategies* people deploy. In this chapter we investigate the extent to which people do indeed have distinct strategies concerning their working lives and examine whether there are any distinctively gendered dimensions to forms of strategic conduct. Our prime argument is that people's attitudes towards the membership of their organisation evoke more complex and emotive ideas than can helpfully be found under

154

the rationalist, instrumental rubric of 'career strategies', and in this respect this chapter picks up on issues raised in Chapter 4. When respondents (male and female) talked about their lives and future plans within the organisation, it frequently became difficult to disentangle their accounts from issues of personal identity and belonging. Individual subjectivities were closely intertwined with organisational membership itself, organisational cultures playing a key role in defining the terrain on which identities form. 'Organisational belongingness' is of crucial importance in explaining the attitudes and values of our respondents.

This chapter begins by considering recent arguments concerning the significance of strategic and instrumental attitudes towards work, and presents some brief evidence that suggests the need for a more complex and nuanced approach. We then discuss each of the sectors in turn, bringing out the way in which organisational cultures and practices have helped to construct the attitudes and identities of employees. It is important, however, not to construct a monolithic picture of employees in these three sectors. We also discuss salient differences, exploring in particular the way in which nursing can sustain a more strategic set of responses to individual circumstances than can banking or local government.

Orientations to work, career strategies and reflexivity

Analyses of workers' attitudes towards their employment have alternated between claims that in capitalist society workers are largely instrumental and uninvolved in their work (for example, Taylor's claims about the need to motivate workers through proper financial incentives), and views that recognise the emotional character of work-based identities (for example, in Mayo's experiments of the 1930s). In recent years the tide has shifted steadily, although not unequivocally, towards the instrumentalist view. Some of these arguments concerning the rise of instrumentalism were related to claims about the declining role of employment in people's identities as consumption-based actitivities have become more significant (see e.g. Saunders, 1990; Warde, 1990; and the discussion in Marshall *et al.*, 1988). They were also related to theoretical arguments concerning the role of agency in social life. One of the central ways in which agency was registered was by exploring the salience of *strategy*. At the most general theoretical level, an emphasis upon strategy was to be found in the work of Giddens (1984: 289), who argues that the study of 'strategic conduct' involves recognising the knowledgeability of actors and their ability to 'make a difference' to a given range of outcomes. From a rather different perspective, Foucault's excavation of the way in which power depends upon the mobilisation of strategies has also been significant and has echoes within 'actor–network theory' (Grint, 1991; Law, 1991). Bourdieu, also endeavouring to find an alternative to determinist structuralist conceptions of social action, claimed that a recogition of individuals' strategies offers an alternative to seeing people simply as rule-following agents (e.g. 1977: 15). Interestingly, however, Bourdieu vacillates on his analysis of strategy. Consistent with his emphasis upon the significance of the 'habitus' (sets of internalised dispositions) as the bedrock of social action, he claims at some points that consciously worked out strategies are less effective than non-calculated ones (see the discussion in Mouzelis, 1995: 112). This immediately raises the question of how it is possible to call something a strategy which is not thought through by actors, and this is precisely the matter on which a major debate now hinges.

For, although the concept of 'strategy' has become widely popularised, its value has been hotly debated within sociology, especially its application in empirical research (see for an overview Wallace, 1993). Some critics of the term, such as Shaw (1993), argue that the concept of strategy should be deployed only with caution since it only has meaning within the specific military context in which the term was developed (where the idea referred to the reflexive and carefully worked out mobilisation of troops and the planning and waging of war). It is, of course, precisely this 'war-like' element which Foucault hoped to stress in his application of the term to power, but there is a real danger that the term is used *a priori* to establish conflict by theoretical fiat rather than through careful scrutiny of empirical evidence. Knights and Morgan (1991) are also critical of many uses of the concept of strategy. They argue that the term is often used by professional groups as a device for advancement and self-aggrandisement since professionals claim to define the 'appropriate strategy' for given problems or issues. We do not find these criticisms especially useful since the social sciences are littered with concepts that have originated in other contexts. The crucial question is whether the concept of strategy can still be used helpfully to explore forms of human agency, and in particular whether it is wedded to an overly instrumental view. Here we are more persuaded by arguments emphasising the way in which the notion of strategy is wedded to rationalist rather than affectual forms of action (Morgan, 1989; Watson, 1991). Thus Crow states that the term can only be usefully used in 'the presence of conscious and rational decisions involving a long term perspective' (1989: 19). It hence involves some degree of consistent and continuous calculation on behalf of the actor.

There is also the issue, which ties closely to the broader themes of this book, of the extent to which strategic orientations are themselves gendered, with suggestions made both by traditionalists and some feminists alike that men are more likely than women to adopt instrumental approaches to career development. Indeed, some feminists have argued that the very concept of strategy rests largely upon masculinist approaches to agency. Edwards and Ribben (1991) claim that the concept depends upon the:

> presence of clear and explicit large scale goals... contained within the concept which implies that activies are directed towards these goals. Activities are therefore assumed to be means–end motivated within rational frameworks. Our attention is thus inevitably drawn towards issues of intellectual cognition, rational choice, and purposive **action**, with a concomitant reduction in our ability to see the relevance to social life of complex emotions and variable qualities of **being**.

Clearly, this is reminiscent of Marshall's and Gallos' construction of gendered binaries in their revision of career theory (see Chapter 4). In what follows we investigate whether men are indeed more strategic than women in thinking about their employment futures, and if so, whether this might be an important factor in explaining their success in reaching senior positions across the three sectors. We also address the question of whether men and women have distinctive career strategies, and if so, what these are.

It is interesting to note, however, that although the concept of career strategy has been widely used it is rarely defined or elaborated. This is especially true in Brown's (1982) influential discussion of 'career strategies'. Here Brown rehearsed the tension between structure and agency within work histories, before indicating how the concept of strategy might fit into the argument:

> An understanding of work histories involves also taking account of the predispositions, preferences, and expectations of the individuals concerned, and such... expectations and preferences will influence the strategy they adopt in the labour market, and may well lead to different strategies being pursued by those who have comparable resources (1982: 125).

Brown then elaborates a distinction between those with career orientations ('who expect and seek some form of advancement during their working life') and those without. For those with career orientations, individuals might either pursue 'organisational' strategies, attempting to climb a career ladder within one organisation, and those pursuing an 'occupational' strategy in which they seek to move from employer to employer. Later, Brown also discussed those pursuing entrepreneurial strategies through forming businesses and the like.

Echoes of Brown's distinctions can be found in the recent work of Kanter (1989, 1993), as well as in Savage *et al.* (1992). It has been suggested that men may be more likely to pursue organisational careers whilst women prefer to pursue occupational ones. However, and this is crucial, rarely has this discussion focused upon the actual stated views of the workers themselves. Rather, the existence of strategies has been extrapolated from the existence of different types of career and patterns of mobility. This is highly problematic. We cannot assume that patterns are the outcome of strategies without investigating further the intent and agency of the workers themselves. However, there has in fact been rather little research exploring whether individuals do deploy strategies and/or the extent to which these are successful.[1]

One recent attempt to think seriously about the dangers of assuming strategic intent is the work of Nicholson and West (1989). They emphasise that the 'career' is a form of a 'narrative' and start with the subjective and autobiographical constitution of 'career', exploring the way in which people make sense of their work histories (ie. *ex-post facto*, or retrospectively). This is certainly the form which most of our interview material about careers takes. Nicholson and West also emphasise the value of examining occupational transitions. They claim that career narratives are stories of transitions – of the punctuations, pauses and turning points that mark work histories – and they conceptualise work histories and careers as chains of transition cycles. Thus for Nicholson and West there are three dimensions to the study of work histories and careers: the analysis of transitions and periods between them; the meaning that career has for individuals; and the ways in which work histories and careers are contextualised within specific organisational or occupational cultures. These are the broad themes that we explore in this chapter. We will examine how far workers attempt to engage reflexively with what they perceive as structures of opportunity and to mobilise available resources to avail themselves of opportunities and rewards associated with these structures. These structures are dynamic, as are the organisational contexts in which individual work-life histories are forged (see Chapters 3 and 4). We invited interviewees to tell their own career narratives, and our analysis picks up on key transition points in their accounts, the meaning that career has for them, and the embeddedness of their occupational stories within organisational cultures.

In attempting to systematise our analysis of these interviews, we use a typology of career narratives that distinguishes *contingent* careers, consisting of changing responses to unfolding opportunities, and *strategic* careers, which approximate more to a notion of planful development. We suggest that it is helpful to conceptualise career narratives as a continuum ranging from contingent to strategic stories, with 'next step' planning occupying a mid-point along that continuum.

Our concern in what follows is to explore the extent to which different types of respondent draw upon contingent or strategic accounts of their careers, and also to explore how such orientations are gendered.

Banking career narratives

In banking it was striking that nearly all the career narratives of our respondents tended to emphasise the *lack* of choice or strategic intent inherent in the banking career and in this respect fell towards the contingent end of the continuum described above. Most respondents, both male and female, gave an image of careers over which they had relatively little control or active choice. Steven, an older bank manager, expressed such views in a particularly acute form:

> I can't say that I have ever made any decision that has affected my job or career because these sorts of things are made, quite honestly they are made for you... I don't think I have ever done anything that has had any effect or setting in a different direction particularly in life, I don't think any, I think it's one of those things that have just happened, a series of things one after the other and it has just rolled on. [Steven]

Steven had reached junior management at a relatively late age, in his late forties, well after most of his male contemporaries. His own account of what he himself defined as a 'failed' career was unable to pinpoint precise reasons for the length of time it took to earn promotion into management:

> When I was much younger and certainly when I joined the bank I wanted to become a manager like everybody else. I think somehow I lost, I lost some ambition somewhere along the line, I don't know whether I was not impressed with some of the others I saw or whether I saw some of them that were always looking over their shoulders... I have always followed the philosophy that if I gave my best to the bank I would be duly rewarded. [Steven]

Steven articulated a sense of loyalty to Sellbank which placed responsibility for job movements largely in their hands and defined himself as the passive recipient of the bank's decisions. This linked into a refusal to articulate a strategic narrative of his career:

> I have not planned [my career] at all. I know it sounds terrible... you go through a natural progression through certain jobs, but when you get to a certain stage, then you are looking for promotion to an appointed (i.e. managerial) position. I got there, I got there just as early as anybody else, but I didn't get that promotion.
>
> **Q:** Was that due to your previous manager?
>
> No, not entirely, it's just one of those things. I can't actually put my finger on it. [Steven]

The culture of banking, with its paternalistic ethos, its emphasis upon loyalty and steadiness, was not one which traditionally encouraged instrumental planning by its employees. Promotion in the bank took place when managers decided that specific individuals were worthy and ready for it. In the words of one manager:

> you sat and waited for a 'phone call and they said 'oh, we have got a job for you at you know Midcity or Dilsbury, you know, or Slieghton, or somewhere' and that was it. [Jeff]

In this climate ambitious employees were constrained. There were no jobs for them to apply for. All they could do was adopt a range of tactics to improve their visibility to those above them, in the hope that this might mark them out as 'promising material'. This goal of visibility could be achieved in a number of ways. If employees passed the Institute of Bankers (IOB) qualifications either extremely well (candidates were placed in national rankings that allowed the outstanding performers to be easily recognised) or extremely quickly, this was regarded as a 'feather in the cap' and could often lead to early promotion. However, the acquisition of such credentials was not in itself decisive. Sellbank's policies on promotion were always flexible enough to allow those who obtained qualifications not to be promoted, and it was not uncommon for those without IOB qualifications to earn promotion.

More generally, visibility depended on 'putting yourself forward', becoming conspicuous to your branch manager since he (and it was always a he) was the most important figure in encouraging and facilitating career progress. This might be done in formal appraisals and meetings with managers, which used to take place once a year but now occur every six months. The format of such meetings has changed along with the culture of Sellbank. Historically, managers wrote brief reports on each of their staff once a year, indicating whether they were suitable for promotion and commenting on a few aspects of the employee's performance. During the 1980s these appraisals became more formalised and were seen as occasions to set targets for staff in the next few months, to rate the employees on six different dimensions of their work performance (with such ratings affecting the final salary), and to suggest possible training courses. These were occasions on which it was possible for ambitious employees to ask about their promotion prospects and to emphasise their ambition to management.

What is particularly important to note, however, is that personality and social factors were always a crucial component in gaining visibility. This related also to the culture of laddishness that male clerks were expected to exhibit. Lively, youthful activity could be seen as a positive feature for new recruits. At one point, in the 1970s, Sellbank explicitly asked managers to refer to the 'personality' of their staff:

> On Sellbank staff reports there always used to be... a section 'personality', they used to mark you for 'personality', I mean how subjective can you get?... I always had been personality plus. At Drawsley Street branch I used to organise the Christmas Party, organise the football team, ...and I think it was felt I had the personality to manage. [John]

One way of thinking analytically about the possibilities open to the ambitious male recruits is to reflect on de Certau's (1984) distinction between strategies and tactics. De Certau argues that strategies are only possible when agents have enough autonomy to plan and control their environment, circumstances which, as we have seen, were historically lacking for bank workers. De Certau goes on to argue, however, that tactics can still be deployed when an agent is restricted by having to operate on a terrain decided by others. Tactics are a 'calculated action determined by the absence of a proper locus... the space of the tactic is the space of the other. Thus it must play on and with a terrain imposed on it and organised by the law of a foreign power...' (de Certau, 1984: 37).

If, traditionally, bank workers have been unable to plan their careers strategically, there is no doubt that in recent years Sellbank has tried to restructure so that 'proactive', instrumental thinking is encouraged amongst its staff. Management posts (but not clerical ones) are now advertised, so that people actually have to decide whether to apply for them rather than simply being promoted directly to such positions. The new management discourse emphasises the need for job movement to be 'self-directed'. Managers are given three month reviews in which they are invited to examine their 'skills portfolio' so that they can attempt to acquire those skills which are necessary for jobs they may wish to move into. In short, Sellbank has tried to remove its paternalistic culture and to encourage forward thinking amongst its staff. In some ways the sort of project they were engaged upon is rather similar to the situation Grey (1994) describes in accountancy, where young recruits are encouraged to pursue the idea of the career as 'a project of the self', in which 'career offers at least the potential for the management of the self through "steps on the ladder", or "moves in the game"' (Grey, 1994: 495). However, at least by the time we did our research, this new culture had not gone very far. A few respondents did refer to the change in the bank's policy:

> I have only been able to plan in the last couple of years because I could see where the opportunities were and how I could get there, because [before] it has been decided really by the bank as to where you could be located and where the next job would be. [Jeff]

In fact it can be argued that the traditional form of career narrative, emphasising the dependence of employees on the bank, has not been fundamentally modified by these new changes. Doug's testimony is an interesting indication of this. Doug was one of the most senior managers whom we interviewed at Sellbank and worked in the newer areas of bank activities, in lending-related actitivies. He can in many respects be seen as one of the 'new breed'. In his early forties, confident and certain of his responses, and a champion of the 'new management style', Doug found it easy to articulate how he had arrived at his current position, and the thinking he had adopted whilst developing his career at Sellbank.

> My personal philosophy is I have not been one of those who have sat down and said, right, that's where I want to be in 10 years time, so to that extent one could say that I am not very career oriented, and therefore my orientations have developed as I have arrived at each job. So one could say that my first aspiration once I had sort of developed through a clerical grade was to get my first management appointment, or accountancy appointment; having got there my next aspiration was I reckon I could do a managerial job, and having got there it developed. If you want, my aspiration has been based on age, so I targetted myself at age 40 to be what was a G5 position, and I was on course to do that until the bank changed the goal posts, right, as it happens I have now achieved a G7 which is a senior management position. [Doug]

Doug did not hide the fact that he was ambitious. He wanted to get on. However, such linear orientation did not involve devising a plan for advancement. Doug had actually joined Sellbank at the age of 18 as an 'A' level entrant and was posted to the usual array of clerical jobs. He passed his exams quickly, however, thus marking himself out as a 'high flyer', and reached the job of accountant at a relatively early age, by his mid-twenties. At this point he decided that a specialised lending job offered him the potential for good career development. He asked to move into this position and was told that this would be possible if he worked effectively in his current job, and in his early thirties he took on this lending position. This sounds eminently like strategic movement. However, what followed was that he was contacted to see if he would be prepared to change direction, by becoming Assistant Manager in a large branch, to which he agreed. Shortly afterwards, again out of the blue, he was telephoned to see if he was interested in applying for a specialised lending job, which he again agreed to. However, he did not enjoy this job, and soon applied for a job as Branch Manager, an application that was successful. However, Doug soon came to realise that branch management was being marginalised within the overall management structure, and managed to secure a release into senior regional management.

Doug's case reveals a number of interesting features. Although from the outside it looks to be a straightforward linear career, based on a steady climb up a job ladder, it was perceived from within in a more disrupted sense, with bad and good jobs along the way. He was largely reactive to developments around him, and it was precisely his willingness to be open to these, often unplanned, openings that allowed him to climb so effectively to a senior post. Indeed, on the occasion when he did deliberately plan a move, into branch management from a specialised lending position, he almost planned himself into a marginalised position. The important point is that Doug was at the heart of the organisational culture of Sellbank and was thoroughly abreast of new developments and trends, with the result that without much conscious pushing he would be phoned up and asked to take on particular jobs. Any independent planning on his part would at best be unnecessary, since he was being smoothly carried up the ladder anyway, and might have been positively harmful if the strategy was wrongly thought out and was not in step with developments within Sellbank. Therefore, although Sellbank tried to emphasise individual skills and abilities as being crucial, there are counter-tendencies that tend to encourage a perpetuation of the older culture of dependence. Such is the scale of change in Sellbank that many staff would rather 'wait and see' what happens.

There were a few respondents (four out of 30 to be precise) who did adopt more explicitly strategic attitudes towards their careers. Strikingly, they all tended to be rather 'foreign', for one reason or another, from the prevailing values of Sellbank. Karen, for example, was a graduate entrant in her mid-twenties who had, at a very young age, reached a junior management position in probably the shortest time possible and who seemed to be on track for rapid advancement. Nevertheless, she evinced considerable uncertainty about her future career within Sellbank:

> I don't know. As yet I don't think I'm as marketable as I could be. I want to do another couple of years within the bank before I would consider moving because I have got to make myself as marketable out there as anybody else really. I mean I did think about going into something like law but I don't really want to go through all the retraining you see. I want to be able to use what I have got to date. One thing I might go into ultimately, is I might go into lecturing, because I really enjoyed doing it; I like to see the academic side of it, that is the problem really. If they give me what I want I will stay. I think it's that sort of basically, if I enjoy what I am doing and if the next job looks interesting I will keep doing it until I have had enough, but as soon as I have had enough and I decide well I don't really like anything else on the horizon, I am unhappy with what I am doing, then I will get out... although I enjoy working for the bank in some ways I don't think it is the be all and end all of life really.

Karen's approach reflects a high degree of uncertainty. Unlike Doug, her career is still very much one in the making. She also exhibited a greater interest in a career strategy not confined to the organisation (although interestingly nor was it an occupational career strategy designed to develop her occupational profile). Her youth, gender and high qualifications marked her out from the organisational culture of Sellbank and also affected her orientation to her career:

> I think being female and a graduate will affect you... I mean some people regard it as my old manager did; he thought it was quite trendy to have me in the area... they could go and show you off at functions and things, and say this is our female graduate... but other management would take a dim view really.

It was not just managers who tended to regard Karen as 'outside' the mainstream organisational culture. Many of the female clerks could also be put out by the presence of a young woman 'high flyer'. Karen pointed out that female clerks:

> just take the view, 'oh she is a bit of an oddity anyway, fancy being 25 and being a manager', you are a bit odd anyway, so they just regard it as being part of your general oddness. But the other managers take the view as well, 'well you haven't done it the hard way, you have just leapt in half way up and it's all right for you'.

The interesting point to recognise here is how Karen's multiple detachment from her working colleagues led her to think strategically. Unlike Doug, whose organisational centrality allowed him to 'jog along', knowing that he would be offered promising jobs, Karen felt she had to plan her way out of her isolated position. She could specify quite clearly what goals she had for her future career:

> **Q:** So what sort of targets do you have... within the bank?

> Well, I would like to go back more into the role that I came from. That sort of role. I would like to work perhaps in a unit which deals with larger corporate lending with perhaps support staff for that, i.e. assessing things all the time, and looking at predispositions, rather than the nitty gritty of whether I should bounce this cheque, and interviewing people complaining about charges, which is not very interesting somehow. I did decide to come to [this current job] because I was told that if I wanted to get on in the bank at some point I had to get out on the sharp edge and prove I could do it, I couldn't go around telling people what to do if I had never actually been out there and experienced what it was like right at the sharp end.

> **Q:** The sharp end being...?

> being the branches, yes the I mean the branches at the end of the day, if you have never been in a branch you are not very credible. And I know that so I did orchestrate a move out here, and I orchestrated it fairly carefully in a way, in that I made sure I went into a branch that had got three managers because some branches have only got two, and I didn't want to get involved in any of the office management side, so what I

really wanted to do is a purely lending role, so I was quite lucky to find this out, so yes, I have engineered it and I did it myself... I intend to engineer myself out of it, mind you.

There is an interesting suggestion here then that strategic thinking is in many respects only necessary for those distant from the cultural assumptions of Sellbank. These mainly included ambitious women and graduates (and especially, as in the case of Karen, women graduates!). Some women engaged in cyclical planning, in that a long period of stasis was interrupted by a specific event which triggered off a decision to plan. Amanda, a junior manager in Sellbank, stated that she had not planned her career for 10 years, but then began planning, in the following way:

> I suppose I started to grow up and decided you know, where am I going, what am I doing, nothing, where do I want to go. I will tell you what it was actually, my husband and I applied to emigrate to Australia and at the time I decided to find out what I could do and I suddenly found out that bank clerks are two a penny and that if I went I probably wouldn't get a job, and then I thought Deborah, that's my friend, she's a Personnel Manager, I could do that, and I started thinking well I could do other things really, and that was actually when it started and I decided to plan it.

Here, a key event in Amanda's life distanced her from Sellbank, made her aware of a world outside the bank and, interestingly, made her more concerned to plan her future. The ability to plan was premised on being able to detach oneself from Sellbank's culture. Interestingly, the few men who talked about planning noted that their plans were normally to avoid promotion. Stuart spoke of:

> about sort of 15 years ago, 15 or 20 years ago, when I was sort of sitting examinations to qualify for promotion, and we (i.e. Stuart and his wife) sort of sat down the pair of us, between us, and said 'look, where do we want this to go'. I mean we personally have got a friend who made quite a big impression on both of us actually, he worked himself into the ground to become an accountant, and he worked so hard that he became an alcoholic and he died, and I thought, 'well God, you

know, if I have got to do this what is the point?', and he made a profound impact on both of us and we both decided well enough is enough. I will get to that sort level within the next few years with no problem and that will be enough... if you aspire to the management side of it you have to devote more of your own time and personality to the bank, which I am not prepared to do.

In short, the stories told by banking workers suggest important qualifications to Marshall's arguments about gendered careers. Men do not need to be 'agentic' if they want to climb the ladder, and it is those men who want to step off the ladder who need to engage in more conscious thought and reflection. Women, by contrast, do need to plan if they seek to rise to senior positions, but such planning may not necessarily be to the advantage of their careers.

Nursing career narratives

Unlike banking, the culture of nursing is much more organised around strategic narratives. This is in itself rather interesting, given Marshall's suggestion that women tend to a more 'communion' oriented notion of career than do men. This difference from banking is partly due to the professional character of the employment. All nurses have at some stage 'planned' to enter nursing as a 'career', because the first step in becoming a nurse is to train in order to be registered. Just under half of the nurses interviewed constructed narratives of planful development that tended towards the strategic, whilst just over half emphasised contingency. Male nurses, to a man, provided accounts of strategic careers, although one account was a lateral strategy, maintaining a number of strategic openings for future developments.

Looking first at the case studies of strategic, planful development, it is interesting to observe the diversity of ways in which women engaged in strategic careers. Women's narratives reveal a complex and rich mix of occupational story-telling (of career journeys) and personal story-telling (of life journeys), often pulling the 'private' sphere into focus alongside or interspersed with the 'public' domain of career journeys. It must be stressed that, although respondents themselves started by defining their own career journeys as either 'planned' or 'unplanned', they nonetheless went on to reveal complex work-life histories, which demonstrated the complex and precarious interrelation of work and non-work factors in the construction of a career (for an extended discussion of this, see Chapter 6). Equally, it is also essential to recognise that the precariousness of nurses' career journeys did not simply reflect the relation between work and non-work trajectories of the self, but was also linked to the organisational context; the structures of opportunity and contraint within which they carved out their nursing careers.

Just over half of the nurses we interviewed provided career narratives that presented their occupational journeys as relatively haphazard and subject to change. Jennifer talked of being 'in the right place at the right time', and Janet of tending to 'go along with what's come up'. These descriptions are evocative of those pursuing successful, although contingent and reactive, careers in banking. However, compared with banking, such reactive and contingent careers did not appear to be so conducive to career progress in the way that was true for men in banking.

The views of women 'returners' in nursing are also interesting. In banking women returning from childcare commitments were no more likely to articulate a strategic set of career narrative than others, largely because they took for granted their lack of prospects. In nursing this was different. Two of the respondents defined themselves as non-planners in the earlier phase of their nursing career, and it was the decision to prioritise family over work, and leave nursing to raise young children, that provided the rationale for *ex-post facto* narratives of the self as 'non-planners'. However, both drew a firm distinction between their attitude then and their attitude now, which was highly strategic. Judith, who had moved in and out of nursing for 10 years, and then taken four years out to have a family, recalled how initially:

> I thought then that I'd have a career in nursing... and I'd enjoy it and I would do it for seven years and I assumed then that I would get married and have a family and settle down and maybe work part time. ...when I

gave up work to have the family I had no intention of coming back. I just assumed that I gave up work to have a family instead of going out to work.

However, full-time childrearing produced symptoms of stress, and Judith returned to nursing part time, soon to find herself accepting the offer of a full-time Sister's post in a specialist unit. Judith's narrative was one of a contingent phase followed by a strategic phase after a brief period away from work altogether:

It all just happened. I think I'm just starting to plan it now. ...it's only now that I've come back into nursing and I quite like it.

These returners provide instances of a 'cyclical' career, with ebbs and flows of contingency, strategy and stillness marking out their career journeys.

In nursing it seems that it is important to plan in order to 'get on'. Let us first consider the case of Margaret, a 35 year old Clinical Nurse Manager in a specialist cardiac unit. Margaret's narrative is one of a planful, linear, instrumental career, located at the strategic planning end of the career continuum, but which projects forward into a work life future that incorporates childbearing and childrearing phases into a long-term career journey. It reveals many of the key tactics used in nurses' career strategies: *credentialism,* through post-qualifying courses to widen or deepen knowledge; *experience gathering,* which is strongly linked to concepts of time, i.e. so long but not too long in one particular nursing role; *skill deepening* which aims to consolidate skills; and *skill enhancement/widening,* which aims to extend the repertoire of specialist skills. Margaret described her career journey as:

planned, and then I changed direction a little bit, but I think that's probably just meant to be. ...[In the future] I'd like to carry on working, and I intend to have a family, but I also intend to carry on working, and I intend to carry on working at this level as a minimum, basically. ...I might want to go into a hospital manager's role, so I suppose I'm planning again now in that clinically I have the skills to move between cardiac and intensive care at this level. ...and I need to do something from a management point of view.

The first phase of her career journey immediately following training consisted of experience gathering, working on a general medical ward and then in theatre. The first key transition tactic (which occurred in staff nurse and senior staff nurse grades) was a credentialling one, studying for a second qualification, and this led to a phase of specialisation in intensive care. The next transition tactic was a job move to be a Sister in regional cardiac unit, and a period of skill widening (to include primary care work with patients). After three years, the next transition was to move to a national centre of excellence in cardiac care, still on a Sister's grade but with a promise (not kept) of promotion to Senior Sister. The non-delivery of a Senior Sister's grade prompted the next transition strategy, which was a Senior Sister's post at another national centre of excellence, incorporating responsibility for intensive care, coronary care and the liver unit. This was followed three years later by a transition event as she left London for personal reasons. The precariousness of nursing careers is revealed by the ensuing downwards spiral, as 'grades out of London seemed lower at the time' and Margaret took a lower graded Clinical Nurse Specialist post in intensive care at a general hospital, but was disappointed at the undemanding nature of the work there, and soon moved to another Clinical Nurse Specialist post on the same grade at Midcity hospital. She was soon promoted to her former grade I and made Clinical Nurse Manager after four months. This series of transition tactics was accompanied by an ongoing credentialling tactic to gain a Diploma in Nursing. Margaret's narrative is a model example a strategic, linear-phased career, punctuated by transition tactics. Indeed, she said that she had always thought strategically about her career, in five year periods, and that she always had a clear idea of her goals.

Diane, who is 27 years old, provided a narrative of planful development in relation to both the past and the future, but hers is a gendered, cyclical, as distinct from purely linear, career narrative, combining planful development phases with a stasis phase. Sandwiched in between two linear, planful work-dominant phases is a projected period of stasis, a family-building phase, although work was not going to be completely sacrificed in this phase, as Diane intended to continue nursing. Nonetheless:

[I'll probably] stay static if I do have a family, for a while. I certainly don't intend to let it stay static for ever.

The bread on the sandwich of this planned career stasis was two periods of linear, planful career journeys, one current, the other projected. Diane had worked as an Enrolled Nurse for five years and had recently converted to State Registered Nurse status. When asked if she had planned her career, she replied:

I've planned it to a certain extent. I always wanted to progress. I actually want to be my own theatre manager within a trauma unit. That's my ideal job, dealing with major injuries of all degrees. So I suppose in some way I've got an idea of what I want to do.

But what did Diane mean by 'planning' a career?

You set yourself objectives. I look at what I think I want and aim towards it, but obviously your perspectives change as you go along, so you keep updating really, and see what's available.

Here we get a strong sense of someone who also responds to changing opportunities, comparable with cases in banking and local government.

Like Margaret, Diane's first career phase consisted of experience gathering working in a dental hospital immediately after qualifying, but the first transition tactic was a move to a general hospital because:

The dental hospital was good experience, but it wasn't exactly very career oriented. My career would just have stayed at an absolute standstill, so the first opportunity I got I moved into the General Hospital, in a main department.

The second phase consisted of more experience gathering. The next transition tactic, after seven years' experience as an Enrolled Nurse, was a credentialling one as Diane studied to convert from an Enrolled to a State Registered General Nurse.

Diane is now making another transition by taking a six-month operating theatre course 'purely so I've got the management and the additional experience of all the areas in theatres', so is once again employing credentialist tactics in planning her career journey. However, this credentialling tactic is setting up the next phase of her career journey, which is to find a Junior Sister's Post and then, within 18 months to three years, to go for promotion to Sister – with the rider that this depends upon whether she is in 'in the right place at the right time'. After that:

> I don't know. I don't try and plan too far ahead, because you never know what life's going to throw at you, but in the next five years I hope to be a Sister.

Diane's career narrative reveals a cyclical journey, consisting of a 10 year work-dominant phase with linear movement, a projected career stasis phase in which childrearing and work commitments are combined but career is imagined in terms of a temporary stillness, followed by a further phase of strategic, linear movement. Diane's cyclical career narrative is strongly strategic and planful.

Both Margaret and Diane reveal the significance of strategic planning (albeit complex and varied) in nursing, which is largely absent in banking. This is in itself interesting since it rather undermines arguments that it is primarily men who are instrumental and strategic in outlook. Nonetheless, a considerable number of women in nursing do adopt a less planned approach to their careers. Veronica, who is 29 years old and has two children, narrates a career story that is contingent and cyclical, although ideally Veronica wanted a strategic and cyclical career. It is also spiralling downwards. The tragic difference between Diane's and Veronica's strategic career narratives is due to the crucial role played by organisational opportunity structures in facilitating or, as is the case here, curtailing gendered strategic careers. Veronica made two rapid transition tactics in the early phase of her career. The first took the form of a credentialling tactic followed by a skill-deepening move to a Staff Nurse post in a specialist unit at a different hospital; the second was three months later when she applied for and got the Sister's post in the specialist unit. The first phase of Veronica's career was planned:

> When I went to do my orthopaedic course I did it in the knowledge that I would want to get a Sister's post at some point after doing it. I wasn't going to do it just for the sake of it ... I wanted a Sister's post at some point. *Now, I just think my career is in the lap of the Gods.* [Emphasis added]

What prompted this shift from a planful, agentic, linear career to a perception of utter contingency, with her career 'in the lap of the Gods'? Veronica worked for two years as a Sister, until the strain of full-time work and looking after her first child led her to reduce her hours to 32. Then after the birth of her second child, Veronica accepted that she would have to put her career on hold, and enter a stasis phase. What she did not anticipate was that she would, in fact, be forced into a downwards spiral and her career would be undone, rather than temporarily static:

> I think all the big changes were made after my second child, whereas with my first child I desperately tried to cling to the lifestyle I already had. Obviously, the first child was a mistake. It wasn't planned, whereas the second one was planned, because I thought well, in for a penny, in for a pound. Let's get the family over and done with and then I can get my career back on course, which sounds very cold and calculating, but...

After the birth of her second child, she requested part-time hours, preferably a job-share, but was told this was out of the question because her G grade Sister's post assumed 24 hour responsibility. She was forced to drop down to an E grade Staff Nurse, working part-time on nights. What is more, she stayed on the same ward where she had been a day Sister and has ended up working under the direction of Sisters who had formerly been Staff Nurses working under her. Veronica's might be described as the typically precarious career of women who seek to maintain a nursing career at the same time as raising small children. It demonstrates the gendered assumptions underlying the notion of 'agentic, linear careers', because Veronica's narrative is that of a typically gendered precarious career:

I was forced into a corner. ... the only option left to me was to go on night duty. I was told 'it will suit you better, I think it will fit in with your family better, and come back when your children are at school or something'. And it didn't feel right from the word go. And I thought well I'll give it a try because lots of women have to do it. Why should I be different? I find it very frustrating to watch other girls run a ward that I used to run. Now I think my career is in the lap of the Gods at the moment. I'm just another Staff Nurse on nights who does nights because she's got a young family.

Veronica's narrative demonstrates a failed attempt to be instrumental (gleaned in her description of herself as seeming 'cold and calculating') in constructing a cyclical career of work-dominant phases punctuated by temporary stasis during a family-building period. It also vividly conveys the precariousness of women's career journeys and how this is linked to organisational inertia – the inability or unwillingness of organisations to accommodate the needs of nurses with childcare responsibilities, and how this, in turn, leads to nurses feeling desparately out of control, without knowing when, and indeed if, it is ever going to be possible to claw one's way back from the 'dead-zone' of part-time work on nights. The 24 hour responsibility condition of G graded Sister's posts might be seen as indirectly discriminatory against women with children, who will be less able to fulfill this condition than men or women without childcare commitments.

There are some similarities and differences between Veronica's narrative and that of another cyclical career provided by Anne. Anne's narrative tells of a career journey that occupies the middle of the continuum – a 'next-step' planner. Interestingly, it was Anne's son who was the unplanned element in her narrative; her nursing career, on the other hand, was planful, but in a 'next-step' way that is more contingent than strategic:

I did originally start training when I was 18, which is quite a few years ago, and I actually left because I became pregnant, and had my son. And then I had to fit in, but I still did nursing, and working things, carrying on. But he was the unplanned aspect. I didn't look at it long-term, being a single parent. I looked at it a step at a time.

Anne has spent the past eight years working full time on nights at Southtown Hospital, but has moved during this period from being a Staff Nurse on a surgical and then a medical ward, to being a Night Sister working a number of different wards. However, Anne views night duty as a 'dead-zone': 'you can't really progress on nights. It's a sticking point'. What is particularly interesting about Anne's long career is that the early phase was contingent, but this has been followed by next-step planning moving from Staff nurse to Sister's posts on nights. Anne is now planning two transition tactics: a credentialling one, studying for a Diploma because she wants to 'go up the ladder'; and a move back onto days. In addition, there is a sense that next-step planning is giving way to a longer-term strategic career, as moving onto days is seen as a way of becoming a Senior Sister, and Anne also imagines an endpoint, which is to be a Director of Nursing.

Typically, women's career narratives reveal career journeys that are seen to have been both planned and contingent – 'A bit of both' is how Gillian, a Director of Strategic Planning at Midcity Hospital, described her career. Gillian has a degree in nursing and distinguished clearly between a linear, planful phase before a career break to raise a family, and a subsequent return to nursing that was not planned. Gillian described how, immediately after graduating:

> I was planning a career. I made certain moves which got me onto the courses I wanted to get on... I actually applied for jobs with the mind that I wanted to know which would actually give me the right experience to get up the ladder.

This planful, linear phase ended when Gillian had children:

> until I had a career break, I think I probably had more plans, and had got more ideas of where I wanted to go and how I was going to achieve it. My return to work was an opportunity, it was not really planned, and since then opportunities have presented themselves to me, ...but it's very difficult, or it has been for me, very difficult having a family and working.

This returner's career narrative reveals distinct linear, planful phase, following by a family-building phase, and then a contingent, or chance, return into nursing, after which further 'opportunities' presented themselves, indicating a contingent or constructed career.

Interestingly, too, Gillian's career narrative is contextualised within a broader sense of achievement. Gillian spoke of 'wanting to pursue a career' and also of 'always feeling that I would want to do something to develop myself, and a career would be part of that'. This demonstrates the ways in which some women are able to integrate activities in the public sphere of employment and the private sphere within an overall project of the self. This is revealed in Gillian's definition of success in terms of having been able to combine career and family-building aspirations:

> if I measure it on the basis that, having had a career break and been able to come back in then, yes, I've been successful. ...one anticipated that you might get married and you may have a family, and..., I had always anticipated that I'd be able to combine the two. I mean, I wasn't more definite than that, and I guess from that point of view I've succeeded in that to a certain extent. So I guess it's worked out roughly as I anticipated.

Finally, did men's career narratives reveal any marked differences from those of women? It would be misleading to portray men's orientations as more instrumental than women's, as we have seen how women nurses engage in a variety of transition tactics, such as job moves and credentialling. Two of the male nurses we interviewed revealed work orientations very similar to those of women nurses, although a third revealed many of the allegedly more typical instrumental and masculine motivations for being a nurse (see Chapter 4).

Bert, one of the few male nurses, recognised that nursing was 'not a normal male career', but there were two quite different kinds of response to the question of whether one's career had been planned or not. Bert noted that:

> Sadly my life has displayed a total lack of any sort of strategy... I haven't consciously pursued a career. Rather I've been fortunate enough to be able to pursue my interests that happen to have led to a career, and

promotions have come along at a time when I've been ready to move, so I've grasped the opportunities that were there. But I haven't thought in terms of 'in two years' time I'll do X, in three years' time I'll do Y'. I've certainly got no ultimate goal other than to keep enjoying what I'm doing, to be stretched constantly, so look for promotions when the novelty starts wearing off in the area that I'm working in.

What was markedly different between the men and the women in nursing was the impact that family life had on their respective work orientations and perceptions of career commitment. We have seen how, for some highly strategic women nurses, family building is conceived as a period of career stasis, when linear, planful development is temporarily put on hold. Precisely the opposite seems to happen for male nurses. There is some evidence that marriage and children promotes a greater sense of attachment by men to their nursing careers, with an increasing emphasis on instrumentalism and 'getting on'. Henry, another Charge Nurse, talked of a distinct shift in career orientations when he and his wife decided they both wanted children 'and knew that we'd have to, if you like, make our careers'. He described how it was at this point that:

I started to structure more into what I was doing, and thinking about achieving different grades and getting to a different position. ...I can't say it was a total long-term plan.

Local government career narratives

Amongst our local government workers we found examples all along the continuum from strategic to contingent careers. However (unlike nursing but in common with banking), strategic approaches to career development in local government were very unusual. Although the notion of planned, strategic career development was associated with being serious about one's career, and ultimate 'success', this was alluded to more in guilt than in actual career narratives. Elaine and Cathy, both in mid–senior management posts by their late thirties commented:

I've never had a 25-year plan. I mean I know I should have really. [Elaine]

No I don't think I've planned it. I think that might be a fault, but no I don't think I did. [Cathy]

It was far more common for career narratives to describe next-step tactical behaviour and contingent careers, in both cases linked to organisational events and to extra-organisational events in individuals' personal lives. We found no evidence in local government to support suggestions that there is a simple gendered division between hierarchical, linear planners (male) and more contingent or cyclical forms of behaviour (female). We did, however, discover a more complex pattern of gendered career narratives linked more to the gendering of organisation than to a straightforward binary gender division in individual career orientations or forms of agency.

Let us begin with those workers who have been most successful, at least in traditional hierarchical terms. By the age of 42, Keith had reached an extremely senior position, which he described as the pinnacle of his career. He had achieved this through a process of conscious planning and was clearly satisfied with his strategic labours:

> **Q:** When you were saying just now that you had this idea that you wanted to [reach the top] by the time you were 35, would you say you planned what has happened to you in your career? Or would you say that it just happened?

Yes, planned to the extent that whilst I've only ever worked for two local authorities... I've always been quite clear that every couple of years I was looking for promotion. It so happened in Grandchester that it was internal until I came to [this authority] and then the same thing happened here. So within two steps [after I got here], effectively I was Assistant Treasurer and Senior Assistant Treasurer as it happened. But, oh yes, I quite clearly saw, there is a kind of recognised path. Sometimes people take longer, obviously, but if you're going for that kind of objective then really it was basically every couple of years from qualifying you go up the different levels of accountancy, and that was what I wanted, mainstream accountancy basically.

Unlike traditional practice within banking, individuals in local government have had to apply for internal jobs and therefore have had to plan when to apply and how to put themselves forward for promotion (which is not to say that there were not, and are not, various informal mechanisms by which people have been encouraged to apply for jobs). As Keith points out, and as we have seen in previous chapters, there were also clear professional hierarchies, at least in accountancy, which the ambitious could identify and attempt to climb. However, amongst those now at the top, Keith remains an exception. He was the *only* senior manager in local government who claimed a strictly strategic approach to his career. Far more often these managers described making short-term, next-step responses to transitional events or, looking back over highly successful linear careers, describing these as totally contingent on extrinsic events. Clearly, this form of behaviour is no obstacle to linear career success in local government.

Harry, another senior manager, provides an antithesis to Keith. Harry was a Senior Housing Manager who begun his career when he simply 'drifted into' the Council as a 16 year old school leaver. At the age of 19 he moved from housing finance, where the opportunities seemed too limited, into rent collection. This work suited him – he liked going to visit tenants – and his application for trainee Housing Officer was sucessful. After this he was 'made up' (i.e. without applying) to District Housing Officer, at which point he became involved in trade union activity. After seven years of this, Harry wanted a change and moved onto a neighbouring authority. Here he got his first opportunity to manage, although he says this was due to *other people's* faith in him rather than because he had been pushing himself forward. During his three years here there were some major reorganisations and:

certain opportunities arose and I was fortunate to secure one of those particular posts so I moved up fairly quickly over a three-year period.

At this time he happened to meet one of the managers from his old authority who implied that there might be job opportunities for him back at Midcity if he was interested. Involved in a dispute with his employer at the time, he put in an application to Midcity, more as a negotiation tactic than a career move, and ended up being appointed to a post far higher than he had reasonably expected to get:

> I just couldn't believe this because I hadn't come to get the job, so when you say did I plan or did it just happen, yes it just happened for all sorts of reasons.

Harry emphasised again that others had more confidence in him than he did himself, and that his rise up the ladder was not something he had planned or expected. After returning to Midcity he was again at the centre of a dispute with managers, which resulted in a total restructuring of the department and eventually, for him, another promotion:

> I was then dis-established from the post and sort of in limbo land for a while and then a new guy came in and... they sort of said 'oh, we'll stick you here' so, well... it just happened really, there was no plan to it.

Harry is clearly well regarded and has been very successful in conventional linear career terms. His case shows the range of influences which may be brought to bear over the life-time of a career and the advantages of responding flexibly to the changing opportunity structure. Many of the key aspects of his career progress were triggered by transitional events. Significantly, much of his career was affected by various disputes with his employers, which hardly suggests that he had a strong sense of individual self-interest over-riding his career.

Harry's narrative is unexceptional. Several other senior staff described their careers in similar terms. Here we take up Jim's narrative shortly after his original career (not in local government) failed in the early 1970s:

it was a question of looking, hunting around the job market... I actually lit on a number of people, people like the County Council, who were hiring property professionals and I ended up [at my previous employer]. From there on in there was no plan attached to it at all. Just, I spent four years with them getting promotion because people disappeared, just that I happened to be there and the right person, and then when I came here in 1978... I just happened to be the right person again.

This process of 'getting caught up in the flow' is repeated over and over again amongst those in intermediate and senior local government positions. Cathy, another senior accountant/manager, claimed, 'It's amazingly evident, when I look back on it, that it wasn't planned', despite having made a hierarchical career move at least every three years during her career. This is not to say that these workers were unreflective about their work or their futures, but that the monitoring of their careers took rather a different form from the classic strategic approach. Rather, most described short-term, step-by-step plans, sometimes within the framework of a very general goal (to reach management team or, even more vaguely, to 'get on') but often with no general goal in mind at all. These people's career choices and actions took place within a series of shifting circumstances and goals.

Christopher provides another good example. He had worked for Midcity for 14 years, since leaving school. At the time of our research he was in a newly established post, on the first rung of the principal officer grades. He described his career as a mixture of his own ambitions:

I wanted to get up as far as I could. I was ambitious but without really knowing what I wanted to do.

and being pushed along by organisational changes (see Chapter 4). As his department became responsible for managing the collection of poll tax, Christoper saw new opportunities. After working with one of the managers he found a new goal:

I thought 'well yes, why not be a manager?' ...So it gave me a little bit of direction, something to specifically aim for if you like, and then I was appointed to my current position about 18 months ago.

Even where individuals have longer-term goals, career narratives are still described in terms of transitional events and contingencies. As Mark, another senior accountant describes:

There was a general idea sort of going through. I started out as a trainee accountant and the logical thing is that you go up and eventually become a Borough Treasurer somewhere, and that's the logical progression. It was never a total, absolute, overriding desire or anything like that and I don't think I've planned my career towards that end. There have been reasons for each career move I've made but I can honestly say that only one really was actually a deliberate career move. All the rest *there were other factors involved, personal factors and things like that.* [Emphasis added]

Whilst Harry, Cathy and Christopher described the transitional stages in their careers in terms of *organisational* events, Mark emphasises the extra-organisational events that have shaped his career. This remained relatively unusual for those in senior posts, and especially for *men* in senior posts. Some now regret this. Keith, for example, insisted on a nuanced response to the question 'Do you consider yourself to be successful?', replying very firmly 'In a *work* sense', and later described the strain that career demands had placed on his personal relationships.

Of course, for others – particularly women in more junior positions – extra-organisational events impinge on their career narratives in far less nuanced ways. Here, as in nursing and banking, we find many women speaking in terms of the continual interplay between home and work: the continuous conflict between demands on their time from children and families and organisational demands. Certainly, childbirth continues to mark a major transitional event, with many women describing this as a point of reappraisal in their career narratives. Maureen worked for local government for seven years before leaving the labour market for four years, during which time she had two children. She is now back in local government in a senior clerical post. Maureen sees the second phase of her career as far more planned than the first. Before her children were born Maureen followed her husband's career around the country, but when the marriage broke up and Maureen was left with the children she began to feel differently:

> I think that's when it became a career, because at that point I felt that I was going to have to be a breadwinner for the family.

Although she subsequently remarried, her commitment to work persisted and she had been promoted four times in the six years since returning to work. Although Maureen's career narrative is strongly shaped by emerging and receding domestic responsibilities, it contradicts popular images of this articulation. Rather than weakening Maureen's commitment to work, childbirth, divorce and even remarriage have all contributed to an enhanced and more tactical approach to her career. Her main tactic involves study during her spare time, in the hope that she will be ready for any opportunities that may arise, although she has few firm ideas on precisely what the opportunties may be. Maureen's case highlights an important finding across both local government and nursing, namely that women may become *more* strategic once they return to work after a career break to have children. This may be linked to a sense of heightened responsibility, as initially in Maureen's case, or to a practical need to become more efficient and organised once overall levels of responsibility rise. However, these cases remain unusual. Most local government women with dependent children are in junior clerical and administrative posts, and most still claim to have unplanned careers. Significantly though, this appears to be more to do with the structural position these women are in, which inhibits progression and renders planning rather pointless, than with characteristics of the women themselves (cf. Kanter, 1977). We will return to this point shortly. Where women with children are not in these junior posts, they describe contingent and next-step career narratives in terms very similar to those of their male counterparts.

Thus far, then, we have emphasised how *few* local government workers devise or deploy long-term or coherent career strategies. We found four exceptions to this. We have already described Keith, who is perhaps the only example of a paradigmatic career strategist. The others who described themselves in these terms actually appear to have more in common with the banking 'outsiders' (see Section 5.2) than with Keith. Furthermore, what they describe as 'strategy' may be more accurately seen as generalised tactics. All three felt that they had had to devise career plans because they were *not* 'caught up in the flow' of career development. One had failed accountancy exams and needed to establish a new line of work. Another wanted to move into surveying work but had failed all his exams at school and had no chance of taking a traditional route via higher education. The last 'planner' was in a similar position, wanting to be a building inspector, but was also a woman trying to enter a totally male-dominated area of local government work. All three spoke of how they planned to gain occupationally related qualifications whilst already working in local government. However, their strategic orientation stopped at this level and did not extend to considering in the long term which jobs to apply for and how to use those credentials. Rather, the impression was given that acquiring credentials would in itself be enough to *get into* the right area of work. However, having achieved this, none of them was confident about the future, and they all continued to modify their goals and to consider other more responsive tactics.

In addition to credentialism we found a number of other generalised career tactics deployed in local government. Cultivating a distinctive or appropriate *personal presence* was one. Claire, a benefits worker, had spent nearly 10 years observing the few men unlucky enough to begin their careers in benefits trying to get out as quickly as possible:

> They come in with their suit and their tie on their first day, and their moustache [referring to the common managerial style in this department] and as soon as you look at them you know where they are going to be in the next 10 years. And they make it. [Claire]

Here we see the quite literal significance of gendered embodiment in career progression. Others tried to do extra work in the hope that they would stand out, and gave this as a recipe for success, claiming that you must:

> set your stall out to achieve what is expected, even more than is expected, of you ...I've always been someone who's worked long hours in order to actually deliver and I felt that I would be letting myself down if I didn't do that. ...People will say, I'm sure, outside this office that the boss will expect you to work 10 hours, 12 hours, X hours, overtime. And yes, up to a point they are right because I think, at a senior level, in this organisation, and in this department in particular ...to do a reasonable job, that is what has to be done. [Keith]

The final 'tactic' mentioned was organisational loyalty. This only surfaced in Southtown where, in the late 1980s, there had been severe recruitment difficulties. However, to describe this as a tactic seems dubious since it is once more a case of staying in place and seeing what happens.

In sum, then, strategic career narratives are rare, tactics are short term and often haphazard, and planning appears, if at all, in narratives mostly as a response to transitional events or life phases. There were a number of reasons why local government workers found it so difficult or inadvisable to plan. Some, such as those in benefits sections and routine clerical work, felt that they were so marginalised from departmental hierarchies as to make planning pointless:

> If you attempt in any way to get out, within the Council, you've got no chance. [Claire]

Almost all of these staff (well over 90 per cent) were women, occupationally segregated into career 'dead-zones' where tactics or strategies seemed meaningless to them. However, despite Claire's observations (above), the few men we spoke to who were stranded in these 'dead-zones' also had difficulties conceiving of escape tactics:

It's the set up, the way the Council is organised. I know about all sorts of things in my job which you would think would help you to get on but it doesn't, it blocks off avenues... It's like my career has come to a standstill. [Neil]

More generally, there was also a sense that the extent of upheaval in local government meant that the future could rarely be foreseen and that it was impossible to plan when jobs and hierarchies were constantly being reshuffled (see Chapter 4). This was also linked to the impact of economic recession, which, in 1991 when we did most of our interviews, was at its worst. We repeatedly came across accounts of the futility of planning, for example:

There's so many changes in legislation and it depends on what happens in the election. You just don't know where you'll be in three years. Southtown authority may not have a Housing Department by then. [Sandi]

It's hard to plan in local government, because things change all the time. If you want to stay in local government you have to accept that you will have to wait. Assess the jobs as they arrive. [Harry]

The gendering of this uncertainty is a complex matter. As we argued at length in Chapter 3, current phases of restructuring appear to be endorsing a new form of masculinity within local government organisations, thus propelling the careers of those men who can deploy that style and image and who are perceived to fit that model. Whilst some women may also be benefiting because of claims about women's 'special' management competencies (Maddock, 1993), these supposed qualities receive only limited endorsement within the new managerialist climate in local government. Furthermore, the uncertainty described above has contributed to reduced funding for, and some would say reduced political commitment to, EO initiatives (widely referred to as more a thing of the 1980s and not 'realistic' in the 1990s) and also leads us to doubt the extent to which women will benefit from current organisational uncertainties.

Linked to the previous point a final explanation for lack of strategic and tactical behaviour concerns the still widespread expectations that careers should be taken care of by organisational rather than individual processes. Although, as we argued in Chapter 3, this does seem to be changing, we repeatedly encountered individuals who were disaffected because they felt the organisation had let them down. Two front-line service staff, in different departments in different authorities, expressed this sentiment:

> It's supposed to be a career. When I first joined the Council I was told that there would be opportunities to go higher, to move on. ...It was a career but after seven and a half years it's not turning out that way. [Neil]

> I'll get no help from the bosses here. Which I'd like. They should be a bit more career minded. [Julia]

Both women and men complained in this way, but again those who felt most let down were those, mostly women, stuck in organisational 'dead-zones'.

Conclusions

In banking and local government most careers were contingent and many consisted of cyclical as well as linear phases. Even the career narratives of those who might objectively have been expected to be strategic (i.e. those who had made frequent and orderly moves up a recognised career hierarchy) revealed considerable contingency, with the deployment of transition tactics at certain key points. Clearly defined career 'strategies' are very rare and, in fact, are adopted most by those who find themselves in unconventional or marginalised positions. In nursing we found clearer evidence of strategic careers and certainly more evidence of transition tactics, usually involving the acquisition of credentials, although these plans may be undermined by current rounds of NHS restructuring (see Chapter 4).

These sectoral differences are particularly interesting in one respect. Strategic and tactical behaviour is most in evidence in a female-dominated sector but is notably lacking in the most male-dominated, traditional career paths of banking and local govern-

ment. These empirical findings certainly undermine any univer-
salist assumptions about women and men, and seem to offer more
in the way of highlighting the complexities and uncertainties of
both women's and men's career narratives. However, and we must
make this clear, we are not claiming that career narratives are
ungendered. In particular the narratives of our staff in banking and
local government simply add grist to the argument about organisational constructions of opportunity for certain categories of worker
– principally men – and the exclusion of other categories – principally women with children. The success of the majority of senior
men in banking and local government was strongly linked to their
gender but not to any sense of masculine strategic behaviour.

One of the implications of our findings is that, on the whole,
individuals did not adopt instrumentalist narratives of their careers.
Talking about their careers raised more complex emotional issues
of belonging (to the organisation, to their working colleagues, to
their families, etc.) and/or detachment. This is an interesting point
in view of the general arguments in this book concerning the
inherently social, and in particular gendered, nature of restructuring
and organisational change. People's views on their own lives and
futures were expressed only rarely in individualistic terms but
much more frequently made references to their organisational
belongingness. In short, people's identities tended to be constructed
in close association to the organisation in which they worked.

Moreover, there are clearly gendered patterns across the three
sectors in the management of transitional events, particularly
emergent childcare responsibilites. Although becoming a father
does impinge on the career narratives of some men, this is usually
expressed in terms of responsibility, particularly financial responsibility, and the need for security and stability. For women, of
course, the implications of such transitional events are usually
rather different. We pursue these points in the following chapter,
which widens out to consider organisational constructions of
'home' and their significance for the gendering of careers.

(Re)presentations of 'Home' and 'Work' in Organisational Life

Introduction

So far in this book we have concentrated on individuals' experience of organisational change and the factors shaping their careers. In Chapter 5 we saw how, for women especially, careers cannot be separated from other life events and responsibilities, in particular becoming a mother. In this chapter we continue to widen our focus by considering more fully individuals' experience of the interplay between life at work, inside their organisations, and life outside work. Of course, and as we will show, these accounts shed further light on processes of organisational change, on career processes and on the gendered dynamics of both.

The idea that 'work' can be cleanly separated from 'home' retains both academic and popular appeal. In our research this notion of *segmentation* was presented as both an organisational and an individual ideal. Certainly, it can be argued that organisations mark off the private as beyond their business or interest. This separation is actively constructed *inter alia* through personnel policies. Provisions for maternity leave and time off for sick dependants, for example, mark out very clearly the extent to which organisations will tolerate the incursion of the 'private' into the 'public' realm of the organisation. Conversely, EO policies mark the extent to which organisations should expect to know about and/or make judgements about individuals' personal circumstances.

191

Initially, then, it seems that the distinctions between 'work' and 'home' are clear. However, beneath this ideal it quickly becomes apparent that the boundaries between 'home' and 'work' are in fact blurred both in individual accounts and in organisational symbols, relationships and identities. Despite individual preferences it is clear that there is, in practice, considerable overlap between 'home' and 'work', on both a daily and a life-cycle basis. Almost all the workers we interviewed described a *spillover* process, in which domestic responsibilities and identities were central to workplace life and, in turn, organisational work, relationships and identities were transferred outside work. Women were most forthcoming and open about this spillover. When women discussed their work histories and plans for their future working lives, they would routinely and without prompting place these in the context of their partners/husbands and children, or decisions about whether to have children. Women articulated a continual consciousness of the gendered specificity of their work histories and talked about deliberate trade-offs and (plans for) managing home/work responsibilities on a daily basis and over the life course. By comparison, the majority of men talked only in vague terms about their lives outside work, and usually only when questioned very directly on the subject.

Of course, the gendered nature of home/work boundaries and interactions has been widely commented on. One of the key issues for women is how organisational constructions of the boundaries operate with male-centred assumptions about the extent to which the private *can* be marked off from the public. Organisational provision of childcare is one way of acknowledging the private responsibilities of workers, and this serves to challenge the boundaries between the public lives of adults without major care responsibilities and the public lives of adults with dependent children or responsibilities towards those with whom they share their private world. However, it has generally proved extremely difficult to get organisations to recognise and make provision for the 'private' responsibilities of participants, and the poor provision of workplace nurseries in Britain attests to this fact. Clearly, organisational policies, practices and expectations endorse some patterns of home life whilst making others more difficult to sustain.

Beneath a superficial layer of segmentation, organisations have shown persistent preferences for a certain pattern of accommodation between home and work life. These preferences, and particularly their androcentric biases, are manifest when we consider the organisational career. The employment careers of many successful men have depended on the establishment of supportive familial and domestic relationships. Kanter (1977) showed how wives were seen as a bonus in the appointment and promotion of male managers, whilst Finch (1983) demonstrates the practical social and moral support that wives lent to the development of their husbands' careers across a range of occupations. Finch even speaks of the 'vicarious careers' of wives. Crompton (1986) has also argued that service class men are facilitated in their career mobility by their wives' domestic servicing activities. In essence, then, it is a particular familial configuration that contributes practically to male bureaucratic careers and is also instrumental in constructing a preferred norm of organisational masculinity, i.e. the heterosexual family man. We have seen in previous chapters how, in banking, it is openly acknowledged that men's home lives have been central to their career prospects. Managerial roles have been and continue to be defined in part through paternal discourses and explicit requirements that organisational men should be married, and even have children, before taking on their first managerial job.

The organisational story for women is very different. If organisational women marry and/or have children, this is regarded unfavourably and perceived as a drain on commitment and loyalty to the workplace, particularly for women in senior, managerial positions (Collinson, 1988). In relation to this, we can see the construction of (at least) two rather different organisational femininities. One defines women as driven by domesticity and emotionality, with only a secondary commitment to the workplace. This typification of femininity serves to rationalise the exclusion of women from a bureaucratic career (Hakim, 1991). The other entails the construction of women as 'social men', as they are expected to behave 'like men' and are perceived as most able to if they are not married, do not have children and are therefore making a primary commitment to organisational life.

However, whilst organisational men are constructed in ways which evoke particular familial and domestic arrangements, 'career women' are expected to spurn familial and domestic commitments in order to meet the practical and symbolic demands of organisational life. In banking the first of these typifications has been by far the most common, whilst in nursing the historical construction of the dedicated nurse, Sister or Matron has been explicitly constructed in opposition to familial and domestic commitments. In local government there is evidence of both typifications, although, of course, the former is dominant, linked to the majority of women who are segregated into routine, non-career posts in organisational 'dead-zones'.

In the rest of this chapter we continue to explore these sectoral specificities, and also to develop common themes across our organisations. We begin with some empirical material from our questionnaire, which seems to indicate that the gendered concomitants of 'home' and 'work' are declining in the contemporary period. To investigate these initial claims we examine the more detailed and nuanced accounts given in interviews, paying particular attention to the different ways in which women and men describe their own experiences and how women and men are placed in relation to discourses of 'home' and 'work' (McDowell and Pringle, 1992). We also explore how the separation between 'home', or the 'private', and 'work', or the 'public', is actively constructed and sustained within organisations. Specifically, this means unpacking 'spurious dualities' (Parkin, 1993: 187) in relation to home/work, private/public and female/male, and making explicit the ways in which these are inflected with gendered meanings and gendered forms of control, both within organisations and within the domestic sphere.

Notions of motherhood, paternalism and the male breadwinner continue to pervade organisational discourses and are revealed through organisational participants' accounts of 'home' and 'work'. Our attention to the significance of motherhood within gendered organisational discourses raises the more general issue of social constructions of the female body and the ways in which these are central to organisational typifications of 'woman'. This is a recurrent, but underdeveloped, theme throughout our discussion of the three sectors in this chapter. In order to expand on this theme we take what is perhaps an unusual step and introduce some new theoretical debates in the final section of this chapter. Integrating debates within feminism and social theory with material 'pulled through' from our empirical study, this final section aims to elaborate on our general theoretical statements about gender, embodiment and organisation made in Chapter 1 and also establish a foundation for our discussion of sexuality and embodiment, which follows in Chapter 7.

Shifting gendered boundaries?

For much of the post-war period thinking about the relationship between 'home life' and 'work life' has been organised around the idea that these are defined as female and male roles respectively. This apparently straightforward conceptualisation of different but complementary gendered spheres of private and public conceals within it some significant assumptions: first, that 'home life' and 'work life' are discrete and distinctive; second, that the different spheres draw on and animate different orientations and characteristics; and third, that men and women tend to possess the appropriate qualities suited to these different spheres. At the same time there has been a steady increase in the number of married women entering paid work. However, far from destabilising gendered representations of 'home' and 'work' life roles, advocates and analysts of married women's increased participation in paid employment initially reworked this association by heralding the era of women's 'dual role' as mothers and wives in the home and paid workers in employment. Married women's employment was made acceptable in the 1960s and 70s by reference to the fact that additional income could benefit families, so women were not necessarily neglecting their families by taking paid work outside the home – particularly as most of this was part time (Jephcott *et al.*, 1962). Thus the 'dual role' ideology served for a period to sustain the gendered ideology of separate spheres whilst, paradoxically, enabling women to inhabit both! It is perhaps worth noting that whilst women's negotiation of the boundaries between 'home' and 'work' life was being reworked, men's identification with the public sphere was not. As some writers (Walby, 1986; Summerfield, 1984) have suggested the construction of part-time work specifically for women, which accelerated in the post-war period in Britain, served to ease shortages in labour supply without undermining men's expectations of linear careers and of the range of services they received from women in the home.

Social and economic change continues apace. More mothers than ever are returning to work, and the time spent out of the labour market is falling. EO policies have been initiated to enhance women's career options and reduce discriminatory judgements made about women. We might, by now, expect to see severe cracks in the gendered discourse of separate spheres, and to see this revealed through organisational participants' understandings of the meanings of 'home' and 'work' and of the relationship between the two, both in terms of the life activities that they prioritise and the utility of gender typifications in describing their own experiences.

Table 6.1 reports the survey questionnaire responses of women and men when asked to evaluate the personal significance of work and a range of non-work activities. Although there are some important differences between men's and women's responses, *gender* differences are less marked than the differences between the *sectors*. Bank workers of both sexes appear to be less work oriented and more home oriented than local government workers and nurses. However, across the sectors men, compared with women, place a similar or slightly higher emphasis on the value of spending time with their children, whilst women are equally as likely as men to place a high value on work, although both sexes rated work as relatively unimportant compared with other activities. More stereotypical is the higher value women place on shopping, homemaking and seeing other family members.

Of course, all of these respondents were in work at the time of our research, so we cannot make claims about those women, or indeed those men, who choose not to work. Nonetheless, these statistics do provide some preliminary indication that a significant change may be taking place.

Table 6.1   **'Are the following activities important to you personally?':**
% claiming 'important' or 'very important'

| | Men (%) | | | Women (%) | | |
	Banks	LG	Nursing	Banks	LG	Nursing
Being with partner★	81	87	73	91	88	89
Being with children★	76	73	70	71	74	69
Being with other family	39	40	29	64	54	48
Work	49	59	65	48	63	63
Socialising	54	53	47	63	55	72
Leisure/sport/holidays	75	64	65	77	67	66
Shopping	11	17	6	40	25	30
Homemaking	40	54	35	69	63	69
N =	89	71	13	111	71	132

★ Only includes those who have a partner and/or children.

Our in-depth interviews provided a more rounded and subtle picture of the meaning of gender roles. All those interviewed were asked to comment on the assumption that women prioritised 'home life' over 'work life' and that men prioritised these conversely. Across all three sectors our respondents recognised the stereotype but typically gave a more nuanced account of their own lives. They pointed to a *shared* commitment to work and home life in the partnerships in which they were involved; to the impact which women's careers are having on the renegotiation of traditional gender roles in the private sphere; and to the subtle ways in which priorities shift during the course of the life cycle for both men and women (but particularly for women); some even went so far as to deny the continuing salience of the notion of gendered roles in the home.

However, although there appears to be a fluidity in people's representation of gender roles in their own and other people's lives, it would be a mistake to think that the general reluctance to endorse gender typifications of 'home' and 'work' life meant that gender-differentiated practices were declining, in either the workplace or the home. As we have seen in previous chapters, women feel that men continue to enjoy organisational career advantages in the organisations, some of which derive from a privileged ability to detach themselves from commitments of time and emotion in the private sphere. As Table 6.2 shows the vast majority of men with dependent children, in all three sectors, were able to rely on their partners to care for the children during the day, which means that their own particular familial and domestic arrangements conformed to the very same gendered expectations from which they sought to distance themselves.

Table 6.2   Childcare arrangements by gender and sector

% of dependent children looked after in the following way	Banks		LG		Nursing	
	M	F	M	F	M	F
Partner	82	17	91	17	89	35
Other family	11	52	3	33	–	16
Other unpaid	5	28	9	50	–	47
Paid childcare	2	3	–	–	11	2

Rather against expectations, Table 6.2 shows that men in banking were slightly *less* likely than men in the other two sectors to rely on their partners to provide childcare during the day, but even here 82 per cent of them did. Nonetheless, men in all three sectors were roughly three times as likely as women to rely on their partners to look after children. However, the proportion of women who were able to rely on partners to provide childcare was not negligible. In nursing, one third of women with dependent children relied on their partners for childcare. There are two possible reasons for this. The first is that nurses working nights or on certain split day shifts may be able to leave children with a partner who is working different hours. The second could be related to male unemployment. Apart from the obvious availability of time, strategies in the face of this, such as men working from home in their own small businesses (an example of which was provided by one high-ranking nurse in Midcity Hospital), may explain men's higher involvement in childcare. However, overall it was still the case that women with children relied most heavily on family and friends for childcare, with paid childcare – even where workplace crèches existed – of negligible importance in all sectors.

We turn now to an analysis of each of the three sectors in which we expand on this disjuncture between widespread claims that 'things are different now' and 'your private life makes no difference to your work life' on the one hand and persistent gender divisions of labour and discursive attachments between female/private, male/public on the other. More specifically, we develop particular sub-themes in each sector. In banking there is particular emphasis on the decline in managerial surveillance of personal life, as well as a fuller discussion of the politics of over-time or taking work home. In local authorities and nursing we focus on the question of motherhood, also briefly considering fatherhood, and explore the practicalities that this raises in the management of home and work. This leads us to consider the ways in which more discursive constructions of motherhood and female emotionality, and especially the nature of female embodi-ment, continue to pervade our organisations.

Banking: separate spheres?

A quarter of banking respondents acknowledged the existence of stereotypical gender roles linked specifically to home and work, but exempted *themselves* from the stereotype:

> Yes, I think there is truth in the statement [about gender roles] but, having said that, myself and my boyfriend are totally the same. The expression we use is 'we work to live and don't live to work' – both of us. So we have both got, I would say, almost identical priorities. You know, home is the most important thing. [Liz]

Another frequent response from bank workers was that, although people were still affected by traditional gender roles, things were changing:

I would think that probably [there are different gender roles] but only
because of traditional values, and I think it is probably moving more away,
where more and more women are taking careers. I think traditional values
were the woman is expected to look after the home, if you like, so
obviously her priorities would then be the home and family, whereas I think
more and more women tend to look to a career as well as the home so
therefore the home is shared by the husband and wife. [Simon]

Others commonly referred to the growing numbers of men
who were interested in leisure or home interests, placing a
lower priority on careers and work than in the old days. A few
respondents went so far as to deny the existence of gender roles
altogether.

At one level, then, there appeared to be considerable fluidity in
perceptions of the gender-differentiated meanings of 'home' and
'work'. However, gendered practices were not necessarily
changing, particularly in households where both partners worked
full time. Many women, and some men, described how it was
women who continued to bear the brunt of domestic work in
these households. Steven denied that women tended to be more
home oriented whilst men were more work oriented, and
described the situation in his household as one where his wife
was strongly committed to her work − but at the same time
doing most of the housework!:

Well, it is certainly not true in my family. I mean if anything it is completely
the opposite. My wife ...I mean it's quite embarrassing when I get home
now, I mean, I might be reading one of my books... and she is probably
preparing for the following working day until midnight... [She] is
completely devoted to her job and puts an awful lot more into it [but] I
don't want to give the impression she hasn't brought up the family...

Q: Who does things like the cooking and the washing?

Of course, she will, oh yes, but at the same time as well. [Steven]

A married female bank manager describes how she is still
expected to plan and manage the domestic sphere:

Well, I think the thing I find quite funny is that, I always think it is quite strange, if tomorrow for breakfast my husband goes to the breadbin to see if there is any bread for toast and it isn't there, he won't have thought ahead and realised that there wasn't going to be any and bought any, whereas I have already made a mental note. ...and it is quite strange because I think, yes, I have very much taken over the traditional wife role. I do all the cooking, all the washing, cleaning, ironing – you name it. [Karen]

Male careers in banking have traditionally depended upon having the right profile in both work and family life. Promotion in bank management has traditionally been dependent upon home circumstances as well as work performance. Bank employees had to be perceived as 'respectable' in order for the public to trust them, and 'respectability' was partly achieved through adopting conventional non-work lifestyles. With the very occasional exception (Crompton and Le Feuvre, 1992) only men were deemed to be eligible for managerial posts and preference was given to family men. As one male clerk recalled:

it was almost a question of the managers in those days could dictate to you when you got married, who you got married to, and whether they envisaged the lending of money so you could set up home. And you had to sort of conform to the style of the bank, you know, 'you are with the bank my son and you can't do anything [out of line]'. I mean, God knows what they would have done if a couple of people had set up home together. ...I mean some of them would have gone absolutely ape. I know when I joined the bank I was questioned as to what my intentions were, whether I was seriously courting, when I was going to get married, who my intended was, what her father did, what school she went to. [Stuart]

And, of course, if stable family men were seen as the stuff out of which bank managers were made, divorce was frowned upon. As one manager, Jeff, recalled:

It used to be, when I joined the bank, any whiff of divorce or anything was a terrible matter and you were transferred to London or somewhere out of the way.

Q: And what was the rationale of that?

Because bankers were perceived as stable, family people, pillars of the community. All that sort of stuff. And to have people talking about divorce and children, no father and one-parent families was just unacceptable. [Jeff]

In banking, then, there have traditionally been quite rigid organisational controls over home and family life. So have we seen an end to these? Although such explicit discrimination no longer exists and most bank staff we interviewed felt that the situation had changed enormously in recent years, a minority were more sceptical and suspected that there were still informal notions of a suitable person for a post.

Respondents recognised that however relaxed the formal policy had become, there might be an informal preference for middle-aged, married men in managerial positions, just as there always had been. Another indication of organisational tolerance of different non-work lifestyles is to be found in the commitment to EO policies. Today Sellbank has a strong formal commitment to not making childbirth and childrearing an obstacle to career progress for women in banking. During the 1980s new career break schemes were introduced to encourage women to retain their links with banking work and it is now one of the largest private sector providers of childcare in Britain. Before the 1980s the very few women who earned promotion in banking all had surrogate male careers and had never had children (Crompton and LeFeuvre, 1992). So to what extent is motherhood still perceived as incompatible with a linear career? None of the female bank managers in our survey had children, and several interviewees referred to the fact that female managers were nearly always childless. Women themselves continued to feel that motherhood was incompatible with the banking career. Suzanne, a middle-ranking manager, was clear on this point:

> The choice is really children or career. ...I couldn't do the job I am doing at the moment with children to the extent and to the working hours that I am putting in. It just would not be feasible. I think I would be a bad mother and I think I would be a bad banker. [Suzanne]

Ambitious younger women adopted a number of ways of dealing with the problems of combining motherhood with career development. A few claimed to have no interest at all in having children and indicated they were all too aware of the difficulties of reconciling the two roles:

> I am getting married in June but I certainly don't intend to have a family.

> **Q:** Why don't you want to have a family?

> It doesn't interest me to be honest. The thought of staying at home all day would drive me nuts. I enjoy my work and I don't want to give it up, couldn't afford to start a family anyway because we need two wages. I like the way it is at the moment and I wouldn't want it to change, maybe in a lot of years time. [Lesley]

Other younger women adopted a mode of thought that distinguished phases in their life, and allocated the possibility of childbearing into a specific phase which had not yet arrived and could therefore be kept away from direct thought. Karen, whom we met in Chapter 5 exemplifies this view:

> I view my life in chunks a little bit, so up until 30 is 'my time', this is the time for me, this is when I try and earn as much money as I can, get in as many foreign holidays as I can, do everything like that really. ... I intended to get married and everything, but the idea was that you know until I was 30 then very much as long as we didn't affect each other too much we did our own thing really. Then when I get to 30 I will have a rethink and if I decide I will have a family... I will do that.

> **Q:** Do you think it will be difficult to combine having a career in the bank with having a family?

> Yes, very, very, very difficult. ...because you have to be committed to
> being here all the time, and you have to work weekends, you have got
> to work late, you have just got to do it. [Karen].

The incompatibility of motherhood being combined with a
'career' orientation showed little sign of being challenged, even
by the women we interviewed. The only significant change is the
fact that a number of mothers now do come back to the bank in
part-time capacities, and later as full timers, and are keen to
resume their employment, but none of those we spoke to had
any desire to be promoted into more senior posts. So, although
there have been some changes in the formal policing of home
life, and in formal policies towards motherhood, we have actually
seen very few changes in the home life patterns of those banking
staff in the mainstream career routes. Although career break
schemes make it possible for women to return to work, their
opportunities for re-engaging with the bank are limited.

It should be added that a number of male managers, especially
those attached to the new management culture, also made reference to their domestic commitments and the constraints these
might pose to their careers. Usually, this was reported in the
context of a refusal to be moved to a job in a different area if it
meant disrupting their children's education. In some cases,
however, it went as far as emphasising their determination to play
an active part in their children's upbringing, even though this at
times seemed to be used as evidence that yet another task could
be achieved by an able manager:

> I am one of the only dads who has helped on a reasonably regular basis
> at the local playgroup, I go in there as a helper, if I have a week on
> holiday I try to make sure that one morning I go in and am a helper.
> ...you know I love my family to bits, I love my kids to bits and I certainly,
> if it came to the crunch, family or work, I would put family first one
> hundred times out of one hundred. [Nick]

Despite this new culture of 'approachable' management,
managers still seem in reality to be expected to work exceptionally
hard. Partly as a result of the intensification of work following

organisational restructuring, overtime was endemic within banking, especially amongst men on senior grades. Nearly all men (88 per cent of our workplace survey) worked overtime. On average this amounted to an extra eight hours per week, either in the office or at home. In contrast, only half of women in banking worked overtime, and then usually just a few extra hours every week. This gender difference can be explained partly by the dominance of overtime amongst senior staff, where most staff are men. For managers the average working week was 50 hours, with a small minority working as many as 65 hours per week. As many as 46 per cent of those who worked overtime said this was necessary simply to do the job, but overtime is also an important indicator of commitment. In corporate banking this is particularly evident:

> Most of the [managers] are here by, say, 8 o'clock in the mornings. You get the odd few who maybe take advantage of their position and maybe leave early, then you get the others who stay on till 7 or 8 o'clock at night. Of course they have got terminals at home as well. Most of them work weekends to get the work done.

> **Q:** So if someone began working here who like yourself left work at 5 in the afternoon would that be seen a bit like, well, she's not really keen?

> Now and again I leave at 5 if I have got something specific to do on the night. Nobody stares at me as go out of the door but if I did it every night and left work behind, it would be seen as though I wasn't too bothered and I didn't want to get on. [Lesley]

Ironically, it was often those managers who claimed to value their family the most whose overtime took on 'heroic' proportions.

> I do wish that I could leave the office and leave the bank behind but it doesn't work like that. But I do personally at this stage try and limit the work I do at home, basically because of the hours I put in I leave home at 6.45 in the morning and never get home before 7.45 at night, so in terms of brain ability at that time of night it just doesn't sink in anyway, so there's no point in trying. If there is anything I tend to take a reading file. [Doug]

It is clear, then, that domestic and familial issues penetrate organisational life, whilst equally – for managers at any rate – organisational life spills over into the domestic sphere. It is not simply that these boundaries are blurred but that they are in the process of being redrawn or reworked. There is some increased tolerance of the incursion of 'home' into 'work' and, at the same time, vastly increased expectations about the incursion of 'work' into 'home'. The gendered meanings of home and work life are clearly undergoing change, although gendered practices in each sphere are not changing apace. In the domestic sphere, women in dual-career households continue to bear the brunt of domestic management and tasks, according to accounts of both men and women in these kinds of household. In the organisational sphere, although organisational controls over domestic lifestyles are less draconian now than they used to be, there was still nonetheless a lingering preference for family men in managerial positions whilst, for women, motherhood (rather than marriage *per se*) continued to be perceived as incompatible with successful managerial careers in banking. These observations are further substantiated when we turn to look at local government offices.

Local government: gender, hierarchy and the presentation of 'home' at 'work'

Like banking workers, staff in local government continue to recognise the normative salience of gender-differentiated attachments to 'home' and 'work', and revealed a multitude of ways in which organisational assumptions and expectations, especially in relation to linear careers, draw on these notions.

As in banking, local government workers commented particularly on how it is discourses about motherhood and organisation which serve to reinforce the notion that women's primary commitment is to home life, whilst their commitment to the organisation comes, of necessity, second. Martin, a senior clerk, had strong views on this:

any normal, decent woman would want to be assured that the upbringing of [her] child is as safe and prosperous as it can be. So I suppose, yes, the woman's perspective would be more home orientated even it she's got a career of her own.

Mark, a manager, made a similar point:

The woman with a family is much more conscious about the impact on that family when she feels she is not giving them the attention that they need and can become quite depressed about it.

Equally, the complementary male social role of breadwinner continues to be endorsed and is an important feature of organisational masculinity. Joan felt that 'it's instilled in men, they've always had to work. They're the breadwinners', and Peter endorsed this:

I don't think I know one man who does not place a high priority on work. ...built into a man is this need for financial responsibility, otherwise what else are we going to do?

'Organisational men' are perceived to be sole providers and, according to Mark (a senior manager), must show themselves to have 'traditional' familial relationships:

The one thing that people do tend to form views on, I think, is on the relationship between husbands and wives and very much whether that relationship is right as they see it.

There are limits to the extent to which familial responsibilities can spill over into work life as far as men are concerned, as Mark reveals in this story of a man from his office who was late for a training course and openly admitted that this was because he had taken his child to school, even though his wife was not in full-time employment:

He was foolish enough to say he's done that. My predecessor apparently blew his top... because he had a wife... and he could see no reason why the wife shouldn't have taken the children to school. ...I

would say he was hen-pecked, that's not quite the right thing, but he
doesn't get his priorities quite right.

Good career men, then, subsume their lives outside work to
their lives at work. Harry reflected on his own career:

I think when you are climbing up the ladder you exclude everything whilst
doing that. I mean if you're high flying you really go for it, and when
you're at the top of that plateau it comes to a period when you ask yourself
what you're doing up there... at some stage you have to reassess your
priorities... there's more than just being at work. ...[but] you certainly can't
do it on the way up... if you do it on the way up that could restrict you
because you have to be somewhat single-minded when you go to work.

Thus we see, as in banking, that a specific form of familial relationship is central to organisational constructions of masculinity.
For women, children are still seen to be incompatible with career
commitment. Considerably embittered by her own experience,
Julia claimed:

As soon as you have a baby here, I think you get looked on as 'oh, she
won't be able to do that so we won't ask her'.

It is not easy for women to step outside the gendered assumptions and expectations that pervade everyday organisational and
domestic life. This is partly because gendered practices persist in
the home, where women continue to bear the brunt of the
responsibility for domestic and childcare arrangements and tasks,
and make the separation of 'home' from 'work' difficult for a
woman to achieve practically. Joan, a clerical supervisor, observed:

the mother always has that niggling worry at the back of her mind even
if she's working, 'Are the kids ok?' 'I've got to do this after work'. 'Are
they being looked after at school?'. I think really a man can just go and
do his job and forget everything at home until he gets back home again.
It's not that easy for a woman, even not just the kids. You're planning
your meals and you're gauging things for your housework to fit in with
everything else, whereas a man is just basically... well, my husband

does the decorating and that ...but it doesn't have to be done. It can wait. Whereas your washing and your ironing have got to be done every week else you're not going to have anything to wear.

In addition to these practical considerations, gendered assumptions about home/work attachments pervade organisational discourse. For women 'home' seeps into 'work' through the notion of the 'good mother', which enters organisational discourses in such as way as to call into question the ability and indeed desirability of female professionalism, commitment and performance. The 'good mother' puts her children first, which means that work comes second. However, for men, 'home' seeps into discourses of organisational masculinity through the notion of men as sole or main economic providers, and it is not expected that 'good fathers' will show a greater commitment to their children than to their work. For organisational men, then, there are none of the same assumptions about prioritising 'home' over 'work' and, in any case, gender roles in the household continue to facilitate men's careers rather than women's. For women with children satisfactory projection of a problem-free, non-interfering home life seems almost impossible; for men with children it is almost imperative.

It is not only that motherhood is assumed to generate problems — regardless of actual circumstances. More generally, female embodiment is assumed to generate problems, through specifically feminine bodily processes such as pregnancy, menstruation and the menopause, again regardless of actual circumstances. As Mills (1989) has remarked:

> Domestic location and biological reproductive capacity are reference points that are constantly drawn upon to restrict/throw doubts on women's ability to be organisationally effective (1989: 35).

Constructions of the female body as problematic and unreliable (compared with constructions of the male body as ultimately reliable, almost mechanistic) form an ever-present subtext within organisational discourses of femininity. In particular motherhood, both actual and potential, continually threatens to disqualify women from organisational opportunities and rewards.

In local government nearly one third of all women felt that managers denied promotions to women on the grounds that they might leave to have children (compared with 43 per cent in banking and 23 per cent in nursing). By contrast, men did not perceive this to be a common problem. Women felt that their promotion chances were diminished by managers' assumptions that reproduction was *by definition* incompatible with organisational commitment. As Serena explained:

> I did come across that. When you go for promotion people say 'Will you be leaving to have children?' 'What do you think you'll be doing in the next couple of years?' You don't really know, but that was a question that was put to me ...and it felt as though, you know, they wouldn't give it to the woman because she'd leave.

These experiences are perhaps one explanation for the fact that women tended to talk to one another about their domestic lives, but not to men about these issues. Men, on the other hand, were far less likely to discuss such supposedly private matters, perhaps because the conventional 'breadwinner' construction of organisational masculinity implies that men should not be experiencing conflicts between home and work, and also because a predominantly male environment precludes such intimate conversations[1]:

> I think the fact that our office is male probably separates the home and the office a bit. ...there's less sharing of home life because men aren't supposed to talk about certain things. [Mark]

These differences between organisational men and women in talking about personal issues also extended to differences in displays of emotion at work. Women appeared routinely to accommodate both personal issues and emotionality into the workplace, whilst men appeared to avoid both personal conversations and displays of emotion, even going as far as to express fears about the incursions of the personal and emotional into the office:

> The one thing I couldn't cope with, and I can't cope with, [is] women crying. Something that comes natural to them but if girls start crying I

think 'oh, I don't know, what are we going to do about this?' It seems to be the easiest way for any woman with a problem to cry. [Harry]

The organisational imperative to conceal emotions was recognised by some employees keen to build careers in management. Claire, working in the almost exclusively female ghetto of benefits, related the willingness or otherwise of men working in her section to reveal personal aspects of their lives to their career ambitions:

There's only two of them [men]. One in particular is that sort [pointing to a photograph of departmental managers] and will eventually make it to the top. But the other one ...goes to the pub and we go over with him. There are men that are OK, but they're not the ones that want to make it. One you can say anything to and he can say anything to you ...whereas the other one is not relaxed [enough] with you ...to say anything about his home life. Because he is so ambitious he doesn't want to get involved in people's lives outside work. [Claire]

Thus there is a sense in which emotion at work is regarded as illegitimate, and indeed that 'emotion' and 'management' are constructed as mutually exclusive categories (Hochschild, 1983). Alternatively, we might see all organisational work as emotional and as a form of emotional labour (Hearn, 1993). Indeed, emotions of dominance and joy can be seen as central to the exercise of organisational power. It may be more accurate, then, to distinguish between legitimate and illegitimate emotions in the workplace and to recognise that some of the emotions associated with masculinity are organisationally legitimated, whilst those associated with femininity are subject to control and defined as inappropriate. The whole area of emotions in organisations has been a comparatively neglected one until recently and, as Hearn (1993) warns, we should be wary of naturalising the gendered concomitants of legitimate and illegitimate forms of emotionality in organisations. Instead:

whilst it is clearly completely inaccurate to equate either organisations or men's action with instrumentality, and women's actions with emotionality, what is of interest is the association of these phenomena within discourses (Hearn, 1993: 156).

As well as being gendered, the issues of sociability and emotion in the workplace have a hierarchical dimension. It seems that juniors discuss their home lives amongst themselves more than their managers do. Juniors are also reluctant to let managers know about the details of their home lives:

> People I immediately work with know I've got children but don't sort of hold that against you whereas people higher up, although they're supposed not to hold that against you, they can sometimes let it cloud their decisions. [Joan]

> I work with a gay bloke and a lesbian ... We're all Council staff and we've got a job to do so we get on with it. Managers might look at it differently. [Neil]

Whilst subordinates may be reluctant to let their managers know about their lives outside work, the reality, of course, is that managers are likely to be in a position to know more about their subordinates than the other way round. This one-way flow of knowledge is an important element of 'management', as Christopher explains:

> In order to carry out our duties, responsibilities, there's this thing about management keeping their distance from staff and I think it is important to have that a little bit. And that's one thing I've found difficult because I like to think I'm quite friendly and I like to talk and have a joke and a chat sometimes... So sometimes I've felt, well, you know, there's one or two cheeky comments or whatever but I suppose I've got to expect that because I've built that sort of a relationship. I've done it on purpose and in some instances to carry out the work... Whereas [the boss], if he were to walk down the section probably no-one would say a word to him.

New to his managerial position, Christopher is clearly finding it a struggle to subjugate his preference for being open and friendly to existing organisational norms of management. He clearly admires and emulates the closed and unapproachable style of the boss but is faced with the contradiction that his own style seems to be a successful way of managing. Nonetheless, faith remains vested in the remoteness of organisational authority.

Our discussions so far, of banking and local government, have revealed some key dimensions of the gendered articulation of 'home' and 'work'. We have seen that this is far more than a question of *practical* accommodation, although organisations clearly contribute to the difficulties experienced here. We have also seen the ways in which gendered assumptions and expectations continue to pervade our organisations and to limit women's careers, whilst enhancing men's careers. Although there is apparently a greater tolerance of both women's and men's lives outside organisationally defined boundaries, this is always accompanied by the caveat 'so long as it doesn't cause any problems'. Women – as the childbearing sex – are assumed to carry potential problems with them, either because pregnancy may be a possibility or because dependent children may make incompatible demands. Thus the female reproductive body is always constructed as a problem.

Nursing

In nursing, where the majority of those interviewed were female (reflecting the gender composition of the nursing workforce), there were nuanced responses to the question of gender-differentiated priorities in relation to home and work lives. A number of the nurses we interviewed were married and/or had children, and their responses were generally more 'feisty' than those of the women in the other sectors. Many recognised that, in general, men and women prioritised home and work life differently, but added various riders, revealing the complex ways in which they, and most of their female colleagues, were constantly struggling to negotiate the competing demands of 'home' and 'work' lives. Men were seen as prioritising their job and their ambitions at work over their home lives, but this was seen by many women nurses as a consequence of men's privileged position within the home compared with women's:

Men measure their success in life on how far they've got in their job and how much money they earn. [Janet]

I think men are better at skipping their responsibilities. It's usually left to the woman to pick up any illness in the family. It's always the women that deal with it, and sickness and problems, or anything like that. It's always the women who seem to deal with that before the men let it impinge on their work life. [Joanna]

Men aren't governed by their home lives. They don't have children. The majority of men are sexist anyway, and the majority of them think that women belong at home raising children. I don't. ...I don't do my own ironing and I don't do the washing. I don't want to. I don't like to be a stereotyped housewife and have never been. [Brenda]

Married or cohabitant women nurses recognised that in dual-career households (of which they all were or had been part) the emphasis tended to be on the man's job, particularly in the career-building phase:

It's hard to have two separate careers going and so the woman seems to give way. [Margaret]

Consequently, women observed how their female colleagues with small children were engaged in a constant struggle to meet the competing demands of motherhood and work:

[with] all the energy that gets invested in their children, they've got to have limited resources for work, although I am impressed here by the number of nurses who have got children and don't let it drag on and take away from their career. ...but they all say, when it comes to the crunch, it's always them that has to sort things out, however good their husbands are. [Joanna]

In addition, there was a life-cycle effect. One ward sister reflected on how later in life there was more possibility of mutual help between male and female partners in combining home and work commitments, but still felt that this was always within the constraints of a dominant emphasis on the man's career. A Director of Strategic Management with three children described how her own priorities in relation to work and home life had shifted during the life-cycle:

I think it varies as you go through your working life. ...When we didn't have children, then my commitment to my work was different, was more of an emphasis on work, and you could fit your family life round it without any compromise. [Gillian]

Many female nurses explicitly declared that they did not conform to gender-stereotypical expectations, but it is also interesting to note that some younger women anticipated a life-cycle shift in their relative prioritisation of home and work, envisage a period of their lives when they would invest more in their home life, specifically motherhood, and relatively less in their careers as nurses. This is rather similar to Karen's view in banking, discussed above. As we saw in Chapter 5, these views were wrapped up in terms of career stasis and conveyed a strong sense of the ebb and flow of the amount of time and energy that women devote over the course of their lives to home and work. However that, as we also saw in Chapter 5, for men the prospect of fatherhood often leads to a stronger (albeit instrumental) attachment to work. This is all confirmation of the trend that it is parenthood, rather than marriage or cohabitation, which leads to decisive shifts in the relative commitment of time and energy to work and home lives by both men and women, albeit in different ways.

As in banking and local government, motherhood assumed a practical significance in terms of the constraints it placed on women nurses' ability to negotiate the boundaries between and competing demands of home and work. The significance of motherhood was also revealed in terms of the disqualifying effect that the 'female reproductive body' has within organisational discourses and practices. Some women nurses were quite explicit about the impact of childrearing on how they apportioned their time, energy and commitment:

I do [prioritise home over work] as regards my child, but before we had children, I fought very hard for a commitment to both, for both my husband and myself. ...there were some difficulties in that my husband worked away from home a lot, so I was there and had to be responsible for it, and that's actually been part of my life ever since. [Beth]

For those nurses who asserted that they did not prioritise home over work, they conveyed a strong sense of the constant conflict between the demands of motherhood and those of the organisation, emphasising that the management and organisation of the domestic sphere, particularly childcare, was left to them:

> No [I do not prioritise home over work life]. I get an awful lot out of my work. I enjoy it. I found it very, very difficult when I first had children... Oh dear, I'm very selfish about it. [Jennifer]

In nursing, as in local government and banking, motherhood and linear nursing careers (or what's left of them) were in constant tension. Again there was evidence of a distinctly gendered discourse about women's ability to do the job and their performance at work if they had home commitments, particularly if they had children to look after. Even when they themselves did not prioritise their home over their work lives, they still felt that they were constantly having to prove themselves:

> You're constantly having to prove yourself, as a woman, as a mother, or whatever. A working mum has positively got to prove that she can cope with it all, that she's superman, that she can do this, can balance the house and the children and a career. [Veronica]

And however hard these mothers worked to prove themselves, however much they believed that women put more into both home and work than men do, there remained a strongly held view that successful women nurses were ones who had chosen to dedicate themselves exclusively to their careers, and prioritised their work lives over and above all else. Veronica felt that those women at the top were more likely to:

> Become totally job oriented and forget everything else... women are still learning how to be the wife and the mother and it's getting the right split, and getting the husband to accept that he's also a father and a husband and a worker.

In addition, one nurse who had children and worked full time actually felt that there was resentment amongst nurses when she moved from a part-time back into a full-time job:

> [they thought] she's got a husband, she's got two kids, she's got a job and she wants this [full-time] job. Let someone else have a crack at the job. [Jennifer]

Forms of discrimination against nurse-mothers were in evidence, and were justified in terms of being 'realistic', as one childless female nurse described:

> you've got to be a bit selective, but it does look as it you are being discriminatory. If I'm getting somebody who can come and do full time for me who hasn't got that kind of commitment to a child, and therefore wouldn't want school holidays off, then I'm more likely to take that person than somebody who has got young children going off to school who'd expect to have the whole of the school holidays off. [Susan]

By contrast, fatherhood carried exactly the opposite connotations. Emma regarded men with children as being 'much more settled and able to get on with the job'. Certainly, it was not thought to be remarkable for a male nurse with two children to be working as a Charge Nurse, whereas it was for a female nurse in a comparable situation. Margaret believed that men did well in nursing careers precisely because they did not have to contend with the competing demands of home and work as women nurses did, because they usually had wives 'who do all the cooking and cleaning', and because they were far less likely than their female colleagues with children to take unpaid leave for family reasons. Indeed, men themselves saw family commitments as increasing their commitment to the organisation, at the same time recognising that these had the opposite effect on women. Male nurses believed that this explained their ability to engage in linear nursing careers with much more ease than women:

> a married man sees his job not only as a job but as a support for the family, but I also feel that he's put more effort into it because of the

career side. You can climb the ladder from this job much quicker.
[Joseph]

Women nurses living in dual-earner households are hampered
in their own careers not only by the lack of any serious attempt
by hospitals to accommodate the specific needs of working
mothers, but also by the refusal of organisations to recognise
men's needs to balance home and work life. Beth, a senior female
nurse described how:

> my husband has worked for companies whose bosses have found it very
> difficult to accept that he's had a working wife, and a wife with a fairly
> senior job, and I know when my husband's been interviewed and been
> offered jobs, they've said 'oh, well, we always need nurses, so there will
> be plenty of jobs [for your wife]. The local hospital's crying out for
> nurses'. They don't seem to ever perceive that you might be fairly senior
> and that there aren't the opportunities, probably not half a dozen jobs in
> the country at any one time.

The problem, then, is organisational responses not just to
women's but also to men's private lives. These are, of course, the
kinds of issue that have recently been put on the policy agenda in
Britain and Europe in the form of a call for 'family-friendly firms'.
    It was not only in the competing demands of motherhood and
work where home life tended to spill over into work life, but also
in conversations on the hospital ward. Female nurses were likely
to discuss their home lives with colleagues, and this was particularly true for nurses on nights, who were often older women
who had worked on the same ward for many years:

> We're very close on nights. I mean you find permanent night staff tend to
> stay a long time... so we are quite close. We exchange personal Christmas
> presents. I would talk to them if I've got any problems... they know my
> family history and I know theirs and we confide in each other. [Jill]

Women nurses needed to talk about personal and emotional
issues precisely because they felt that they couldn't separate their
work from their home life. However, they felt that their male

colleagues did not disclose as much about their home circumstances as women did:

> When they go to work, they go to work and they don't seem to know each
> other as well. You can work with a man and you will not know that he is
> married or unmarried, or whether he's got children, or whether his wife is
> pregnant. It seems to be something that's not OK to talk about. [Beth]

Male nurses were much less likely to discuss private issues in
the public domain of the workplace:

> you have to probe it because they see it as a weakness and therefore
> they're not probably going to come up front and say 'look there's a
> problem at home' or whatever it is. [Gillian]

Male nurses clearly shared some similarities with their counterparts in banking and local government, especially in relation to
how their presentations of home life at work tended to be highly
controlled and strategic, rather than a routine and integrated part
of daily work life. The strategic projection of heterosexuality was
one reason some male nurses made disclosures about their private
lives outside work, particularly given the popular stereotypes
about gay men being attracted to nursing as a career:

> If a man isn't married, their whole sexual orientation is brought into
> question. ...people think they're gay. [Beth]

All the male nurses we interviewed volunteered early on
during the interview that they were not gay, making conscious
reference to popular stereotypes, but dissociating themselves
from these. As Henry put it, 'we're just regular guys'. However,
a more oblique way for male nurses to establish that they are
not gay is to reveal details about their private lives in workplace conversations. Thus the significance of men disclosing
details of their home lives in nursing was not primarily linked
(as in banking and local government) to projecting an image
of a conventional, organisationally favoured 'family man'
lifestyle of aspiring managers, but contained a distinctive sub-

text concerning male sexuality and whether they were gay or heterosexual.

However, strategically projecting an image is rather different from engaging in long-term relationships with colleagues that draw upon detailed and intimate knowledge of individuals' lives outside work. Henry described how, although he felt it was essential that female nursing staff knew him as a person in order to build up trust, there were clear limits to his revelations:

> They knew about my wife and they know about my children. They know basically that I'm trying to move house. ...I do talk because they have to know me, they have to trust me and part of that trust is letting them get close enough to me to be able to do it. ...[but] certainly nobody gets beyond that point where they may know about my children being ill. They certainly wouldn't get into my personal home life, because that's where, if you like, I draw the line. ...I guess it's unfair in some ways, because I ask them to always make sure that if they have a problem at home that they tell me. Yet I don't tell them. [Henry]

Gendered bodies and organisations

The idea that there should be as little spillover as possible from employees' homes into their work lives has strong currency across the three sectors of banking, local government and the health service. There is also a discernible shift away from a formal adjudication of workers' domestic and family circumstances, indicating a loosening of organisational controls over employees' private lives. This has contradictory consequences for the gendering of organisation. Whilst, on the surface, it appears to stop discrimination on the basis of personal characteristics and individuals' choice of lifestyle outside the workplace, by constructing the image of a universal worker whose personal needs and specific identities are separable from organisational concerns, it nonetheless also serves to obscure what was previously more apparent, i.e. the preference for managers to be middle class, white, male and heterosexual. This is apparent in banking and local government organisations, although it takes a different form in nursing, where it is traditional organisational preferences for nurse managers to be single, white and female that have loosened.

Nonetheless, we have argued that, particularly in banking, the absence of an explicit preference for certain characteristics means that it is no longer acknowledged that those workers who do not conform to these preferred characteristics are less likely to get on. In addition, we have suggested that the ability of workers to project a satisfactory arrangement between their home and work lives is still gendered. In particular, we have shown how organisational assumptions about motherhood and the female reproductive body serve to weaken women's ability to distinguish and separate 'home' and 'work', 'private' and public', in the management of their identities within organisations. We have also explored how naturalist discourses about emotionality and womanhood function to position women as organisationally inferior to men, as women are constructed as emotion-full, compared with masculine emotion-lessness (Parkin, 1993), which underpins the alleged rationality of organisations.

This raises some interesting questions about the evocation of the gendered body in constructions of 'home' and 'work', 'private' and 'public', in organisational discourses and practices. More generally, this leads us to stress the importance of embodiment in organisational analysis. Concepts of modern organisations are shifting away from an emphasis on these as functional, goal-directed systems of rational action, towards a recognition that they might be premised on a particular construction of the male body and historically specific associations between masculinity and rationality (Pringle, 1989a,b). Acker (1990) argues that supposedly abstract gender-neutral organisational forms are actually premised on the male body, particularly on male sexuality, conventional male control of emotion and restricted male involvement in procreation, and that these characteristics are normalised, only to be represented as intrinsic, gender-neutral characteristics of 'organisation'. From this perspective we can see how, by definition, men in organisations will match all the requirements of a working life free from emotion, sexuality and family ties – although, paradoxically, men's embodiment *per se* is rendered invisible in this discourse of organisation precisely because we are presented with abstracted and disembodied notions of 'organisation'.

Conversely, female embodiment is antithetical to 'organisation'. Menstruation, pregnancy and breastfeeding, and the menopause, as well as women's supposed irrationality and emotionality, are rendered organisationally inappropriate, women's bodies being literally 'matter out of place' and 'suspect, stigmatised and used as grounds for control and exclusion' (Acker, 1990: 152). Women's bodies properly belong elsewhere, in the 'private' sphere of home and family, rather than the 'public' sphere of organisations. The meaning of these differences, such as the fact that women menstruate and men do not, and individual experiences of gendered embodiment, such as pregnancy, are shaped by social values and expectations (Martin, 1987) at the same time as being material, physical and biological experiences and processes (Shilling, 1993). Recognising the gender-embodied nature of organisations and the socially constructed significance of men's and women's bodies for their participation in organisations is helpful in thinking about the gendering of organisation. Nonetheless, we must heed Connell's (1987) warning concerning the similarities between men and women, whilst not exaggerating the similarities that women share with each other, and men share with each other. Thus we suggest that 'organisation' is not constructed on the basis of *the* male body (as Acker, 1990, 1992 implies) but *a version of* male embodiment.

Frank (1991) proposes a typology of four body usages: the communicative body, the dominant body, the mirroring body and the disciplined body. It is the last of these, the disciplined body, which corresponds most closely to Acker's conceptualisation of the male bodily foundation of organisations. According to Frank the disciplined body presents itself as highly controlled and predictable, lacking desire, isolated within its own performance even though this performance might be part of a collective institutional activity, and disassociated from itself. Although Frank is not centrally concerned with issues of gendered embodiment, it is apparent that the disciplined body conforms most closely to a form of male body usage. Frank suggests that it is the communicative body which is primarily a female type of body usage and, indeed, the characteristics of this type of body usage are quite different from those of the disciplined body. The communicative body is unpredictable, contingent, productive of desire and relates to others, especially sexually, and is aware of itself and the ongoing reproduction of the body in daily life – it epitomises the form taken by women's body usage, according to Frank.

We have strong reservations about this argument. The element of uncontrollability clearly refers to menstruation, pregnancy and childbirth as unique aspects of female embodiment. However, these aspects are far from uncontrollable, although women's *own* control over them may be restricted by limited availability of birth control, stigma and legal controls over abortion, etc. These kinds of assumption, together with Frank's notion that men achieve the disciplined body, amount to the incursion of gendered naturalistic assumptions into Frank's typology of body usages. Nonetheless, whatever the intricacies of arguments about the gendering of Frank's types of body usage, we can nonetheless see that the notion of the female body as 'communicative' is a powerful one within organisational discourse. Most obviously, women are seen as a risk and unsuitable for training, management, etc. because there is always the possibility that they might get pregnant and have a baby. Worse still, women can do this 'in private' and it cannot be (directly) controlled by organisations. All women up to middle age are therefore suspect. Once in middle age the perceived uncontrollability of women's bodies continues through reference to the menopause. If ideals of bureaucratic organisation are constructed on the assumption of a disembodied, universal worker, clearly both women and men will be expected to conceal actual bodily states. Because men are not really disembodied, this may be hard work! However, for women the work is even harder. This is partly because – in general – women's bodies undergo more transformations than men's bodies, through menstruation, pregnancy and the menopause, symbolically linking women more closely with private and organisationally inappropriate identities. Martin makes the point eloquently:

> Because of the nature of their bodies, women far more than men cannot help but confound these distinctions every day. For the majority of women menstruation, pregnancy and menopause cannot any longer be kept at home. Women interpenetrate what were never really separate realms. They literally embody the opposition or contradiction between the worlds (1989: 197).

However, more than any actual differences in terms of male and female embodiment, the major imperative to concealment is the way in which women's bodies are constructed: first, as uncontrollable, controlling 'the woman *in* the body' (Martin, 1989; emphasis added); and second, as inherently weak and unstable. The evocation of women's bodies in organisational discourses occurs along a number of dimensions. However, it is the *reproductive body* that assumes particular importance, and it is constructed as the kernel of difference within the shell of disembodied equality between men and women in organisations. Cockburn (1991), in her study of men's resistance to women's equality in three organisations, refers to the 'domestic disqualification clause' evoked in organisational discourses and practices. In particular, it is the prospect of maternity which functions to 'keep women in their place' within organisational discourses and practices, as a married female nurse described:

> As a married person without children taking interviews I was always asked when I was going to start a family and I'm sure a man is never asked that. ...Now that I have got a family, the only thing that is to my advantage is that I can say 'well, I've taken my maternity leave. I'm not going to take any more'. [Veronica]

More generally, female embodiment is evoked in organisational constructions of women as unpredictable, unreliable and unsuitable. Because the discourses framing women's bodies construct them as inferior, unstable and inherently weak (Ussher, 1989), the imperative to conceal menstruation, pregnancy and the menopause is strong (Martin, 1989). A senior male housing manager confirms this point in his efforts to account for gendered career patterns in his department:

> The other thing I have noticed is that women tend to have problems around their mid-40s to the mid-50s that can often kic into touch. I mean, hysterectomies can knock you straight up in th ar and men don't have hysterectomies. ...It does strike me, when you look at it in the long term, that there are always going to be problems with women ...unless their chemistry changes. [Harry]

Male aggression and impatience towards women in organisations can be expressed through calling up female embodiment precisely in order to put women in their place by reminding them that they are, ultimately, bodies out of place in a male world. A junior woman working in a traditionally male occupation described a typically antagonistic interaction with her male colleague as follows:

> 'I don't believe in ... women doing this job', he said to me one day and he's still like it. He don't think I can do it. You know, the other day I got up to go to the toilet because of a woman's problem or something and it's 'Where are you going? What have you got to go to the toilet for? Why can't you go later?' And I get this all the time. I came out of the toilet the other day – rushed to the toilet, I didn't tell him I was going. It was about 4 o'clock in the afternoon ...dead as a dodo and I walked out and I heard him having a real go. Men. They don't understand why some women have to. Don't they? [Julia]

In the hospital we listened to nurses' accounts of the routine evocation of female embodiment by male superiors with throwaway statements such as 'oh, it's that time of the month' or 'she's not got a man at the moment' to neutralise nurses' anger or assertiveness. So the evocation by men of women's reproductive, menstruating or sexualised body can be used as a means of reasserting male authority over women. Conversely, there is the nursing uniform, which one nurse described as her 'protection'. Another nurse commented how wearing a uniform enabled women to assume authoritative positions more easily as 'uniform' clothes literally conceal gendered embodiment:

I think in nursing and especially as a Ward Sister, it you really want to you can still hide behind your uniform and your hierarchy, and it actually doesn't matter whether they're a male or female. [Andrea]

It becomes particularly important for women to conceal their bodily processes from men precisely because these can be turned back on women in disabling ways. Talking about bodies, families, sex and emotions was most common where the office was all or predominantly female, as we saw above. Martin (1987) suggests that women's shared embodiment in the face of institutional hostility to women's bodies, and women's shared collusion in secrecy, may form the basis for female resistance to oppression in workplaces. This suggestion would seem to be confirmed by the following comment:

Q: Are there any problems working in mixed sex groups?

Going to the loo when you've got a period I should think. Very practical. You know keeping your handbag with you when you go out or stuffing things in your pocket, or whatever. Or if you need to borrow something. I mean its very basic. Just little things that make it difficult. And I think, from my experience, women can keep a secret better than men can. If you say something you know it won't go any further. The element of trust is much stronger between women. [Christine]

It is implied here that shared embodiment is connected to trust and intimacy and thus that women's bodies may be a basis for female sociability. Perhaps this is so where internal bodily processes are concerned. Conversely, the surface appearance of women's bodies is sometimes the basis of feminine competition and division. However, there are also occasions, probably rare, on which women deliberately discuss their embodiment in front of men:

some women would only talk about women's problems in front of women. Whereas they won't say anything to men. Because I think men should know what we have to suffer, personally, if you go on about it and say it in front of them as often as you can, its drummed into them. [Cathy]

Refusing to conceal bodily processes in this way may also be seen as a form of resistance to the disciplined (male) bodily basis of organisations.

It is apparent, then, that male and female embodiment is evoked in complex ways in organisational discourses and practices. Of course, both men and women in organisations are embodied, but it seems that women's bodies are explicitly linked to the private, the familial, the domestic, whilst men's bodies are discursively obscured. Our attention to the significance of motherhood as the social consequence of the reproductive body has shown us how the female reproductive body continues to restrict women's opportunities in the workplace. Indeed, it might be argued that the reproductive body of the woman serves constantly to disqualify or exclude her, whilst the sexualised body of the woman provides one of the means whereby she is included (Cockburn, 1991; Adkins, 1992, 1995), qualifying her for certain front-stage and subordinate organisational functions, such as presenting an 'attractive' front in reception areas. Evocations of female embodiment in terms of reproductive and sexualised bodies serve to mark off women as different from men, in the sense of lacking competencies or possessing special sexually specific ones. Significantly, discourses of equality require the woman to adopt behaviours and attitudes that are comparable to or the same as men's, and these discourses effectively erase or deny the body of the women, whilst discursively obscuring the body of the man. So it is the disciplined, concealed male body that provides the underpinnings for 'organisation' and the standard against which women must strive to be 'the same'. The strategic dilemmas associated with the politics of 'sameness' versus 'difference' in gender politics at work (Bacchi, 1992) are grounded in precisely this concealment of the male body within the organisational standard against which women must measure their 'sameness', and it is therefore no wonder that the 'difference' of embodied women constantly threatens to disrupt the equality agenda in the workplace. In the next chapter we turn to explore the sexualisation of workplace cultures, and once again point to the embodied underpinnings of everyday workplace interactions, developing a notion of a three-dimensional 'politics of the body'.

7 Organised Bodies: Gender, Sexuality and Workplace Culture

Introduction

In earlier parts of this book we drew attention to the way in which restructuring involved redefining the qualities of staff members. This frequently involved rethinking the gendered, familial and sexualised properties of employees. In this chapter we explore more systematically how sexualised discourses were invoked in our organisations, and we use this material to take further our analysis of the relationship between the 'gender paradigm' and the 'sexuality paradigm', which we alluded to in Chapter 1. The former, the 'gender paradigm', emphasises the notion of a corporate patriarchy or systemic sets of relations of male dominance and female subordination within organisations, whilst the latter, the 'sexuality paradigm', focuses on localised and strategic deployment of power and sexuality through organisational discourses. There is a legacy of tension between these two approaches. Analyses of sexuality and organisations have been strongly influenced by Foucault and, consequently, have tended to emphasise sexuality in a way that appears to sideline or even displace the category of gender. Furthermore, some feminist writers remain strongly critical of the diffuse conceptualisation of power in the 'sexuality paradigm' (Walby, 1990; Adkins and Lury, 1996; Adkins, 1995). Conversely, the 'gender paradigm' has been criticised for an over-emphasis on structural and universalised forms of power and for a lack of attention to human agency and the diverse forms which this can take (Pringle, 1989a; Callas and Smircich, 1992).

It should be noted at the outset that the differences between the two paradigms reach beyond a simple question of whether 'gender' or 'sexuality' is the primary category of analysis to broader theoretical considerations about the nature of power; to structure, culture and human agency; and ultimately to questions of epistemology. Of course, these two paradigms should not be reified, but with some notable exceptions (especially Cockburn's work, which we discuss below) a clear tension between them persists. A particularly clear example of this continuing strain concerns the 'pleasure' and 'danger' of sexuality, specifically heterosexuality, for women at work. On the one hand those working within a more agentic, less structuralist perspective emphasise the possibilities which there may be for women to redefine male-dominated notions of sexuality, thus allowing women to derive pleasure from sexualised forms of workplace relations (Pringle 1989a; Cockburn, 1991). On the other hand there are those who believe that heterosexuality is so imbued with patriarchal power relations as to render such a shift both theoretically and politically impossible (Adkins, 1992, 1995).

In this chapter we are particularly concerned to draw upon the insights of both the gender and the sexuality paradigms in order to explore the everyday interactions between women and men in contemporary organisations, and in turn to understand some of the more elusive ways through which gendered organisational hierarchies are sustained. Integrating analysis from both accounts is not a straightforward matter given the deep differences between them. Furthermore, we find drawbacks in both approaches. We remain particularly wary of the tendency within the 'sexuality paradigm' either to subsume gender within the category of the sexual (see Witz and Savage, 1992, for a development of this argument) or to 'retire' gender as part of the social or economic, whilst valorizing sexuality as part of the cultural (Adkins and Lury, 1994). Furthermore, we refute these fixed boundaries and have no interest in claiming finite primacy for either gender or sexuality. Rather, like Acker (1992), we see sexuality as part of the on-going production, and deployment, of gender. We also see gender as part of the on-going production and deployment of sexuality.

One way of retaining a focus on both gender and sexuality without 'retiring' either is to operationalise a notion of the 'lived body' as the materiality of both gender and sexuality. So it is by developing insights from recent research and writing on embodiment that we seek to develop an embodied perspective on gender and organisations as an exciting and fruitful way of building on the strengths of both paradigms. A bodily-informed feminist sociology of organisations may offer a way through and beyond the paradigmatic counterposition of 'gender' and 'sexuality' in organisations.

Embodied organisations

We have already discussed the significance of the body in recent analyses of organisation in Chapters 1 and 6. We simply want to recap and develop a few points here. The ideal type of bureaucracy, stemming from Weber and well-represented in popular images of contemporary organisations, does not admit the body. In this account the very representation of bureaucratic organisation in terms of a rational system of action entails a radical denial of the body (Bologh, 1988; Pringle, 1989a; Morgan and Scott, 1993). However, as Acker (1990) argues, even this apparently disembodied model of organisation makes certain assumptions about the bodily attributes and capacities of organisational members. In particular, Acker (1990) emphasises assumptions about distance from the processes of childbearing, i.e. naturalising the (lack of) capacities of the male body. Furthermore, the daily practice of organisation entails the spatial distribution of bodies in ways which draw upon their gendered and sexualised qualities, mobilising specific masculinities, femininities and sexualities in the performance of specific organisational tasks. For example:

> The practice of locating 'attractive' women at reception or frontage areas is a clear illustration of the interplay between gender, bodies and power in formally rational bureaucracies (Morgan and Scott, 1993: 16).

Recent feminist studies of workplace organisations have introduced concepts of 'emotional' (Hochschild, 1983) and 'sexual' (Adkins, 1992, 1995) labour to analyse the ways in which women's emotions and bodies are implicated in the performance of their work (see also Fineman, 1993; Lash and Urry, 1994; and Chapter 3 in this book). What we are witnessing is a gradual displacement of the notion of work or labour as an abstract, disembodied capacity and the recognition that real jobs and real workers are embodied (Acker, 1990, 1992). More specifically, it is women's bodies which are most often involved in this way (Cockburn, 1991). Women are more commonly obliged to engage in sexual banter with male customers and observe explicitly sexualised dress codes in order to comply with gender-specific, unwritten 'contracts' of employment (Adkins, 1992, 1995).

As we argued in Chapter 1, once we 'see' bureaucracies as embodied systems of social relations the mutual articulation of gender and sexuality becomes clearer. Both gender and sexuality are inscribed on, marked by and lived through bodies. Both everyday interactions and the structural design of organisations are informed by, draw upon and work through dynamics of gender, sexuality and embodiment. Through this conceptualisation we are seeking to avoid seeing 'sexuality' as occupying only the domain of the cultural, and to avoid using 'gender' only to invoke the more systemic properties of the structural. Similarly, we would argue that there is a recursive and dynamic relationship between organisational structures and cultures. The recursive nature of the structural context and interactional content of organisations works through participants' own knowledge and understanding of organisational rules, procedures and injunctions. Because participants do not 'leave their bodies behind' when they 'go' to work, and interact as embodied agents, part of this knowledge and understanding is an embodied one.

This chapter is not explicitly, or indeed only, structured around an exploration of 'embodiment' in the organisations we studied. Instead, it is led by the major issues that our interviewees raised when asked about sexuality in everyday organisational life, or when they introduced issues relating to gender, sexuality and embodiment without being explicitly asked to do. It is interesting to note the degree of awareness of, and willingness to talk about, sexuality revealed by interviewees. This point reinforces the paradox of organisational life: that organisation presents itself as a desexualised public space but is sustained by the privileging of certain forms of sexuality (male heterosexuality) and the mobilisation of particular aspects of female sexuality in discrete organisational spaces or particular organisational roles. Sexuality in organisation, it seems, is not there and yet is there at the same time. It is, as Hearn and Parkin (1983, 1987) have argued, one of the best kept organisational secrets around which there is a 'booming silence'.

Amongst the staff in our banks, hospitals and local authority offices, sexuality was always discussed in gendered and almost always in heterosexual terms. Very few staff indeed spoke of homosexuality, with the main exception of the male nurses who were all concerned to confirm their own heterosexuality. Lesbian sexuality rarely emerged as a topic of conversation. Elaine, the only 'out' lesbian we encountered, was able to describe the embedded nature of gendered heterosexuality particularly well, through the eyes of a stranger:

> A lot of men, particularly men who are more senior than me, find it difficult to know how to treat me. Like, they don't know whether to treat me as one of the boys. They don't know whether it's worth trying to treat me as they would other women in the organisation, who they know to be heterosexual, they have a really difficult time... That's true of senior women too. [One heterosexual woman] she was flirting with me as if I was a man, and I found that bizarre.

This articulation of 'strangerhood' was closely echoed by one of the very few 'out' gay bank workers who spoke of his position in the bank in the following way:

> I think they treat me as a bit of a joke, yes, not quite male not quite female... I mean they [other staff] tend to portray this picture of some great bruiser, but when they talk to me and see that I have got two eyes and a mouth and ears the same as they have it doesn't seem to bother them. [Ken]

This heterosexualisation of workplace cultures was bounded by a 'hegemonic masculinity' and an 'emphasised femininity' (Connell, 1987). The central feature here is an orientation towards accommodating the interests and desires of heterosexual men. This is routinely evident in everyday talk and interactions. Hierarchies of authority and mechanisms of control could, in various ways and to different degrees, evoke the boundaries of the body through sexualised and gendered markers to 'position' and 'control' organisational men and women. We were particularly intrigued by evidence of clear managerial notions of 'productive' (hetero)sexuality in both banking and local authority cultures – evoking Marcuse's (1978) early analysis of the commodification of sexuality within capitalism. In addition, we draw attention to female strategies of empowerment, in the face of disempowering heterosexual discourses. These emerge particularly in the context of hospital ward culture and nursing hierarchies, where women seek ways to establish themselves as authoritative subjects *vis-à-vis* male nurses whilst male nurses, in turn, seek non-hegemonic forms of assuming authoritative subject positions *vis-à-vis* women. We are thus able to provide further grist to the mill of Pringle's (1989a) argument that familial, as well as sexualised, discourses come into play in gendered organisational relationships. In nursing particularly, gendered familial or kinship discourses provide a significant resource in the regulation of workplace interactions between embodied participants.

Pringle's work (1989a) demonstrates how secretaries are represented not simply as women, but in more complex sexualised or familial terms: as wives, mothers, spinster aunts, mistresses and *femmes fatales*. The 'sexy secretary' discourse clearly constructs the secretary–boss relation in terms of female sexuality, whilst the 'office wife' discourse evokes patriarchal, familial imagery to construct both the nature of the secretaries work and the power relation between bosses (husbands) and secretaries (wives). It has also been suggested that organisational participants expand the familial analogy to include quasi-kinship relations as ways of positioning gendered subjects in bureaucratic locations, thus encompassing references to father/daughter, mother/daughter, mother/son, brother/sister relations and so on (Eisenstein, 1991). The motif of the patriarchal family has proved a powerful one in describing the construction of authority relations between doctors and nurses in the Victorian hospital, where the authority of the doctor over nurses and patients was analogous to that of the husband over his wife and the father over his children (Gamarnikow, 1978).

In the remainder of this chapter we use new empirical material to investigate how gendered hierarchies and interactions are under-pinned by discourses of gender, sexuality and the body. Whilst looking at the multifaceted ways in which this occurs in hospital wards, local authority offices and bank branches, we develop Cock-burn's (1991) notion of 'a politics of the body'. With this phrase Cockburn draws our attention to the material and the socially constructed nature of embodiment, as well as its simultaneously gendered and sexualised character. Although Cockburn herself continues to operate within a feminist structuralist paradigm, her work represents a rare example of an attempt to overcome some of the tensions between the 'gender' and 'sexuality' paradigms. Whilst maintaining her focus on the corporate patriarchy and the systemic patterning of male dominance and female subordination within organisational contexts, she also explores new agendas emanating from post-structuralist concerns. Cockburn identifies male discourses of difference (as negative representations of women in terms of their problematic relation to power and authority) and of differentiation (as positive representations of women as tractable and willing subordinates), which she links through to a sexual poli-tics and a politics of the body. We use these distinctions to elaborate on some of the differences between our three sectors.

In the concluding section of this chapter we build on some of the themes emerging from our empirical material and suggest an analytical framework which might enable us literally to 'flesh out' this concept of a politics of the body by identifying its verbal, spatial and physical dimensions.

Ward work and ward talk: strategies of sexualisation and counterstrategies of resistance

Nurses described three rather different ways in which gender, sexuality and a politics of the body underscored workplace interactions and hierarchies. The first related to the 'body work' of patient care provided by nurses. One nurse described how men, in particular younger men, operate with strongly hetero-sexualised notions of nurse–patient interactions. Younger men, she observed, were 'nervous about having their bodily needs sorted out by another man'. Another nurse articulated the subterranean level of heterosexualised nurse–patient interactions – male sexual fantasies:

> Nurses fulfill the intimacies that other women wouldn't, and perhaps it's because men like... bits of them being touched, and there's a fantasy about nurses.

The other two distinctive sets of relationship here concern interactions between staff in hospitals: on the one hand those between nurses, and on the other those between nurses and doctors. It is these relationships on which we concentrate here.

The vast majority of nurses are still female and, given the division of labour between doctors and nurses, most of the day and night hospital wards are run by women. This poses some interesting questions about gender, sexuality and the workplace. Studies of mixed sex and predominantly male workspaces, such as the boardroom, office or factory floor, have identified the dominance of masculinist cultures (Kanter, 1977; Collinson and Collinson, 1989). In relation to the sexualisation of organisation, it has been claimed that this leads to the dominance of a male sex drive discourse (Collinson and Collinson, 1989) framed in terms of a distinct form of heterosexual masculinity. Is this discourse still dominant on the ward? Or do female-dominated workspaces generate alternative forms of sociability? Female nurses certainly described female-only workspaces as distinctive. Female work groups were described as being emotional, intense and even 'bitchy', with a certain amount of 'backbiting', but also as fairly open, sharing environments within which women shared information about non-work matters. Differences between female and male workplace cultures were evoked by nurses and these were often elicited through reference to the ways in which interactions were altered by the presence of male nurses:

I think that if you have a predominantly male environment with one female the swearing would be reduced, and I think it's the same in a predominantly female environment with a male, then the conversation would change. They wouldn't be talking about female subjects all the time.

having worked a lot of my career in just single sex groups, you get on. I mean a certain amount of bitching does go on, but I don't think it's meant in a malicious way, because people just get on with it, but if you've got men working with you then you might be a little more cautious of what you're saying.

Thus, the hospital ward is a workplace where male nurses are, in the words on one nurse, 'strangers in a female world', whilst another nurse recognised that 'it must be very frightening for them, actually, to come into an all female working environment'.

Indeed, these feelings were so strong that some nurses were unsure of why men should want to be nurses in the first place and invoked strong associations between physical caring and femininity. There was also a widespread suspicion of men's motives for becoming nurses, criticisms of male working style and a strong feeling that the embodied presence of male nurses necessitated alterations to established female sociability on the ward, most particularly to the sexualised elements of ward talk. Heterosexual talk was a common source of pleasure and camaraderie between women in female-only wards, and women nurses were described as capable of having 'quite raucous conversations'. The presence of male nurses was perceived to transform this sexual talk into a potential source of danger, and nurses were wary about sharing 'a good laugh and a joke' with them. Women also perceived that they might not be able to control the sexualisation of ward talk when men were present, and cited an example of:

one male nurse here, and he makes these sort of jokes, you know, sexual innuendo jokes and it [the atmosphere] is different.

A ward sister also spoke of the need to be aware of any innuendo or double meaning when dealing with male rather than female nurses from a position of authority. It was certainly not the case, then, that female sociability assumed a desexualised form, but more the case that the pleasure women derived from sexualised talk tipped over into a potential source of danger once a male nurse was present. This sense of danger relates to women's perception that they might not be able to control the sexualisation of ward culture when men were present. If female sociability is replaced by a masculine sex drive discourse (Collinson and Collinson, 1989), women may find it harder to adopt authority positions, instead being routinely positioned in ways subordinate to men.

Whilst the physical entry of male nurses into this female space is not automatically welcomed, neither are they automatically excluded unless they deploy unacceptable forms of masculinity, particularly sexism or sexual harassment. There is a clear onus placed on male nurses to refute the suspicions raised by their presence on the ward by negotiating non-hegemonic and more acceptable forms of masculinity. To this end it appears that male nurses are prepared to carry out considerable 'relational work' and that, in return, female nurses will also work to ease the accommodation of men into ward life. Both of the male nurses who were interviewed at Midcity Hospital revealed an acute sensitivity to these issues and indicated how they both had to work hard at their own particular brand of masculinity in order to work successfully with all-women teams. Indeed, Bert, a male Charge Nurse, drew an explicit contrast between the female sociability of the hospital ward and the distasteful dominance of the male sexual drive discourse in the local authority office where he had worked for some years. He described office males as 'totally obsessed with bloody football... standard male, Sun-reading, page 3 "oh look at the knockers on her" types'. Their sense of humour was crass and crude compared with that of the women nurses with whom he now worked and described as 'witty and more pleasant'.

For both male and female nurses, especially for female nurses, one common way of negotiating a successful relationship that avoided the pitfalls of hetereosexualisation was to invoke familial and kinship discourses. The nurses we interviewed provided numerous examples of gendered workplace relationships built around analogy with familial or kinship relations such as brother/sister, mother/son and uncle/niece. These discourses offer women a range of 'subject positions' through which they can position themselves in relation to men as equal or authoritative, and through which men can position themselves in non-hegemonic masculine roles, both subordinate to female authority and in positions of authority themselves. Sometimes female nurses linked this to homosexuality, invoking the gay male nurse as representing a non-hegemonic and acceptably familial form of masculinity, and the gay male nurse was described as 'getting on better with women' as well as 'like a brother to us'. Henry also described how, in his early days nursing, he was helped a lot by women and represented this in terms of being 'mothered', whilst now his position of authority over female Staff Nurses was represented by all concerned using kinship terms, 'I'm not their dad. I have been known as Uncle for a long time'.

The use of familial imagery to represent work relations between embodied women and men is one way in which female nurses facilitate the integration of male nurses into a female ward culture, carefully containing the heterosexualised elements of ward life. Sexual banter still occurs but more commonly with women 'ribbing' male nurses, who are in turn expected to accept sexual banter at their expense. As we shall see when we examine banking and local goverment, this contrasts with heterosexualised discourse in organisations dominated by male sociability, which routinely privileges men's sexuality and in which women find it more difficult to occupy subject positions, especially those of an authoritative or egalitarian nature.

The pattern of relationships between nurses and doctors is strikingly different, illustrating how gender, sexuality and a politics of the body are implicated in workplace interactions and hierarchies in varying ways. Unlike gendered nurse–nurse relationships where, as we have seen, nurses sought to limit and contain the sexualisation of ward life, it was widely agreed that the nurse–doctor relationship was routinely (hetero)sexualised and drew upon hegemonic forms of masculinity and emphasised femininity.

At its most benign the sexualisation of the doctor–nurse relationship was described in terms of doctors being 'friendly', or as doctors and nurses 'playing each other up', and was tinged with 'Mills and Boon' type notions of romance. However, this could also be experienced as undermining, humiliating or threatening, tipping into either a verbal or physical politics of the body, which shaded into harassment. In particular, female nurses described the ways in which male doctors used heterosexualised language and conversation, usually to draw attention to nurses' physical embodiment, and also used physical acts to establish their power and authority. Female nurses gave many examples of such occurrences, with senior medical staff often cited as the worst problem. One nurse vividly described her initiation into the routine eroticisation of nurses' bodies by a senior member of the medical staff:

> My very first day, I went and worked in a theatre, and the Senior Registrar stopped the whole theatre to admire my legs, and I was mortified... he made all the students stop... I felt acutely, acutely embarrassed, because I'd had attention drawn to me and I was new, I was very new, ... I could not believe it. [Beth]

Even after this, Beth went on to describe how although this doctor always talked about her legs whenever they worked together, she 'eventually got used to it', accommodating it as 'just his way'. Similarly, male medical staff would routinely deal with nurses deemed to be too assertive (i.e. challenging medical judgement) with verbal reference to nurses' bodies, for example 'you're being arsy because it's the time of the month' or the reference to one nurse as 'needing her tits twisting', said in anger front of a number of members of the medical and nursing staff.

In contrast, then, to the use of familial discourses that enable female nurses to hold authoritative or equal relationships with male nurses, the nurse–doctor relationship is characterised by hegemonic forms of masculinity, and heterosexualisation of nurse–doctor relationships is accepted as a routine part of everyday life, as this comment clearly illustrates:

> When doctors think they have a right to touch you, I think still that if you tend not to notice, that's good, but if you actually go into hysterics and

draw attention, I think that makes you feel as bad yourself. But I don't know how many other people react to being touched, because we're all touched by doctors. But I wouldn't have said that's a big problem. It's part of everyday life, as far as I'm concerned.

Thus nurses accommodate themselves to an imposed masculinist hierarchy by adopting an 'emphasised femininity' – heterosexual, passive/submissive, object not subject – in their relationships with doctors. This is evidenced by the fact that nurses rarely made formal complaints and, indeed, the boundary between acceptable and unacceptable heterosexualisation was blurred. When nurses tried to articulate the point at which they became uneasy, they found it difficult:

it's when it just goes over, and it's very difficult to pin-point. I think it's body language and it's how close they stand, …all those little nebulous things… the arm slipped round the waist, or the shoulder, or the standing close behind you.

Thus when female nurses attempt to differentiate something approaching sexual harassment from the routinely accommodated 'politics of the body' that underpins the doctor–nurse relationship, they could be said to be describing the breakdown of this order. In the case above it is violation of the spatial politics of the body – bodily integrity – which is constituted as harassment. This point links into disputes about the 'pleasure' and 'danger' of sexuality in the workplace, and particularly to Adkins' (1992, 1995) criticism of both Pringle's (1989a, b) and Cockburn's (1991) notion of the empowering potential of sexuality, once the boundaries of a body politics are set on women's terms rather than imposed by men on women. Adkins (1992, 1995) is particularly critical of the implicit distinction here between a 'coercive' heterosexuality, which is male-dominated, and a 'non-coercive' form, which is not necessarily structured by or through gendered power relations. She insists that male dominance structures both forms of heterosexuality and that it is better to see 'coercive' and 'non-coercive' heterosexuality as occupying a continuum in which both 'sorts' may be equally structured by male dominance. As we saw above, female nurses routinely distinguish between 'acceptable' and 'unacceptable' forms of sexualisation of doctor–nurse relationships, but nonetheless the fact that they find some forms of sexualised encounter acceptable certainly does not imply that they necessarily find these desirable or pleasurable. However, we cannot discount the possibility that nurses may sometimes perceive some of these acceptable interactions as pleasurable. Certainly, as we will show in the following sections on banking and local government, many women see such interactions in these terms.

What emerges from this discussion of nurse–nurse and doctor–nurse relations is that of a wholly different 'politics of the body' governing these two relationships. Where sexualised comments on the appearance or body of a female nurse by a male nurse, or unwanted touching, would absolutely not be tolerated, the same actions by a male doctor would be accepted as part of the bodily order of that relationship. The tacit parameters of heterosexuality in workplace relations between male and female nurses (in terms of what was deemed acceptable or unacceptable behaviour) were drawn quite narrowly and clearly, and on women's terms, so were more likely to be informally sanctioned or formally resisted if contravened. The tacit parameters of heterosexuality in doctor–nurse relations, by contrast, threw the net of acceptable sexualisation much more widely, and there were no examples of formal resistance cited by the nurses we talked to. We suggest that there was a wholly different conception of a politics of the body governing male–female nurse–nurse and doctor–nurse relations.

But what about the experiences of male nurses, who are literally 'odd men out' in gendered and sexualised hierarchies between doctors and nurses? As a male nurse 'out of place' in these hierarchies, one male nurse reflected on how a physical politics of the body can also enter into power games between men:

[The male Consultant] does not believe that men should be nurses, …[but] he tends to treat me more like his houseman or senior houseman than he does a nurse. If I do a round with him it's a very technical round. He relates to me on a different level. Female nurses he treats badly. …he feels less secure with me, *plus he's smaller than me, so I use that. I stand over him and look down at him.* [Henry, emphasis added]

Henry then went on to describe how he had 'more trouble with the female Registrars'. In a manner which makes the sociologist rather redundant, he described how establishing authority on the ward is more problematic for female medical staff, particularly when it is over a male nurse:

> she's flexing her power. She's using that power and she's perhaps not getting away with it in the way a bloke would. But the same mechanisms would be tried first – 'you will do it because I am the doctor, because I say so, because it's me who say's so'. Is that a male or a female thing, because that's what they are as well isn't it? Is it the same thing? Because that power thing about the doctor – 'I'm the doctor, you're the nurse' – is that control or is it 'I'm a man, you're a woman, you will do as I say'? [Henry]

In other words female Registrars may experience problems with establishing their authority, both generally and over male nurses in particular because workplace authority relations are overlaid by patterns of male power and female subordination.

Conversely, if the 'doctor–nurse game' relies on doses of hegemonic masculinity and emphasized femininity to sustain it, then it cannot be played by the standard rules between same-sex players. Another Charge Nurse observed how doctors and nurses:

> not quite chat each other up, but react as male to female as well as doctor to nurse... [so he did not have] the introductory avenue of the little bit of sexual politics to get into the conversation. [Bert]

Nonetheless, being the 'odd man out' was not all negative, especially when the male consultant, exasperated with being unable to get some information he wanted from a female nurse, went up to him and said 'thank goodness, a Y chromosome to talk to'!

Local government: the body politics of the office

Although local government as a whole continues to be marked by pervasive occupational segregation, the white collar workers in our Housing and Finance Departments worked in open-plan, mixed-sex offices. Widespread preference was strongly expressed for these mixed-sex spaces. Single-sex groups were associated with gender-specific, 'difficult' forms of sociability that disrupted efficient work. For example, it was claimed that, left to themselves, men tended to be 'laddish' and engage in overtly sexualised and often crude conversations that impeded concentration on work. Equally, groups of women were felt to talk incessantly about non-work related issues, which often related to personal relationships, bodies and self-presentation, such as dieting and clothes:

> With women they're all sort of comparing themselves all the time. Women always feel in competition with each other... 'oh, she's prettier than me' – that sort of thing. ...It's just clothes in our office. That's the be-all-and-end-all of their lives. And weight. They're all on bloody diets. [Tracey]

Contrary to popular suggestions that members of mixed groups will distract each other and not get on with their work, this was seen as more of a problem with *single-sex* work groups. Michael summed up the main problem with single-sex groups thus:

> Probably lack of control. They might go too far. Lose concentration on what you're meant to do. At the end of the day you're meant to be here to do a job of work, not to enjoy yourself.

Neither junior staff nor managers liked single-sex work groups, rejecting what they both saw as unpleasant and problematic sociabilities liked to male-only and female-only spaces. Female staff pointed to a 'bitchiness' amongst women-only groups, a point also raised in nursing and banking. Interestingly, this activity was highly stigmatised, and although there was consensus that it was widespread, it is invariably described as something which *other* women engage in! Pringle argues that women bitch when they are spatially segregated because they are perceived as 'lacking' and needing men to:

save them from drowning in this sea of female nastiness. ...Women alone are seen as trivial, incompetent, directionless, snivelling, pathetic (1989b: 237).

But we found that, just as the presence of men in women-only office spaces was welcomed by women, the presence of women was also seen by men as a welcome addition to all-male spaces, introducing a 'more rounded perspective' and a 'more balanced' atmosphere into work groups. So there was a sense in which men-only groups also perceived themselves as 'lacking'. A female presence was commonly described as toning down 'obsessively sexual' male sociability and injecting elements of mutual support and friendship lacking in male-only spaces:

> I used to work in an all-male section and it was all-male talk. Everything was pushed and catered towards the male way of life so to speak. ...Down to the pub and a few bevvies and talk about women and what you'd like to do and what you wouldn't like to do, etc. etc. But when you come into a male/female situation a lot of that goes out of the window, you know. You change the way you talk and the attitude you have towards people. ...I've changed as a person working with women and men rather than just being in an all-male section. [Neil]

Thus spatially mixing men and women is seen as a way of curbing the excesses of unruly single-sex groups. There is a clear sense here of a 'productive' heterosexuality in organisational life. This rests on a form of self-discipline that comes into play when embodied women and men work alongside each other and modes of heterosexualised interaction are called up which appear to enhance organisational productivity and control. In particular, the presence of women is thought to tone down the unruly sexuality of men, transforming a subterranean, non-productive and disruptive male sexuality into an organisationally legitimate mode of heterosexualised interaction in office spaces. Thus we see a notion of an acceptable level of heterosexualisation of office culture, which brings into play heterosexualised discourses of difference between women and men and an essential complementarity between the sexes. This in turn articulates a mode of managerial or bureaucratic control.

This self-censored, mixed-sex sociability is far from being de-sexualised, and indeed both men and women claim to derive pleasure from some form of mutually acceptable and enjoyable level of office talk, often referred to as 'banter'. This point once again raises some important and complex issues to do with the danger and pleasure of sexuality at work. Sexual banter was described largely as a positive aspect of mixed-sex working spaces. Keith argued:

> I mean, it's all about balance. And I do believe the majority of women are looking for that balance. There's extremes in both camps but I believe that the majority want balance. So, you know, you can have a bit of a joke and it'll have a bit of a connotation and vice versa and, you know, there's nothing wrong with that.

He felt that sexual banter was crucial to a working relation-ship, although we do not know what his secretary felt about this:

> [My secretary] and I have a bit of banter every now and again. ...we can have a laugh and a joke and pull each other's leg a bit and say things and that's just fine. You know you don't go beyond that line, nothing like that.

Women also spoke positively about sexual banter and about how the spatial proximity of men and women working together relieved the boredom of office work and injected sexual 'jouis-sance' into the working environment:

> There's a lot of flirting. ...I think they flirt because they fancy other people and because they're bored. [Sandi]

> I mean it's just there, isn't it? I suppose for a lot of people work and social life is separate so, even if they are married or have boyfriends, it's still a thrill at work. [Tracey]

Women, then, may claim enjoyment, but the authenticity of this is denied by some writers who argue that workplace sexuality, like workplace relations generally, is male defined and controlled and therefore denies women any real power or pleasure (Adkins, 1995). Unlike Adkins we do not wish to completely foreclose the potential for women's pleasure in this way, and we consider this further in the conclusion to this chapter. Nonetheless, there is certainly evidence that women's participation in sexual banter may often be defensive:

> When I'm pushed too far I can be very aggressive back. ...I mean like they used to have the lads' chat or whatever about sex or whatever, and they used to say 'whoops, sorry Tracey' and I'd say 'oh, I've heard worse'. Or I'd sometimes come out with something worse and they're like 'oh, all right' [shocked into silence]. [Tracey]

Although women are by no means completely passive recipients of sexual banter, and frequently give as good as they get, these contributions are often defensive and responsive in the face of comments from male co-workers. In these cases there are distinctly patriarchal parameters to sexual banter in the office.

Although we have noted how the heterosexualised dynamics of mixed-sex groups were widely believed to contribute to bureaucratic control, the 'office affair' was nonetheless perceived as a distinct threat to this control and was frowned upon. There was clearly a residual fear that bureaucratic rules might be abused or professional judgement compromised if co-workers were having affairs. One woman who had had a relationship with a male colleague described how:

> At one time we were both off sick at the same time, without knowing, and I actually almost had a disciplinary over it because basically they didn't believe that we weren't together having a good time... I know that for a time there was a certain attitude towards me seeing Dave, and he knew it as well. ...Definitely from the management point of view attitudes changed towards us. [Sandi]

There was clearly a notion that actual sexual relationships, as distinct from the 'productive', but virtual rather than actual, heterosexualisation of office workspaces through sexual banter, flirting, etc., violate the supposed impartiality of bureaucratic rules, procedures and hierarchies. There was also evidence of managerial strategies clearly designed to reassert the implicit rules of sexualised workplace encounters by segregating transgressing bodies at work. These rules define appropriate spatial–sexual parameters to gendered workplace interactions, revealing a distinct spatial politics of the body in the workplace:

> One of the managers at Christmas was having an affair with one of his staff and he was sent packing for a couple of weeks and, when he comes back, the girl is moved and everything is smoothed over and no-one's said nothing about it. [Neil]

A further aspect concerns the presentation of the body and the ways in which bodies can be physically invoked through modes of dress. Unlike hospital ward culture, where all participants wear uniforms, women in offices were required to engage in considerable body work in terms of how they presented themselves at work:

> I still struggle with what to wear to work sometimes, you know... like if I know I'm going in to see the Director about something or I'm going to the management team to do a presentation, or whatever, then I'll dress in one way. Well, I have my armour that I put on. Then, if I'm just having a normal day, I'll put something else on. But always I'm conscious that I have to think about it. [Elaine]

It can be a minefield for women, who frequently find themselves in a no-win situation of attractive = sexual = unprofessional versus unattractive = asexual = professional, as the following comments by a male office worker illustrate all too brutally:

> The things women wear to work? I don't take notice of the women here that much. Only because they're not very good looking, most of them... I don't know. It's more sexual when you're looking at a woman and the

way she's dressed as opposed to professional. The way I dress at work is related to my professionalism. ...But with a woman if she's dressed all plain and frumpy [she'll get ignored], but if she's a bit more sleek, a bit more legs, it would be like 'what's going on over there?' It's more sexual, it's not so professional. [Alex]

Woolf (1990) points out that all the choice of outfits in the world will not overcome this dilemma, given workplace requirements for femininity and the equation of femininity with sexual availability.

This analysis of the body politics of office space in local government suggests one or two points of contrast with hospital ward culture, as well as bringing some new elements into play which will be picked up in the analysis of heterosexual office culture in banking. First, female local government workers' descriptions of female-only work groups tended to be overwhelmingly negative compared with those of female nurses, who were more likely to invoke their positive aspects. Nurses appeared to endorse much more of distinctive female sociability, with women nurses working productively with other women, than did female office workers. Second, however, women in both sectors articulated the fragile nature of boundaries between the 'pleasure' and 'danger' of working with men. In office culture the dangers were described mainly in terms of the verbal politics of a body, as office talk initiated by men could easily call up a woman's embodiment in such a way as to disempower her and challenge her authority or competence. Indeed, the only two examples of harassment we came across in local government took this form. In local government, like nursing, we found clear evidence that women deliberately toned down their topics of conversation when in the company of men, attempting to preclude the danger of their verbal sexualisation of women. Also as in nursing, although to a lesser degree, we found that men, too, monitored their conversations and behaved in ways which they deemed more 'appropriate'.

Finally, what emerges most strongly out of the analysis of office culture in local government is the shared understanding

by male and female staff and managers alike of an organisationally 'productive' sexuality, as forms of heterosexualised workplace
interactions that are perceived as enhancing the productivity and
discipline of work groups. This office culture of heterosexuality
is also present in bank branches and draws upon discourses of
difference and complementarity to steer an uneasy course
between the pleasure and productivity of heterosexuality at
work, and its attendant dangers and threats to the perceived
impartiality of bureaucratic forms of control.

Banking: embodied subordinates and disembodied superiors

In banking, whilst the majority of bank clerks are female, a
distinctive female work culture centred around an exclusive
female sociability has not emerged as it has in nursing. As in
local government offices, mixed-sex groups (often with women
in the majority) were the norm and were preferred to single-
sex work groups by both staff and managers. Left to themselves,
it was suggested, men would lark around and not concentrate on
work, whereas women (or 'girls' as female clerks are nearly
always referred to by men, in a tellingly diminutive way) would
talk incessantly. Very similar patterns of office flirtation were
discussed by respondents in banking as local government,
although on male-defined terrain:

> When I first joined I was told there were three topics of conversation,
> beer, sex and football, and I would have to say this is pretty much true.
> Yes, there is quite a lot of flirtation... traditionally we have always been
> behind the scenes, we worked as a closed unit... so I think it has tended
> to lead to incestuous relationships, if you like, within the branch.
> [Neville]

However, what emerged much more strongly in banking than
in local government was conscious and deliberate managerial
mobilisation of notions of complementarity between the sexes,

hinging on heterosexuality, as part of a managerial strategy to control subordinates in the workplace. Male and female managers alike emphasised the positive effects of mixed-sex work groups, thus introducing again the notion of a 'productive' workplace heterosexuality. Interestingly, a female manager felt that the presence of men countered the unproductive features of female sociability, whilst a male manager described how the presence of women curbed the excessive features of male sociability:

> if you get a whole bunch of women together it could be absolute chaos and you probably wouldn't get anything done for hours. They need a little bit more discipline. ...I think they [women and men] complement each other. I think men stop women talking all day. [Karen]

> to be brutally honest, it you are working in a team where you have got women working with you, I suppose that you are more respectful. I think the dirty joke syndrome doesn't start, if you know what I mean – the foul language. If there is any, it's toned down... so I have to say it has probably got a calming effect on the men. [John]

In many ways this managerial endorsement of heterosexual sociability is extraordinary in the context of banking. Traditionally, personal relationships at work were prohibited, mainly on the grounds of a threat to security if two bank workers formed a relationship. If any sexual liaison, or even sexual interest, was known about, the bank would move one partner, usually the woman, to a different branch. In recent years this policy has been relaxed and some banks have even produced advertisements showing their staff going out together socially. Despite this apparent shift there are two important caveats. First, bank management still expects to control heterosexualised interaction in the branch to its own specifications and to this end will conduct surveillance over 'inappropriate' sexual liaisons in the bank:

> [a relationship] can cause issues amongst other staff that there is a bit of lovey-doveyness going on. Then, as manager, you have got to speak to them... [Doug]

Managers continue to deploy strategies which enable them to manage sexual liaisons amongst staff. Since the majority of managers are male, there is a tendency to locate such relationships within the masculine sex drive discourse (Collinson and Collinson, 1989):

> I had a manager about two years ago. ...he rang me to tell me about one of the girls on his staff. He's a divorced guy. He says 'can you transfer her?' I said 'why?' He says 'I'm going out with her'. I said 'you dirty bastard'. She's a nice young girl. In fact, she's leaving. She's going to university. [Giles]

Thus bank management openly colludes in the sexualisation of the bank environment only as long as it conforms to definitions of productive sexuality and is not perceived as a threat to bank 'organisation'. Whilst the sexual dynamics of mixed work groups were widely perceived to contribute to good working relationships, morale, and ultimately bureaucratic control, the formation of consummated relationships was seen as causing potential problems. Thus, as in local government, actual sexual liaisons continue to be seen as violating the supposed impartiality of bureaucratic rules, although in practice they were also extremely common.

Q: What about flirtation?

Um, heh, heh, well look let's put it like this, I married a woman from the bank... I reckon there must be a third of them out there who have married people from the bank. When I was recruited two years ago I said to some of these girls, 'its a good place for the meat market'. I mean I could look at every branch and say there's somebody there going out with somebody else. [Giles]

The second caveat in relation to bank managers' collusion in the heterosexualisation of workplace culture concerns the way in which managers deploy the heterosexualised discourse of complementarity as a means of control over subordinate, clerical staff, but not in relation to their own managerial sociability. In short, it is a managerial discourse which positions male and female clerks but which refuses to include itself. The gendered and sexualised body is absent from manager's own accounts of themselves. It was striking how male managers strove to represent women as managers as 'no different'. Effectively, women managers were required to fit into what were assumed to be a gender-neutral set of management attributes and into pre-existing patterns of male sociability that characterised the managerial culture in banks:

> [Women] are one of the [management] team and I do try and treat them as one of the lads, and I don't mean one of the lads in terms of male/female. But, look, it you want equality we are going to have to have equality. [Doug]

This illustrates only too well that it is, in fact, (dis)embodied male rationality which marks the tacit norm to which women managers must approximate, thus providing grist to the mill of Acker's (1990, 1992) argument that organisational discourses and practices have 'naturalised' the capacities of male bodies. It also reveals how the naturalised male body occupying the higher echelons of organisational life is the 'disciplined body' (Frank, 1991) – highly controlled or regimented, lacking desire, isolated in its own performance and dissociated from itself.

Whilst male managers represented their women colleagues in ostensibly gender-neutral terms, which effectively assumed that women would assume male qualities but not 'be' either male or female, women bank managers were very aware of their position as 'strangers' in a male-defined female culture (cf. Marshall, 1988). This provides something of a contrast with the accomplishment of ward nursing, where it was male nurses who assumed the status of 'strangers' in a female work culture. However, women managers, no less than male nurses, also felt that they were able to deploy this difference with positive effect:

> I think women do stand out more. As I say, like at this dinner last week, I mean we were bound to stand out. There were five long tables, and there was one woman, one on each. I mean, we are going to stand out,

aren't we? But you see, I try and take advantage of that so I wore a red suit on the basis that all the men I knew would be in grey and dark. So I did stand out and, yes, the speaker did come over and speak to me at the end. ...That is part of playing the game, isn't it? [Karen]

The practice of sharing the women out amongst the men by seating one at each table is significant in itself, but the overt manipulation of the physical presentation of the organisational body is interesting. It serves to illustrate how embodied participants can call up their embodiment through ways of presenting the body. In this case the choice of a red dress is evoking a number of associations between red and the womanly body. The contrast between the evocation of the distinctive womanly body in the red dress with the mass of manly bodies uniformly clad in dark suits introduced a moment of female 'jouissance' into the social situation – but on the woman's or the men's terms?

However, there are constant flip-sides to the assertion of embodied difference in organisational contexts. The 'pleasure' of female sexuality can easily flip into 'danger' as embodied difference can be turned back on women in such as way as to disempower them. There is no doubt that women as well as men in banking spoke favourably of the ways in which flirtations make working environments more 'pleasurable'. Flirtations and, despite managerial concern, full-scale office affairs were seen as routine elements of mixed workplace culture. One woman clerk admitted that their absence meant 'a sort of flat working relationship', whilst another clearly articulated their pleasurable dimensions and how these enhanced workplace productivity:

it's just flirtation. Just in fun and people getting on with each other. There are obviously romances going on and they perhaps do split up. But, I mean, as long as the work itself is done and not affected then it makes people tick and get on and do things. [Penny]

However, uneasiness about the flipover point between a negotiated and imposed bodily order, between 'flirtations' and 'sexism', is also revealed by the accounts of women clerks. Although some women did admit to enjoying an atmosphere in which office flirtation existed, there was a substantial minority who expressed unease about the heterosexualisation of office culture. However, like nurses, women clerks operated with notion of negotiated and non-negotiated forms of sexualisation in the workplace, where the former took the form of a collective consensus, whilst the latter arose from the individual transgressions of individual men, which were understood and defined as sexual harassment. Interestingly, when women bank clerks pinpointed examples of sexual harassment, these were events which occurred mainly in non-work spaces such as the office party, or in a secluded office where a woman had become especially vulnerable. However, it was quite clear that some men operated with quite different understandings of what constituted the acceptable and unacceptable boundaries of workplace heterosexuality, regarding 'groping' women at office parties as falling within the bounds of the acceptable, whilst women did not. Equally, a minority of male respondents operated with a distinction between negotiated and non-negotiated heterosexualised encounters that complied more with women's understanding of the boundary between pleasure and danger:

> I would have thought that everywhere men and women meet there is a certain amount of flirtation or horseplay or whatever you like. If it doesn't exist, then obviously it would be a strange world. ...I think it can make working life better if there is a slight heated, jokey environment, as long as it doesn't become oppressive or what might be termed harassment. As long as it is mutual, then I can't see anything particularly wrong with it. [Suzanne]

Thus the pleasurable side of heterosexualised discourse evokes the desiring, playful body in work relations between embodied women and men as peers and co-workers, who mutually call up their embodiment in the course of getting their work done. However, lurking beneath both men's and women's awareness of the constant danger of heterosexualised discourses is the potential of men to physically, spatially or verbally 'abuse' the female body in ways which diminish or disempower women in the workplace. In addition, as in hospital ward culture, there was evidence of women flipping a heterosexualised discourse into a familial one, precisely because the former curtails the potential for women to take up authoritative subject positions whilst the latter, the familial discourse, permits women to position themselves as authoritative superordinates in relation to men.

Organised bodies

Gender relations between embodied men and women at work are regulated through heterosexualised discourses, which mark out legitimate and illegitimate modes of sexualisation in the workplace and are underpinned by a bodily politics. However, there are two quite distinct heterosexualised discourses that come into play: one foregrounds sexual difference in constructing authority relations between men and women; the other is also built on difference but foregrounds sexual complementarity in constructing colleague relations between men and women.

The former discourse of difference was much more in evidence in relations between doctors and nurses, in which nurses routinely accommodated themselves to sexualised workplace encounters with doctors, which were underpinned by a verbal and spatial politics of the body. By this we mean that doctors routinely called up women's embodiment as a way of asserting their authority over nurses, i.e. a verbal politics of the body, as well as violating women's bodily integrity by contravening accepted notions of spaces between bodies, i.e. a spatial politics of the body. We saw how nurses had a clear sense of sexualised and embodied workplace encounters that they routinely accommodated into everyday work routines, but how they also described situations about which they felt uneasy ('the arm slipped round the waist, or the shoulder, or the standing close behind you'). What emerges clearly from our material on typically gendered doctor–nurse relations is how differences between power and authority may be expressed and experienced as spaces between bodies, and how nurses' bodily integrity, i.e. the space around their bodies, was routinely transgressed by superordinate males but accommodated by nurses. It was also common for doctors to assert their authority over nurses by making derogatory, and indeed complimentary, remarks about women's bodies, so nurses also accommodated themselves to a routine verbal politics of the body. In short, the sexualization of nurse–doctor relations was routinely accepted as part of the everyday reality of hospital ward or theatre workplace culture and perceived as a collective, rather than an individual, phenomenon. The edges between sexualised interactions and 'sexual harassment' were extremely fuzzy. Nurses' understanding of what constituted 'sexual harassment', as distinct from a routinely accommodated bodily politics, tended to be in terms of an individualised encounter between a doctor and a nurse, as 'actually getting at *that* nurse, rather than at the sex as a whole'.

The discourse of difference as complementarity was much more in evidence in bank and local authority offices, where the heterosexualisation of workplace culture rested on an implicit notion of the 'productive' mobilisation of heterosexuality in mixed-sex workspaces. This heterosexualised discourse of complementarity was unequivocally endorsed by managers and subordinates alike as a feature of workplace culture amongst subordinates. This was not, however, the case in nursing, and we have suggested that this is because heterosexualised discourses of difference and complementarity are both equally restrictive in terms of providing women with the possibility of assuming authoritative subject positions *vis-à-vis* men. This is because the prevailing discourse of heterosexuality, whether it takes the form of difference or complementarity, implies a hegemonic masculinity and emphasised femininity, which empowers men and disempowers women and hence renders female patterns of authority and control in the workplace at best problematic and at worst impossible. We observed how interactions between female and male nurses and between some bank workers were conducted more commonly within familial or kinship discourses, rather than sexualised ones, because women are then able to establish themselves as competent and authoritative subjects in relation to men in the management and accomplishment of nursing work. This contrasted starkly with how the heterosexualised discourse of difference served to mark out authoritative subject positions for doctors and subordinate ones for nurses.

Returning for the moment to the issue of the significance of the discourse of complementarity in banking and local authorities offices, this certainly does suggest interesting ways in which dominant discourses of sexuality in organisation are shifting – albeit in complex ways. Clearly, the disembodied, rational male actor assumed to inhabit the bureaucratic office is revealed once more as an idealised fiction. Men's own accounts of men-only office work groups describe forms of masculinity inimical to labour productivity. This, however, is a complex matter, because superordinate men clearly developed a self-conception that was gendered but presented as desexualised. Whilst it is clear that Frank's (1991) description of the 'disciplined' body may be the ideal-typical form of male embodiment within the bureaucratic workplace, it seems to be a form of male embodiment that is worked at rather than easily assumed (see Chapter 6 for elaboration of this point). The notion of a 'productive' heterosexuality seemed to hinge particularly on the presence of real, embodied women as curing the excesses of masculine embodiment in the workplace – as tipping them towards something approaching the ideal-typical 'disciplined' body.

What emerged in all three workplaces was the problematic issue of the 'pleasure' and 'danger' of sexuality at work. In nursing we came across very few expressions of sexual pleasure in workplace interactions. Rather, we have described the combination of preclusion, in nurses' relationships with one another, and an accepted level of unwelcome harassment, in nurses' relationships with doctors. In banking and local government expressions of pleasure were far more common. Although earlier we concentrated on the fragile nature of such pleasure, on the possibilities for a flip-over into harassment, we do not wish to reinterpret or deny these expressions as inauthentic or necessarily oppressive. As Segal (1994) argues, we believe there is a need to move beyond received notions of both male and female sexuality, to open up possibilities for a re-examination of heterosexuality. In particular, Segal (1994) claims that the fixed assumption of male/active and female/passive needs to be reviewed, both in terms of heterosexual acts themselves and in terms of the broader psychic and social meaning of heterosexual relationships. She claims that vulnerability and passivity are commonly central components of male heterosexuality, whilst we must see female heterosexuality as something that women *do*, rather than something that is done to women. Through this redefinition Segal hopes to transcend the 'choice' between seeing heterosexuality as *either* dangerous *or* pleasurable, a development which seems vital if we are to explore further the nature of gender, sexuality and organisation.

In the final part of this conclusion we wish to develop some of the points made throughout this chapter about the 'politics of the body'. Part of the experience underscoring gendered workplace interaction and hierarchies of power and authority is an embodied experience. This experience is best conceptualised through the concept of a politics of the body, or body politics, in organisational life. We propose that it is helpful to work with an understanding of three different dimensions of a body politics of organisational life, as different ways of understanding the tacit rules governing inter-actions between embodied, gendered participants.

First, there is a *spatial* dimension, which describes the rules governing spaces between bodies or their integrity in organisa-tional life. Indeed, there is a sense in which job hierarchies them-selves can be understood not simply as ordered spaces between jobs, but also as spaces between bodies. There is, then, a symbolic space between bodies as they are arranged into hierarchies within organisations. However, the concept of a spatial dimension of a body politics can also refer quite literally to the spatial proximity between embodied organisational members and to the spatial distribution of men and women between different locales within organisations. Spatial distribution works through the notion of the segregation or location of men and women in different locales in organisations. Spatial proximity works through the idea of 'personal space', which evokes the assumption of bodily integrity, the bounds of which will be much more tightly defined in workplaces than in other locations, such as the dance hall or the night club, and raises the possibility of the invasion of that space by others. Sometimes contact between bodies is incorpo-rated into the routine of a job, such as in the case of the relationship between nurses and patients, and doctors and patients. Crucially, it is this spatial dimension of a body politics of the workplace that has been one of the implicit reference points in definitions of 'sexual harassment' of women by men at work. The definition of sexual harassment as an explicitly sexualised, unwanted and threatening form of contact initiated largely by men is frequently experienced in terms of a violation of women's bodily integrity and thus of the norms of spatial proximity in organisational cultures.

The second dimension of a politics of the body is a *verbal* one, which describes the 'calling up' of embodiment in the language of organisational participants. The womanly body is routinely called up in many jobs, especially where part of the bargain women strike with employers is to respond to or initiate 'sexual banter' with customers. The calling up of women's bodies through language most often means men assuming the right to make indirect or direct reference to clothes or eroticised parts of women's bodies. Importantly, sexual harassment has been defined as incorporating instances of 'verbal harassment', which describes threatening and unacceptable instances of the verbal sexualisation of women by men (cf. Stanko, 1989).

The third dimension of a politics of the body is a *physical* one. Routinely, this is a politics of the presentation of the body, of how we dress and what this signifies, as well as of our comportment and demeanour. Some women's jobs describe explicitly sexualised presentations of the body whilst others demand that women observe 'feminine' codes of dress which nonetheless do not function to 'sexualise' them too much. However, this is also experienced in terms of body size, shape, etc., and an awareness of this, as well as bodily comportment and acceptable or unacceptable ways of carrying or using our bodies in organisational encounters. This dimension draws attention to the internal work done by organisational members when 'conducting' their bodies in the workplace.

We have suggested, then, and sought to substantiate these suggestions with the understandings of organisational participants themselves as revealed to us during the course of interviews, that analyses of gendered interactions and hierarchies in organisations might, quite literally, be 'fleshed out' by a concept of a politics of the body consisting of three dimensions: the verbal, the physical and the spatial. However, these dimensions are not discrete but are interrelated, so, throughout our analysis, we have sought to introduce these various dimensions of 'organised bodies' in such a way as to reveal the interplay of the institutionalisation and discursive construction of gender, sexuality and embodiment in workplace organisations.

Conclusions

Throughout this book we have elaborated on some of the many complex and contradictory ways in which gender was embedded in the organisations which we studied. Whilst we found many similarities, we also found many differences – both between the sectors and within the sectors – and the dynamism of gendered symbols, relations and identities in our organisations became increasingly obvious to us. Of course, from an embedded perspective on gender and organisation, such variation and change is precisely what one would expect. In our conclusion we will return to the question with which we began this book: how far has there been a remaking of gender relations in the organisations we have studied, and what are the broad implications of our research for debates concerning the changing position of men and women in the workforce?

There is a general consensus that the 1980s saw a massive restructuring of organisations in Britain. Although there is no consensus about how such change can be conceptualised, with varying theories of the flexible firm (Atkinson, 1984), post-Fordism (see Amin, 1994) and disorganised capitalism (Lash and Urry, 1987), and the idea of a new form of 'enterprise culture' (e.g. du Gay, 1996) on offer, there is no doubt that this picture of a major restructuring was borne out in our case studies. In terms of gender there seemed clear evidence of a shift from an ascriptive gender order in the past 20 years, and we have argued that this trend heralds an important departure from long-standing historical forms of gendered inequality within organisational hierarchies. As we have shown above, in both banking and nursing, organisational hierarchies were traditionally anchored in familial gendered attributes, with a clear and direct association between managerial authority and forms of familial masculinity and feminity. Thus the bank manager's role was linked specifically to his fatherly qualities, and women were barred from promotion to such jobs. In nursing the 'sisterly' and 'matronly' authority of senior nurses was evident from the job titles alone. In local government this association was somewhat more muted, but in practice the professional hierarchies that dominated the various departments were largely composed of senior men, and we found plenty of evidence that an authoritarian paternalism had pervaded career processes and managerial discourse. In all three organisations restructuring has hit hard at these traditional notions and has replaced familial and gendered discourses of management and organisation with an *ostensibly* gender-neutral management based on performativity. It is important to recognise that, at least in principle, it has become more possible for women in banking and local government, and men in nursing, to move into senior positions. *In this respect* there has been an undeniable decoupling of gender (as well as age) from organisational position, and this is a historical shift of considerable importance.

Having made this point, it is immediately necessary to make some qualifications. Whilst in the organisations we studied there were significant numbers of women employees in senior posts, they remain a small minority in banking and local government. The evidence from our case studies indicates all too clearly that men and women remain highly unequally distributed across the organisational hierarchy. In the organisations we studied there are extremely few junior men, excepting those at the start of their careers, whilst very large proportions of junior positions are filled by women who remain there throughout their careers. Furthermore – and rather against the expectations of one of the authors (Savage *et al.*, 1992) – the 'organisational career' continues to have some vitality, even though it has undeniably changed in nature. To repeat, at the time of our research it was still eminently possible (indeed probable) for men to work their way up from lowly positions in their organisations to senior positions, and across our organisations there were only small numbers of men aged over 35 who had not moved into management positions.[1] It is therefore clear that the gains which women have made do not appear to have been made at the expense of men, and this raises the possibility that the inroads made by women in the 1980s were only possible in the context of the general expansion of professional and managerial jobs in Britain (see more generally Butler and Savage, 1995). The possibility referred to by Crompton and Jones (1984) of increasing competion for promotion between men and women as the latter become more ambitious does not appear to have taken place. At the time of our research the small numbers of women who had been able to 'climb the ladder' had not prevented large numbers of men from doing the same. It is also worth making the point that the sector in which the organisational career had been most radically changed – indeed where the recently established bureaucratic career had been seriously truncated – was nursing: a traditionally female career route!

However, although the organisational career – especially in banking and local government – continues to allow promotion opportunities for many workers, that is not to say that there has been no change. In Chapters 3 and 4 we described how organisational careers have fragmented as professional and managerial employment has become more specialised. There is evidence of some re-segregation of careers between men and women, with women being concentrated either as operations managers or lending managers in banking, and in secondary hierarchies in local government. As we have also seen, in an organisational culture where established career routes and expectations have been challenged, it is still those workers who are able to embody the most central values of the organisation who are more likely to get to the top, and these tend to be men.

In nursing, the gendering of career in the context of successive rounds of NHS restructuring has also been complex. The relatively late creation of a linear, hierarchical nursing career where management functions displaced clinical ones the higher up the hierarchy one moved, heralded the rapid masculinisation of the nursing career in the 1970s and early 80s. What is particularly interesting about the more recent round of NHS restructuring is that this has flattened out the nursing career and centred it more around clinical skills combined with managerial ones in the higher graded work on wards and in clinical directorates, and this raises the question of whether this will lead eventually to the de-masculinisation of the nursing career. Certainly, in the new NHS, there is considerable evidence of a culture clash between the values of nurse professionalism and the new managerialism that has characterised the last 10 years of NHS restructuring, and of a gendered subtext to this, which equates the new managerialism with a more 'macho' management culture in the NHS. However, at the same time, there was also evidence of new opportunities for women, some of whom were being tempted back into nursing after career breaks as hospitals sought to utilise their skills and experience in innovative postitions, where they could be 'change mistresses' in the rapidly changing work of hospital and community nursing.

It cannot be doubted that the shift away from a directly ascriptive gendered culture is one which has profound implications for the dynamics of the organisations we studied. Amongst other things the traditional gender order offered a device for legitimising organisational hierarchies, and for justifying who got to the top and why, and the passing of this has affected the ways in which organisations can try to win the consent and support of their employees. Here our research has indicated a number of important themes. First, all three sectors have seen a shift towards a 'perfomance-related' management hierarchy, in which managers justify their position, pay and privileges not in terms of their gender, age, ethnicity, experience or seniority, but in terms of their ability to carry off certain objectives. This may seem obvious, but it marks the rise of a new 'performative' management culture based around values of competitiveness, specialist skills, dedication and 'getting things done' (see more generally Kerfoot and Knights, 1993; du Gay, 1996). This culture is one in which women can participate, since it is not directly associated with a particular gender. It is however, a culture that depends on a particular configuration of the relationship between home and work, and which valorises the independent, lone individual with no other commitments. This has the *de facto* effect of making it difficult for people, especially women, who value other aspects of their lives, or who have domestic responsibilities they do not wish to or are not able to avoid, from playing a leading role in the organisations concerned. These difficulties stem only in part from the practical or material conflicts between domestic and workplace demands on time and energy. As we saw in Chapter 6 women's domestic commitments (not men's), and furthermore female embodiment (not male embodiment), are *assumed* to present problems, to be in conflict with organisational and career demands, whatever the material circumstances. The construction of the new management culture based on an ethos of 'competitive individualism' tends to endorse an emergent masculine hegemony, based on the idea of the active, freestanding (male) individual. As well as having gendered implications, it also has clear social class connotations, being identified closely with graduates who are well versed in performance-based skills, learnt – in part – through examination and assessment procedures.

It is in relation to this newly emergent image of these ideal properties which organisations require from their senior workers that many women and a few men consciously decide that they do not want to take part in organisational career hierarchies (see Halford and Savage, 1997). As we have seen in all three sectors, especially in banking and nursing, but even in local government where the situation is slightly better, childbearing has a fundamental impact on the way in which women are perceived. It is extremely rare for women with children to move into senior posts, and women across all three sectors saw themselves as having to make a stark choice between children and careers. We found evidence that some women with children – although we should stress they were in the minority – do not seek such promotion, a few being content and most resigned to temporary or even permanent stasis in their careers. However, these feelings need to be placed in the context of the organisational cultures, which make it clear that they must choose between motherhood and careers, so that there is no option of trying to combine these elements. Occasionally, however, we came across women for whom motherhood had galvanised their ambitiousness. Indeed, seeing the difficulties before them had led them to formulate *more* clearly defined career tactics.

There is a distinct irony here which is worth pulling out. One of the traditional reasons for women being discriminated against in promotion ladders was the claim that they were primarily centred around domestic interests and were not regularly committed to the labour market. Whatever the truth of this claim in the past, there is no doubt now that the vast majority of female employees do have a persistent interest and commitment to the workplace, and that many women with children are keen to combine their domestic work with paid employment. This commitment may not always be recognised by others, but even where it is recognised, long-term commitment to an organisation is no longer regarded as being an essential qualification for management. The redefinition of managerial and professional authority around a 'performance culture' entails the notion that participation in it is a Faustian gamble that will not interest those people who tend to prefer security of employment and regular work commitments (the sort of people who under the 'old regime' would have been deemed eminently suitable for management positions). Promotion into management is taken to be something of a leap into the dark. Steady, permanent commitment to an employer is not regarded in itself as a key attribute, but it is rather the willingness to transform oneself, to retrain, and possibly lose one's job security, that is seen as the key for getting on. In other words, although the vast majority of women have demonstrated their commitment to the labour market, such commitment has now been downgraded as a criterion for promotion to senior positions.

This leads us to another major shift in the gendered cultures of our case study organisations, the close relationship between sexualised cultures and workplace culture. The point we want to emphasise here is that the traditional gender order rested primarily on familial idioms, which as we saw in Chapter 7 tended to distance themselves from sexualised discourses. The father figure branch manager and the matronly nurse were supposed to exclude sex and sexuality from their workplaces. We have seen how in all three sectors, however, sexualised discourses play a large role in working interactions, and the organisations

themselves are tolerant of such cultures and indeed even acqui-
esce or support them. This marks a major break from the past. We
have seen how such cultures are organised around constituting
the workplace as an arena of constructive heterosexuality in
which mixed-sex work teams 'pull together'. It is once again
worth emphasising that this emergence of mixed-sex workplaces
marks a very important break from traditional single-sex workplaces marked by occupational sex segregation, and appears to
mark a notable shift in gendered relations. It is clear, however,
that the construction of the workplace around notions of
productive heterosexuality has led to a variety of conflicts and
tensions, and we have explored some of the resistance that our
respondents highlighted. The point we wish to emphasise here is
that a shift seems to have taken place. Whereas in the past sexuality seems to have been understood as an undesirable feature of
organisational life that should be minimised and controlled,
notions of heterosexual complementarity are today openly sanctioned by managers as a device for policing workplace life.

In sum, restructuring in our organisations has diverse implications for the gender order. We want to insist that the breakdown
of the traditional masculine hegemony is not simply cosmetic
and does allow women to participate in more senior organisational positions. However, it is vital to place these trends in a
wider context and to recognise counterveiling currents that are
constructing a new form of male dominance based around
images of the competitive, performative, skill-based manager who
is not overburdened by domestic responsibilities. Women can
enter the new management culture, but only by accepting these
key tenets and abandoning many orthodox claims to femininity,
notably motherhood. This is something which only a minority of
women were prepared to do.

This relates to an interesting observation revealed by our
survey and also our in-depth interviews. Managers tended to be
less happy with their jobs than did more junior workers, and
women managers tended to be most unhappy of all. This can
readily be understood in view of the isolation that many women
managers describe, being constantly marked out as different from
'normal' (male) managers by both managment and staff alike.

There is another important issue here. Many of these women were still relatively young and spoke readily of the difficulty they faced in linking work commitments with other desires and interests. It remains unclear from our research whether this vanguard of professional and managerial women will continue to involve themselves in management and professional work, or whether they will choose to 'opt out'. The gender order is still very much being negotiated.

This brings us to an important point concerning the frailty of the new management culture. At the time of our research it was clear that the new management culture had not become a legitimate one for the vast majority of workers. Therefore, although we have some sympathies with the work of writers such as du Gay (1996) who have explored the discursive construction of work identities around notions of the enterprise culture, we also want to insist on the significance of resistance to such changes. du Gay himself acknowledges the way in which many workers try to resist new managerial discourses through the adoption of various 'tactics' of resistance. However, he tends to see managers (especially younger managers) as largely uncritical bearers of new management ideas. In our work we found remarkably few respondents, at any level of the organisation, who were totally uncritical of their organisations and spoke unreservedly in support of new management ideas. Of course, most people had to accept that top-down endorsement of a new culture or new style of management shaped the terrain on which they had to work, and in this respect du Gay's arguments that employees were forced back on tactical forms of resistance has an important element of truth. However, it may well be the case that the difficulty of establishing new management discourses may mean that if they are to be enduring they need to fall back on more widely accepted gendered stereotypes. It is an interesting fact that those men most supportive of the new 'enterprise culture' also tended to endorse gendered notions of management, in which men were deemed best able to 'carry things off'. We may therefore see, in the longer term, the apparently gender-neutral language of new management merge with older, and more established, gender imagery.

When thinking about the roots of this resistance, we are led to a recognition of the need to see organisations as historically constituted processes. Our research showed time and again that the views that respondents had developed of their organisation had emerged during the entire course of their attachment to them, which sometimes extended over 20 and 30 years. New ideas could not sweep away the histories that individuals bore and which had been formed in close association with the organisations themselves. Although restructuring is tied up with redefining the nature of the qualities people are supposed to bring to their work, which means that restructuring is bound up with daily routines and work, it is not something which was successfully imposed from on high (although this is not to say that there are not attempts to do so) but was open to resistance and contestation. Restructuring is bound up with people's identities and values, and provokes reflection and discussion. Because it is so bound up with people's own lives, this makes it a messy, unpredictable and uneven process.

Appendix: Details of Interviewees

This book draws extensively on in-depth interviews carried out with employees in the three sectors. This appendix provides brief details on the respondents, listed alphabetically by anonymised names, which can be used for reference purposes during the book. The need to respect anonymity limits the extent of detail we can provide, but these portraits should convey a sense of the people involved.

Banking

Amanda: a junior manager in a small branch in Midcity. In her late 30s. Married, no children.

Doug: a high-flying senior manager in a Midcity specialist unit. In his early 40s. Married with children.

Jane: a secretary, in her late 40s, Jane worked at one of the specialist units in Midcity. Single, no children.

Giles: a specialist manager, in his early 40s, worked from a regional office in Midcity. Married with children.

Jeff: a medium-graded manager, working in a specialist lending capacity in a Midcity branch. A graduate, now in his early 40s. Married with children.

Joe: a senior clerk in his early 30s based in Midcity and posted to different branches to cover for staff shortages and holidays. Single, no children.

John: a manager of a medium-sized urban branch in Midcity, In his late 30s. Married with children.

Karen: a junior manager in a branch of Midcity. Graduate trainee in her mid-20s. Married, no children.

Ken: a specialist manager in a large branch near Southtown. In his early 30s. Single, no children.

Lesley: a junior clerk in her early 20s, recruited to a management trainee programme, and based at a specialist unit in Midcity. Single, no children.

Liz: a junior clerk based in a branch near Southtown, in her mid-20s. Single, no children.

Neville: a young male security clerk in a specialist unit in Midcity. Single, no children.

Nick: manager of a large branch near Southtown, a university graduate in his mid-30s. Married with children.

Nigel: a senior clerk in his mid-20s, working in Southtown. Single, no children.

Pat: a part-time secretary working at a large branch near Southtown. Married with children.

Penny: a part-time clerical worker, in her mid-30s. Married with children.

Sara: a junior clerk from an Asian background based at a large Midcity branch, in her mid-20s. Married, no children.

Simon: a senior clerk working in a specialist lending unit at a branch in Midcity. Single, no children.

Steven: a sales manager based at an urban branch in Midcity, in his early 50s, who had only just earned his promotion after a long period in clerical work. Married with children who had left home.

Stuart: a senior clerk in a Midcity branch, in his mid-40s. Married, with children who had left home.

Suzanne: a lending manager in her early 30s, working from a large urban branch. Married, no children.

Vanessa: a senior securities clerk in her early 30s, working from a specialist unit in Midcity. Married, no children.

Nursing

Andrea: an H grade Senior Sister in an elderly care unit at Midcity Hospital, where she had worked for 5 years. Married with grown-up children.

Anne: an F grade Night Sister at Southtown Hospital, after working nights at Southtown for eight years and before that as a Staff Nurse on medical and surgical wards. Single parent with one child.

Brenda: an F grade Sister in Casualty at Southtown Hospital, where she had worked for 20 years.

Bert: an H grade Charge Nurse in the intensive care unit at Midcity Hospital. After qualifying and working as a Staff Nurse, he spent 8 years at university doing a degree, Masters and PhD. Whilst also working part time as a nurse, began to train as an accountant but then decided to return to nursing full time.

Beth: an I grade nurse manager in theatre at Midcity Hospital. Beth was aged 39, married with one child and had worked as a nurse for 18 years.

Diane: a Staff Nurse in theatre at Midcity Hospital, aged 27, who had started as an Enrolled nurse but converted to State Registered Nurse.

Emma: a staff nurse at Southtown Hospital.

Gillian: a Director of Strategic Management at Midcity Hospital, aged 45. Married with three children. Gained a nursing degree in 1969, but moved into administration and lecturing, working part time when the children were young, before moving back

Henry:	to full-time work. a G grade Charge Nurse, who had been nursing for 12 years. Married to a midwife and had two children.
Janet:	a Sister in the renal unit at Midcity Hospital. She had been a clerical worker before entering nursing. Single.
Jennifer:	an H grade Senior Sister at Midcity Hospital, in intensive care, full time. Married with two children.
Joanne:	an H grade Project Nurse at Midcity Hospital, aged 38 and single. She had worked in nursing for 15 years and moved from an F-graded Sister's post to a newly created project nurse post three years previously.
Joseph:	a Senior Staff Nurse in theatre at Southtown Hospital. Married with one child.
Judith:	a G grade Sister at Midcity Hospital, 36 years old. Married with two children. Worked as a nurse, as well as briefly in computing and bar work, over a 14-year period, and had four years out of nursing to look after her children.
Margaret:	an I grade Clinical Nurse Specialist at Midcity Hospital, aged 35. Married, no children. She had worked as a clerk before entering nursing, and had progressed from Staff Nurse to Clinical Nurse Specialist in 10 years.
Samantha:	a Staff Nurse at Southtown hospital, 27 years old and single.
Sarah:	an Enrolled Nurse, working part time on nights at Southtown Hospital for 22 years. Her husband was retired.
Susan:	an I grade Senior Nurse at Southtown Hospital, working as an Operations Manager for the Community Care Directorate. Single. Worked at Southtown Hospital for 25 years.
Veronica:	a grade E Staff Nurse working part time on nights at Southtown Hospital. She was 29 years old. Married with two children and used to be a full-time G-graded Sister on the same ward.

Local government

Alex:	a surveyor at Southtown. Pursued an active programme of day release for post-entry qualifications. Single and lived alone.
Bob:	an accounts clerk with Midcity. Had worked for the authority for 18 years. Left school with no qualifications and worked for several employers. In his early 50s. Married with grown-up children.
Cathy:	a CIPFA accountant, Cathy had worked for Midcity since graduation. In her late 30s. Single, no children.
Christine:	a junior housing officer in her mid-40s. Left school with 'O' levels and followed varied career including a career break of several years. She had four children and lived with the youngest.
Christopher:	a junior manager at Midcity. Worked for the Council since leaving school after 'A' levels. In his early 30s. Married, no children.

Claire: a benefits assessor at Midcity, aged 25. Married with a pre-school child. Had worked for Midcity since leaving school with GCSEs.

Elaine: a principal officer involved in staff development, Elaine was a latecomer to the local government sector. An out lesbian, Elaine lived with her partner and children from a previous marriage.

Harry: a Senior Housing Manager in his early 50s, had always worked for local government. Married, with one young daughter.

Keith: a Senior Finance Manager at Midcity. Keith entered CIPFA training as a graduate and achieved rapid career advancement. Married, with several children.

Neil: a front-line services clerk in the Finance Department, had worked for Midcity since leaving school with GCSEs. In his mid-20s, single and lived with his parents.

Jim: a professional surveyor in his 50s. Had a variety of jobs before joining Southtown. He had been in present, senior position for many years. Married with grown-up children.

Joan: a Junior Manager in the Housing Department at Southtown. Left school with no qualifications and had had a mixed career, working for several employers. Had two children and took a career break.

Julia: a front-line services clerk in the Housing Department at Southtown, in her early 20s. Separated with one young child, Julia had not taken a career break.

Mark: a senior accountant at Southtown. Entered CIPFA training as a graduate. In his mid-30s. Married with children.

Maureen: a benefits assessor at Southtown. Married with children.

Michael: a junior clerk in the Finance Department at Southtown. Mixed career before entering local government. In his early 30s. Single.

Peter: now a systems analyst in the Finance Department at Southtown, had initially trained to be an accountant. In his late 20s. Single and lived alone.

Sandi: A Junior Housing Officer in her mid-20s. Left school with 'A' levels and worked for a housing association. Single, lived alone.

Teresa: an accounts clerk with Midcity, had worked in hotel management after leaving school. In her late 20s. Married, no children.

Martin: a senior accounts clerk. Worked for Midcity since the 1970s. In his 40s. Single and lived alone.

Melissa: a systems analyst. Worked in local government since completing a postgraduate degree (non-vocational). In her early 30s. Married, no children.

Stanley: a senior surveyor. Worked for Midcity since the 1960s. Married with grown-up children.

Serena: a junior clerical worker in the Housing Department. Worked for Midcity since leaving school at 16. Married, no children.

Tracey: a surveyor. Worked for Midcity since leaving school after GCSEs. In her mid-20s. Married, no children.

Notes

Preface

1 These Acts respectively made it unlawful to pay women and men different rates for doing the same job or to discriminate against either sex in access to employment, eduction or training, or access to services or premises. Both Acts have been subject to various amendments, most notably the 1984 amendment to the Equal Pay Act, which allowed equal pay claims to be made between different jobs that might be considered 'of equal value'.

Chapter 1

1 For a fuller discussion, see Witz and Savage (1992) who argue for a 'gender paradigm' for the study of bureaucratic organisations as historically and spatially specific ways of organising, and Mills and Tancred (1992) where the development of this debate is set out in a chronologically presented collection of reprinted papers.

2 We should make it clear here, however, that we find distinctions between formal and informal aspects of organisation difficult to make. Rather, we believe that the formal and the informal are thoroughly intertwined with one another, making firm distinctions pointless. We elaborate on this point throughout our book.

3 Weber acknowledged that the features of bureaucracy that he identified established an 'ideal-type' bureaucracy and that, in practice, bureaucracies would conform to this ideal to varying degrees. Nonetheless, he maintained that the core features of bureaucracy would be widely recognisable.

4 cf. Walter Benjamin's observation that, 'Whoever has emerged victorious participates to this day in the triumphal procession in which present rulers step over those who are lying prostrate' (1970: 258).

Chapter 2

1 We should point out here that there has been considerable theoretical debate in recent years concerning the value of regarding otherwise disparate forms of economic activity as part of a 'service sector' (see e.g. Walker, 1985; Urry, 1987). We do not attach any particular theoretical significance to the concept of services, except that it points, in descriptive fashion, to the fact that a considerable amount of 'work' is directed to a body of consumers. The relevance of this will be suggested in later chapters.

2 The term 'local areas' is chosen deliberately to avoid some of the reductive associations linked to the concept of 'locality'. See Duncan (1987), Duncan and Savage (1989, 1990), Cooke (1989) and Warde (1989).

3 The exclusion of manual staff was not an easy decision to make. We finally did so since we could not hope to cover both manual and white collar workers, and we felt that we could explore the dynamics of gender and career more

fully amongst white collar staff. We would not want to limit 'career' to only its hierarchical linear meaning, nor did we want to exclude this type of career path, which, as things stand, is rooted in white collar and not manual work. Furthermore, manual work is more sex segregated than white collar work, with less opportunity for exploring the gendering of everyday workplace interactions. Undoubtedly, however, the gendering of careers in manual work is a neglected topic – especially amongst writers on gender and organisation – and one which we would like to see explored further.

4 The Chartered Institute of Public Finance Accountants.

5 Throughout this section the precise numbers of individual employees have been suppressed in order to maintain confidentiality of the organisation.

6 Nurses may qualify either as a Registered General Nurse (RGN), which takes three years, or as an Enrolled Nurse (EN), which takes two years. We decided to include only Registered General Nurses, and not Enrolled Nurses, for two reasons. First, there is no longer a separate EN training, and second, unless she or he attends a conversion course to RGN, the EN's role is 'to assist', and there is a clear, and low, ceiling to her or his career.

7 'Unit' refers to the new units of hospital management within the NHS. This is often a single hospital, but may be two or more hospitals combined.

8 The higher number in banking was due to the fact that Sellbank chose to distribute the questionnaire to more staff than we had asked. The resulting returns were controlled to ensure that they conformed to the overall sampling strategy described below.

9 All references to interviews include the anonymised name of the respondent. Brief details of these respondents are included in the Appendix.

Chapter 3

1 As explained in Chapter 2, all quotations from the in-depth interviews are attributed to anonymised respondents, brief details of whom can be discerned from the Appendix.

2 We focus on these issues in more depth in the next chapter, when we look specifically at the impact of restructuring on the nursing career.

Chapter 4

1 The only other member of the board in this position was the Director of Estates.

2 Forty per cent of men are at the highest Grade I, compared with only 13 per cent of women nurses in our sample. This means that, at the top rung of the nursing hierarchy, the ratio of men to women is 1:3, compared with a ratio of 1:9 overall. This is not simply a function of longer service.

Chapter 5

1 A recent exception is Anderson *et al.* (1994) and McCrone (1994) who have explored the salience of various types of household strategies in their research in Kirkcaldy.

Chapter 6

1 Although, as we discuss in Chapter 7, all-male offices were strongly associated with discussion about sex.

Conclusions

1 We must remind the reader here that our study of local government only included white collar workers. Among manual workers the position is, of course, totally different.

Bibliography

Abercrombie, N. and Urry, J. (1983) *Capital, Labour and the Middle Classes.* London: Unwin and Allen.

Acker, J. (1973) Women and social stratification: a case of intellectual sexism, in J. Huber (ed.) *Changing Women in a Changing Society.* Chicago: University of Chicago Press.

Acker, J. (1990) Hierarchies, jobs, bodies: a theory of gendered organizations, *Gender & Society*, **5**:390–407.

Acker, J. (1992) Gendering organizational theory, in A. J. Mills and P. Tancred (eds) *Gendering Organizational Analysis.* London: Sage, 248–60.

Acker, J. and Van Houten, D. R. (1974) Differential recruitment and control: the sex structuring of organisations, *Administrative Science Quarterly*, **19**(2):152–63.

Adkins, L. (1992) Sexual work and the employment of women in the service industries, in M. Savage and A. Witz (eds) *Gender and Bureaucracy.* Oxford: Blackwell, 207–28.

Adkins, L. (1995) *Gendered Work: Sexuality, Family and the Labour Market.* Buckingham: Open University Press.

Adkins, L. and Lury, C. (1996) The Cultural, the Sexual and the Gendering of the Labour Market, in L. Adkins and V. Merchant (eds) *Sexualizing the Social Power and the Organization of Sexuality.* Basingstoke: Macmillan.

Althauser, R. P. and Kalleberg, A. (1981) Firms, occupations and the structure of labour markets: a sociological analysis, in I. Berg (ed.) *Sociological Perspectives on Labour Markets.* New York: Academic Books, 119–49.

Amin, A. (ed.) (1984) *Post-Fordism: a reader.* Oxford: Blackwell.

Anderson, G. (ed.) (1988) *The White Blouse Revolution.* London: Croom Helm.

Anderson, M., Bechhofer, F. and Kendrick, S. (1994) Individual and household strategies, in M. Anderson, F. Bechhofer and J. Gershuny (eds) *The Social and Political Economy of the Household.* Oxford: Clarendon Press.

Arthur, M., Hall, D. and Lawrence, B. (1989) *Handbook of Career Theory.* Cambridge: Cambridge University Press.

Atkinson, J. (1984) Manpower strategies for flexible organisations, *Personnel Management*, August 28–31.

Bacchi, C. L. (1992) *Same Difference: Feminism and Sexual Difference.* London: Allen & Unwin.

Bagguley, P., Mark-Lawson, J., Shapiro, D., Urry, J., Walby, S. and Warde, A. (1990) *Restructuring: Place, Class and Gender.* London: Sage.

Barrett, M. (1980) *Women's Oppression Today: Problems in Marxist Feminist Analysis.* London: Verso.

Beck, U. (1992) *The Risk Society.* London: Sage.

Becker, G. (1965) A theory of the allocation of time, *The Economic Journal,* September: 493–517.

Beechey, V. (1977) Some notes on female wage labour in capitalist production, *Capital and Class,* **3**:45–66.

Beechey, V. (1987) *Unequal Work.* London: Verso.

Benjamin, W. (1970) Theses on the philosophy of history, in *Illuminations.* London: Fontana.

Berle, A. and Means, G. (1932) *The Modern Corporation and Private Property.* London: Macmillan.

Beynon, H., Hudson, R., Lewis, J., Sadler, D., and Townsend, A. (1989) 'It's all falling apart here': coming to terms with the future in Teeside, in P. Cooke (ed.) *Localities: the Changing Face of Urban Britain.* London: Allen and Unwin.

Bologh, R. (1990) *Love or Greatness: Max Weber and Masculine Thinking – A Feminist Inquiry.* London: Unwin Hyman.

Bourdieu, P. (1977) *Outline of a Theory of Practice.* Cambridge: Cambridge University Press.

Brenner, J. and Ramas, M. (1984) Rethinking women's oppression, *New Left Review,* **144**:33–71.

Brown, H. (1992) *Women Organising.* London: Routledge.

Brown, R. (1982) Work histories, career strategies and the class structure, in A. Giddens and G. MacKenzie (eds) *Social Class and the Division of Labour.* Cambridge: Cambridge University Press.

Burrell, G. (1984) Sex and organisational analysis, *Organisation Studies,* **5**(2):97–118.

Burrell, G. and Hearn, J. (1989) The sexuality of organisation, in J. Hearn, *et al.* (eds) *The Sexuality of Organisation,* London: Sage.

Butler, J. (1990) *Gender Trouble: Feminism and the subversion of identity.* London: Routledge.

Butler, T. and Savage, M. (1995) *Social Change and the Middle Classes.* London: University College London Press.

Callas, M. (1992) An/other silent voice: representing Hispanic women in organisational texts, in A.J. Mills and P. Tancred (eds) *Gendering Organisational Analysis.* London: Sage.

Callas, M. and Smircich, L. (1992) Using the 'F' word: feminist theory and the social consequences of research, in A. J. Mills and P. Tancred (eds) *Gendering Organisational Analysis.* London: Sage.

Carpenter, M. (1977) The new managerialism and professionalism in nursing, in M. Stacey and M. Reid (eds) *Health and the Division of Labour.* London: Croom Helm.

Cavendish, R. (1982) *Women on the Line.* London: Routledge & Kegan Paul.

Certau, M. de (1984) *The Practice of Everyday Life.* London: University of California Press.

Chapman, T. (1990) The social mobility of women and men, in G. Payne and P. Abbott (eds) *The Social Mobility of Women.* London: Falmer, 25–37.

Chodorow, N. (1978) *The Reproduction of Mothering: Psychoanalysis and the New Sociology of Gender.* London: University of California Press.

Chodorow, N. (1989) *Feminism and Psychoanalytic Theory.* London: Yale University Press.

Clegg, S. (1989) *Frameworks of Power.* London: Sage.

Clegg, S. (1990) *Modern Organisations.* London: Sage.

Cloke, P., Philo, C. and Sadler, D. (1991) *Approaching Human Geography.* London: Paul Chapman.

Cochrane, A. (1993) *Whatever Happened to Local Government?* Buckingham: Open University Press.

Cockburn, C. (1983) *Brothers: Male Dominance and Technological Change.* London: Pluto Press.

Cockburn, C. (1991) *In the Way of Women.* London: Macmillan.

Collinson, D. (1988) *Barriers to Fair Selection: A multi-sector study of recruitment practices.* London: HMSO.

Collinson, D. and Collinson, M. (1989) Sexuality in the workplace: the domination of men's sexuality, in J. Hearn *et al.* (eds) *The Sexuality of Organisation.* London: Sage.

Connell, R.W. (1987) *Gender and Power.* Oxford: Polity Press.

Cooke, P. (1983) *Theories of Planning and Spatial Development.* London: Hutchinson.

Cooke, P. (ed.) (1989) *Localities: The Changing Face of Urban Britain.* London: Allen and Unwin.

Coyle, A. (1988) The limits of change: local government and equal opportunities for women, *Public Administration,* **67**:39–50.

Cressey, P. and Scott, P. (1992) Employment, technology and industrial relations in the UK clearing banks: is the honeymoon over?, *New Technology, Work and Employment,* **3**:83–96.

Crompton, R. (1986) Women and the service class, in R. Crompton and M. Mann (eds) *Gender and Stratification.* Oxford: Polity Press.

Crompton, R. (1989) Women in banking, *Work, Employment and Society,* **3**(2):141–56.

Crompton, R. (1993) *Class and Stratification.* Oxford: Polity Press.

Crompton, R. (1995) Women's employment and the 'middle classes', in T. Butler and M. Savage (eds) *Social Change and the Middle Classes.* London: University College London Press.

Crompton, R. and Jones, G. (1984) *A White Collar Proletariat? Gender and Deskilling in Clerical Work.* Basingstoke: Macmillan.

Crompton, R. and LeFeuvre, N. (1992) Gender and bureaucracy: women in finance in Britain and France, in M. Savage and A. Witz (eds) *Gender and Bureaucracy.* Oxford: Blackwell.

Crompton, R. and Sanderson, K. (1990) *Gendered Jobs and Social Change.* London: Allen and Unwin.

Crow, G. (1989) The use of the concept 'strategy' in recent sociological literature, *Sociology,* **23**(1):1–24.

Crozier, M. (1964) *The Bureaucratic Phenomenon.* London: Tavistock.

Davidson, M. and Cooper, C. (1992) *Shattering the Glass Ceiling: the woman manager.* London: Paul Chapman.

Davies, C. (1990) *The Collapse of the Conventional Career.* Project Paper One, English National Board for Nursing, Midwifery and Health Visiting.

Davies, C. (1992) Gender, history and management style in nursing: towards a theoretical synthesis, in M. Savage, and A. Witz (eds) *Gender and Bureaucracy.* Oxford: Blackwell.

Davies, C. (1995) *Gender and the Professional Predicament in Nursing.* Buckingham: Open University Press.

Davies, C. and Rosser, J. (1986) *Processes of Discrimination: a study of women working in the NHS.* London: HMSO.

Davis, K. and Moore, W.E. (1945) Some principles of stratification, *American Sociological Review,* **10**:242–9.

Department of Environment (1972) *Local Authority Management Structures.* London: HMSO.

Devine, F. (1992) Gender segregation in the engineering and science professions: a case of continuity and change, *Work, Employment and Society,* **6**(4): 557–75.

Diamond, J. and Speeden, S. (1993) Look Who's Wearing the Emperor's New Clothes. Paper presented at the 9th Urban Change and Conflict Conference, Sheffield, September.

Dominelli, L. (1991) *Women Across Continents: Feminist Comparative Social Policy.* London: Harvester Wheatsheaf.

Duncan, S.S. (1987) What is locality?, *University of Sussex Working Paper in Urban and Regional Studies,* No. 35.

Duncan, S.S. and Savage, M. (1989) Space, scale and localities, *Antipode,* **21**(3): 176–206.

Duncan, S.S. and Savage, M. (1990) Space, scale and locality: a reply to Cooke and Warde, *Antipode,* **22**(1): 67–73.

Edwards, R. and Ribben, J. (1991) Meanderings around 'strategy': a research note on strategic discourse in the lives of women, *Sociology,* **25**(3):477–85.

Eisenstein, H. (1991) *Gender Shock: Practising Feminism on Two Continents.* Sydney: Allen and Unwin.

Elcock, H. (1982) *Local Government: Politicians, professionals and the public in local authorities.* London: Methuen.

Elcock, H. (1991) *Change and Decay? Public Administration in the 1990s.* Harlow: Longman.

Evans-Pritchard, E. (1967) *Witches, Oracles and Magic Among the Azande.* Oxford: Clarendon.

Evetts, J. (1992) Dimensions of career: avoiding reification in the analysis of change, *Sociology,* **26**(1):1–21.

Evetts, J. (ed.) (1994) *Women and Career: Themes and issues in advanced capitalist countries.* London: Longman.

Ferguson, K. (1984) *The Feminist Case Against Bureaucracy.* Philadelphia: Temple University Press.

Fielding, A. (1995) Migration and middle class formation in England and Wales 1981–91, in T. Butler and M. Savage, *Social Change and the Middle Classes.* London: University College London Press.

Finch, J. (1983) *Married to the Job: Wives' incorporation into men's work.* London: Allen and Unwin.

Fineman, S. (ed.) (1993) *Emotion in Organisations*. London: Sage.

Finer, H. (1945) *English Local Government*. London: Methuen.

Flynn, R. (1992) Managed markets: consumers and producers in the National Health Service, in R. Burrows and C. Marsh (eds) *Consumption and Class: Divisions and Change*. Basingstoke: Macmillan.

Fogarty, M., Allen, A. and Walters, P. (1971) *Women in Top Jobs: Four studies in achievement*. London: George Allen and Unwin.

Foucault, M. (1977) *A History of Sexuality*, Vol 1. Harmondsworth: Penguin.

Frank, A. (1991) For a sociology of the body: an analytical review, in M. Featherstone, M. Hepworth and B. Turner (eds) *The Body: Social processes and cultural theory*. London: Sage.

Fuss, D. (1989) *Essentially Speaking*. London: Routledge.

Gallos, J. (1989) Exploring women's development: implications for career theory, practice and research, in M. Arthur *et al.* (eds) *op. cit.*

Gamarnikow, E. (1978) Sexual division of labour: the case of nursing, in A. Kuhn and A. Wolpe (eds) *Feminism and Materialism*. London: Routledge.

Gatens, M. (1990) A critique of the sex/gender distinction, in S. Gunew (ed.) *A Reader in Feminist Knowledge*. London: Routledge.

Gatens, M. (1996) *Imaginary Bodies: Ethics, Power and Corporeality*. London: Routledge.

Gay, P. du (1996) *Consumption and Identity at Work*. London: Sage.

Giddens, A. (1984) *The Constitution of Society*. Oxford: Polity Press.

Giddens, A. (1990) *The Consequences of Modernity*. Oxford: Polity Press.

Gilligan, C. (1982) *In a Different Voice: Psychological theory and women's development*. London: Harvard University Press.

Goldthorpe, J., Llewellyn, C. and Payne, C. (1980) *Social Mobility and the Class Structure of Modern Britain*. Oxford: Clarendon Press.

Goodwin, M., Duncan, S. and Halford, S. (1993) Regulation theory, the local state and the transition of urban politics, *Environment and Planning D, Society and Space*, **11**:67–88.

Grey, C. (1994) Career as a project of the self and labour process discipline, *Sociology*, **28**(2):497–8.

Grint, K. (1991) *The Sociology of Work*. Oxford: Blackwell.

Gunew, S. (ed.) (1991) *A Reader in Feminist Knowledge*. London: Routledge.

Gutek, B. and Larwood, L. (eds) (1987) *Women's Career Development*. London: Sage.

Gyford, J. (1985) *The Politics of Local Socialism*. London: George Allen and Unwin.

Hakim, C. (1979) Occupational Segregation: Comparative study of the degree and pattern of the differentiation between men's and women's work in Britain, the US and other countries. Department of Employment Research Paper, HMSO.

Hakim, C. (1991) Grateful slaves and self made women: fact and fantasy in women's work organisations, *European Sociological Review*, **7**(2):101–21.

Halford, S. (1991) Feminism, Politics and the Local State. Unpublished PhD Thesis, University of Sussex.

Halford, S. (1992) Feminist change in a patriarchal organisation: the experience of women's initiatives in local government and implications for feminist perspectives on state institutions, in M. Savage and A. Witz (eds) *Gender and Bureaucracy*. Oxford: Blackwell.

Halford, S. and Savage, M. (1995) Restructuring organisations, changing people: gender and restructuring in banking and local government, *Work, Employment and Society*, **9**(1):97–122.

Halford, S. and Savage, M. (1997) Rethinking restructuring: agency, identity and embodiment, in R. Lee and J. Wills (eds) *Space, Place and Economy: States of the Art in Economic Geography*. London: Edward Arnold.

Hall, M. (1989) Private experiences in the public domain, in G. Burrell and J. Hearn (eds) *The Sexuality of Organisation*. London: Sage.

Harre, R. (1969) *The Principles of Scientific Thinking*. Chicago: Chicago University Press.

Hartmann, H. (1979) Capitalism, patriarchy and job segregation by sex, in Eisenstein, Z. (ed.) *Capitalist Patriarchy and the Case for Socialist Feminism*. New York: Monthly Review Press.

Hearn, J. (1993) Emotive subjects: organisational men, organisational masculinities and the (de)construction of emotions, in S. Fineman (ed.) *Emotion in Organisations*. London: Sage.

Hearn, J. and Parkin, P. W. (1983) Gender and organizations: a selective review and critique of a neglected area, *Organization Studies*, **4**(3):219–42.

Hearn, J. and Parkin, P. W. (1987) *'Sex' at 'Work': The Power and Paradox of Organizational Sexuality*. London: Sage.

Hearn, J., Sheppart D.L., Tancred-Sheriff, P. and Burrell, G. (eds) (1989) *The Sexuality of Organisation*. London: Sage.

Hill-Collins, P. (1990) *Black Feminist Thought*. London: Routledge.

Hirst, P. (1984) Review article: Witches, relativism and magic, *Sociological Review*, **32**(3):573–88.

Hochschild, A. (1983) *The Managed Heart: Commercialisation of Human Feeling*. Berkeley and London: University of California Press.

Hoggett, P. (1991) A new management in the public services?, *Policy and Politics*, **19**(4):243–56

Hoggett, P. and Hambleton, R. (1987) *Decentralisation and Democracy: Localising public services*. Bristol: School for Advanced Urban Studies, Occasional Paper 28.

hooks, b. (1982) *Ain't I a Woman*. London: Pluto Press.

Hunter, D.J. (1994) From tribalism to corporatism: the managerial challenge to medical dominance, in J. Gabe, D. Kelleher and G. Williams (eds) *Challenging Medicine*. London: Routledge.

Jackson, R. (1958) *The Machinery of Local Government*. London: Macmillan.

Jackson, W.E., (1964) *Local Government in England and Wales*. Harmondsworth: Pelican.

Jephcott A, with N. Seear and J. H. Smith (1962) *Married Women Working*. London: Allen and Unwin.

Johns, E. (1973) *The Sociology of Organisational Change*. Oxford: Pergamon.

Kanter, R. (1977) *Men and Women of the Corporation*. New York: Basic Books.

Kanter, R. (1983) *The Change Masters: Corporate Entrepreneurs at Work*. London: Routledge.

Kanter, R. (1993) *Men and Women of the Corporation*, 2nd edn. New York: Basic Books.

Kerfoot, D. (1993) An infinite number of 'monkeys': gendered jobs in Supabank. School of Business and Economic Studies, discussion paper, Leeds University.

Kerfoot, D. and Knights, D. (1993) Management, masculinity and manipulation: from paternalism to corporate strategy in financial services in Britain, *Journal of Management Studies*, **30**(4):659–78.

Knights, D. and Morgan, G. (1991) Management control in sales: a case study from the labour process of life insurance, *Work, Employment and Society*, **4**(3):369–89.

Knowles, R. (1971) *Modern Management in Local Government*. London: Butterworth.

Laffin, M. and Young, K. (1990) *Professionalism in Local Government: Change and challenge*. Harlow: Longman.

Lash, S. and Urry, J. (1987) *The End of Organised Capitalism*. Oxford: Polity Press.

Lash, S. and Urry, J. (1994) *Economies of Signs and Spaces*. London: Sage.

Law, J. (1991) *Power, Action and Belief: new directions in the sociology of knowledge*. London: Routledge.

Layder, D. (1993) *New Strategies in Social Research*. Oxford: Polity Press.

Leach, S., Stewart, J. and Walsh, K. (1994) *The Changing Organisation and Management of Local Government*. Basingstoke: Macmillan.

Leonard, P. (1995) Gender/Organisation/Representation: A critical and post-structuralist approach to gender and organisational theory. Unpublished PhD Thesis, University of Southampton.

Levinson, D (1978) *The Seasons of a Man's Life*. New York: Ballantine.

Levitt, R. and Wall, A. (1992) *The Reorganised National Health Service*, 4th edn. London: Chapman and Hall.

Leyshon, A. and Thrift, N. (1993) The restructuring of the UK financial services industry in the 1990s: a reversal of fortune?, *Regional Studies*, **9**(3):223–41.

Llewellyn, C. (1981) Occupational mobility and the use of the comparative method, in H. Roberts (ed.) *Doing Feminist Research*. London: Routledge.

McCrone, D. (1994) Getting by and making out in Kircaldy, in M. Anderson, F. Bechhofer and J. Gershuny (eds), *The Social and Political Economy of the Household*. Oxford: Clarendon Press.

McDowell, L. and Pringle, R. (1992) Defining public and private issues, in L. McDowell and R. Pringle (eds) *Defining Women: Social Institutions and Gender Divisions*. Milton Keynes: Open University Press.

McDowell, L. and Court, J. (1994) Missing Subjects: Gender, power and sexuality in merchant banking, *Economic Geography*, **70**(3): 229–51.

Mackay, L. (1989) *Nursing a Problem*. Milton Keynes: Open University Press.

MacKinnon, C. (1979) *Sexual Harassment of Working Women: a case of sex discrimination*. New Haven: Yale University Press.

Maddock, S. (1993) Barriers to women are barriers to local government, *Local Government Studies*, **19**(3):341–50.

Mallaby, G. (1967) Committee on the Staffing of Local Government Report. London: HMSO.

Marcuse, H. (1978) *One Dimensional Man*. London: Routledge.

Mark-Lawson, J. and Witz, A. (1986) From 'family labour' to 'family wage'? The case of women's labour in 19th-century coal mining, *Social History*, **13**(2):151–74.

Marshall, G., Newby, H., Rose, D. and Vogler, C. (1988) *Social Class in Modern Britain*. London: Hutchinson.

Marshall, J. (1989) Re-visioning career concepts: a feminist invitation, in M. Arthur *et al.* (eds), *op. cit.*

Martin, E. (1987) *The Women in the Body*. Milton Keynes: Open University Press.

Massey, D. (1984) *Spatial Divisions of Labour: Social Relations and the Geography of Production*. London: Macmillan.

Massey, D. and Meegan, R. (1982) *The Anatomy of Job-Loss: The how, why and where of employment decline*. London: Methuen.

Massey, D., Quintas, P. and Wield, D. (1992) *High Tech Fantasies: Science Parks in Society, Science and Space*. London: Routledge.

Mills, A. J. (1989) Organisation, gender and culture, in A. J. Mills and P. Tancred (eds) *Gendering Organisational Analysis*. London: Sage.

Mills, A. J. and Tancred, P. (1992) *Gendering Organizational Analysis*. London: Sage.

Mincer, J. (1962) Labour force participation of married women: a study of labour supply, National Bureau of Economic Research, *Aspects of Labour Economics*. Princeton: Princeton University Press.

Mohan, J. (1988a) Spatial aspects of health care employment in Britain 1: Aggregate trends, *Environment and Planning A*, **20**(7):295–310.

Mohan, J. (1988b) Spatial aspects of healthcare employment in Britain 2: Current policy initiatives, *Environment and Planning A*, **20**(2):203–17.

Morgan, D. (1986) Strategies and sociologists: a comment on Crow, *Sociology*, **23**(1):25–30.

Morgan, D. and Scott, S. (1993) Bodies in a social landscape, in S. Scott and D. Morgan (eds) *Body Matters: Essays in the Sociology of the Body*. London: Falmer.

Morgan, Gareth (1986) *Images of Organisation*. London: Sage.

Morgan, Glenn (1990) *Organisations in Society*. Basingstoke: Macmillan.

Mouzelis, N. (1995) *Sociological Theory: what went wrong?* London: Routledge.

Murgatroyd, L. (1982) Gender and occupational stratification, *Sociological Review*, **30**(4):574–602.

Murgatroyd, L., Savage, M., Shapiro, D., Urry, J., Walby, S. and Warde, A. (1985) *Localities, Class and Gender*. London: Pion.

Nicholson, P. and West, M. (1989) *Managerial Job Change*. Cambridge: Cambridge University Press.

O'Reilly, J. (1992a) Where do you draw the line? Functional flexibility, training and skill in Britain and France, *Work, Employment and Society*, **6**(3):369–96.

O'Reilly, J. (1992b) Subcontracting in banking: some evidence from Britain and France, *New Technology, Work and Employment*, **3**:107–15.

Owens, P. and Glennester, H. (1990) *Nursing in Conflict*. Basingstoke: Macmillan.

Pahl, R. (1995) *After Success*. Oxford: Polity Press.

Parkin, W. (1993) The public and the private: Gender, sexuality and emotion, in S. Fineman (ed.) *Emotion in Organisations*. London: Sage.

Passmore, J. (1990) Customer care – cultural change at Welwyn Hatfield, *Local Government Studies*, **16**(5):1–8.

Pawson, R. (1993) Social mobility, in D. Morgan and L. Stanley (eds) *Debates in Sociology*. London: Macmillan.

Pendelton, A. (1991) Barriers to flexibility: flexible rostering on the railways, *Work, Employment and Society*, **5**(2):241–57.

Pfeffer, J. (1989) A political perspective on careers: interests, networks and environments, in M. Arthur *et al.* (eds), *op. cit.*

Pinch, S. (1989) The restructuring thesis and the study of public services, *Environment and Planning A*, **21**:905–26.

Pollert, A. (1982) *Girls, Wives, Factory Lives*. London: Macmillan.

Poulantzas, N. (1973) *Classes in Contemporary Captialism*. London: New Left Books.

Pringle, R. (1989a) *Secretaries Talk: Sexuality, Power and Work*. London and New York: Verso.

Pringle, R. (1989b) Bureaucracies, rationality and sexuality: the case of secretaries, in J. Hearn, D. L. Sheppard, P. Tancrid-Sheriff and G. Burrell (eds) *The Sexuality of Organisation*. London: Sage.

Pulkingham, J. (1992) Employment restructuring in the health service: efficiency initiatives, working patterns and worforce competition, *Work, Employment and Society*, **6**(3):397–421.

Reskin, B. F. and Roos, B. (1990) *Job Queues, Gender Queues: Explaining Women's Inroads Into Male Occupations*. Philadelphia: Temple University Press.

Reskin, B. F. and Padavic, I. (1994) *Women and Men at Work*. London: Pine Forge Press.

Ressner, U. (1987) *The Hidden Hierarchy: Democracy and equal opportunities*. Aldershot: Avebury.

Robson, W. (1954) *The Development of Local Government,* 3rd edn. London: George Allen and Unwin.

Roper, M. (1992) *Masculinity and the British Organisational Man since 1945*. Oxford: Oxford University Press.

Rubery, J. and Fagan, C. (1995) Gender segregation in societal context, *Work, Employment and Society*, **9**(2):213–40.

Saunders, P. (1990) *A Nation of Homeowners*. London: Unwin Hyman.

Savage, M. (1991) Restructuring and current changes in banking: a background paper, mimeo, Dept of Sociology and Social Anthropology, Keele University.

Savage, M. (1992) Women's expertise, Men's authority: gendered organisation and the contemporary middle classes, in M. Savage and A. Witz (eds) *Gender and Bureaucracy*. Oxford: Blackwell.

Savage, M. (1993) Career mobility and class formation: British banking workers and the lower middle classes, in A. Miles and D. Vincent (eds)

Building European Society: occupational change and social mobility in Europe, 1840–1940. Manchester: Manchester University Press.

Savage, M. (1996) Social mobility and the survey method: a critical analysis, in D. Bertaux and P. Thompson (eds) *Pathways to Social Class: qualitative studies in social mobility*. Oxford: Clarendon Press.

Savage, M. and Witz, A. (eds) (1992) *Gender and Bureaucracy*. Oxford: Blackwell/*The Sociological Review.*

Savage, M., Barlow, J., Dickens, P. and Fielding, T. (1992) *Property, Bureaucracy and Culture: Middle class formation in contemporary Britain*. London: Routledge.

Sayer, A. (1984) *Method in Social Science: a realist approach*. London: Hutchinson.

Sayer, A. (1989) Post-fordism in question, *International Journal of Urban and Regional Research*, **13**:666–95.

Scott, J. (1979) *Corporations, Classes and Capitalism*. London: Hutchinson.

Segal, L. (1994) *Straight Sex: The Politics of Pleasure*. London: Virago.

Shaw, M. (1990) Strategy and social process: military context and sociological analysis, *Sociology*, **24**(3):465–74.

Shilling, C. (1993) *The Body in Social Theory*. London: Sage.

Silverstone, R. (1980) Accountancy, in R. Silverstone and A. Ward (eds) *Careers of Professional Women*. London: Croom Helm.

Spellman, E. (1988) *Inessential Woman*. London: The Women's Press.

Stanko, B. (1988) Keeping women in and out of line: sexual harrassment and occupational segregation, in S. Walby (ed) *Gender Segregation at Work*. Milton Keynes: Open University Press.

Stanyer, J. (1976) *Understanding Local Government*. Glasgow: Fontana/Collins.

Stoker, G. (1990) Regulation theory, local government and the transition from Fordism, in D. King and J. Pierre (eds) *Challenges to Local Government*. London: Sage.

Stone, I. (1988) *Equal Opportunities in Local Authorities: Developing effective strategies for the implementation of policies for women*. London: HMSO.

Strauss, A. (1989) *Qualitative Analysis for Social Scientists*. Cambridge: Cambridge University Press.

Strong, P. and Robinson, J. (1990) *The NHS: Under new management*. Milton Keynes: Open University Press.

Summerfield, P. (1984) *Women Workers in the Second World War*. London: Croom Helm.

Super, D. (1957) *The Psychology of Careers: An Introduction to Vocational Development*. New York: Harper & Row.

Thompson, P. (1978) *The Voice of the Past*. Oxford: Oxford University Press.

Thrift, N. (1987) The geography of the late twentieth-century class formation, in N. Thrift and P. Williams (eds) *Class and Space*. London: Routledge.

Turner, V. (1969) *The Ritual Process: structure and anti-structure*. London: Routledge.

Urry, J. (1987) Some social and spatial aspects of services, *Society and Space*, **5**:5–26.

Urry, J. (1990) Work production and social relations, *Work, Employment and Society*, **4**(2):271–80.

Ussher, J. (1989) *The Psychology of the Female Body*. London: Routledge.

Walby, S. (1986) *Patriarchy at Work*. Oxford: Polity Press.

Walby, S. (1990) *Theorizing Patriarchy*. Oxford: Blackwell.

Walby, S. and Bagguley, P. (1991) Gender Restructuring: A comparative analysis of five local labour markets. Lancaster Regionalism Group, Working Paper 28, University of Lancaster.

Walby, S. and Greenwell, J., with Mackay, L. and Soothill, K. (1994) *Medicine and Nursing: Professions in a changing health service*. London: Sage.

Walker, R. (1985) Is there a service economy? The changing capitalist division of labor, *Science and Society*, **49**:42–83.

Wallace, C. (1993) Reflections on the concept of strategy, in D. Morgan and L. Stanley (eds) *Debates in Sociology*. London: Macmillan.

Warde, A. (1985) Spatial Change, Politics, and the Division of Labour, in D. Gregory and J. Urry (eds) *Social Relations and Spatial Structures*. London: Macmillan.

Warde, A. (1989) Recipes for pudding: a comment on Duncan and Savage, *Antipode*, **22**(1):60–7.

Warde, A. (1990) Introduction to the sociology of consumption, *Sociology*, **24**(1):1–4.

Warde, A. (1992) Notes on the relationship betwen production and consumption, in R. Burrows and C. Marsh (eds) *Consumption and Class: Divisions and Change*. Basingstoke: Macmillan.

Warren, J.H. (1952) *The Local Government Service*. London: George Allen and Unwin.

Watson, W. (1990) Strategy, rationality and influence: the possibility of symbolic performances, *Sociology*, **24**(3):485–98.

Webster, B. (1985) A women's issue: the impact of cuts, in *Local Government Studies* March/April, 19–46.

Westwood, S. (1984) *All Day, Every Day: Factory and Family in the Making of Women's Lives*. London: Pluto Press.

Witz, A. (1992) *Professions and Patriarchy*. London: Routledge.

Witz, A. (1994) The challenge of nursing, in J. Gabe, D. Kelleher and G. Williams (eds) *Challenging Medicine*. London: Routledge.

Witz, A. and Savage, M. (1992) The Gender of Organisations, in M. Savage and A. Witz (eds) *Gender and Bureaucracy*. Oxford: Blackwell.

Woolf, J. (1977) Women in organisations, in S. Clegg and D. Dunkerley *Critical Issues in Organisations*. London: Routledge & Kegan Paul.

Woolf, N. (1990) *The Beauty Myth*. London: Verso.

Wright, E. O. (1979) *Class, Crisis and the State*. London: New Left Books.

Wright, E. O. (1985) *Classes*. London: Verso.

Zeitlin, J. (1989) Theories of women's work and occupational segregation, *Journal of the Society for the Study of Labour History*, **54**(1):6–9.

Zeitlin, M. (1974) Corporate ownership and control: the large corporation and the capitalist class, *American Journal of Sociology*, **79**(5):1073–119.

Index

287